MARCHING TO
THE FAULT LINE

MARCHING TO THE FAULT LINE

THE 1984 MINERS' STRIKE AND THE DEATH OF INDUSTRIAL BRITAIN

Francis Beckett and David Hencke

CONSTABLE • LONDON

Constable & Robinson Ltd
3 The Lanchesters
162 Fulham Palace Road
London W6 9ER
www.constablerobinson.com

First published in the UK by Constable,
an imprint of Constable & Robinson Ltd, 2009

A copy of the British Library Cataloguing in
Publication data is available from the British Library

ISBN: 978-1-84529-614-8

Printed and bound in the EU

Mixed Sources
Product group from well-managed
forests and other controlled sources
www.fsc.org Cert no. SA-COC-1565
© 1996 Forest Stewardship Council
FSC

CONTENTS

LIST OF ILLUSTRATIONS

London during the 1926 general strike. © *Topham Picturepoint/ Topfoto.co.uk* (0235642).

Miners greet the announcement of the strike, March 1984. © *Peter Arkell.*

Attacking the police vans carrying strike breakers. © *Peter Arkell.*

A wounded miner, Yorkshire. © *Peter Arkell.*

Police arresting picketers. © *Topham Picturepoint/ Topfoto.co.uk* (0814365).

The Battle of Orgreave. © *Peter Arkell.*

Arthur Scargill and Mick McGahey at the 1984 Trades Union Congress. © *David Mansell, The Observer Ltd.*

Arthur Scargill and TUC General Secretary Norman Willis, 14 October 1984. © *The Associated Press Ltd.*

Neil Kinnock, Arthur Scargill and Ron Todd at a Labour Party rally. © *Roger Hutchings, The Observer Ltd.*

Margaret Thatcher at the 1984 Conservative Party Conference. © *Peter Arkell.*

Coal Board chief Ian Macgregor. © *Hulton Archive/Getty Images* (73116464).

Striking families at Christmas, 1984. © *Peter Arkell.*

Women on the picket line in Yorkshire. © *Peter Arkell.*

Whittle miners' wives support group on the picket line. © *Peter Arkell.*

NUM chief executive, Roger Windsor. © *Topham Picturepoint/Topfoto.co.uk* (0468540).

Print union leader Bill Keys. © *Andrew Wiard.*

Betteshanger Colliery, Kent. © *Topham Picturepoint/Topfoto.co.uk* (0021138).

A closed down mine, Durham, 1987. © *Peter Arkell.*

Winding gear broken up and recycled, 1989. © *Peter Arkell.*

PREFACE

Britain before the great miners' strike of 1984–5 and Britain after it are two fundamentally different places, and they have little in common. The full story of this turning point in our history has not been written before, because documents were not available and people were not willing to talk. Much of what is in this book has never been made public.

We could not have told it without the help and generosity of several people.

A talented young journalist, Dan Johnson, was our principal researcher, conducting some of our most important interviews. Because of his deep knowledge of mining communities, and because he was brought up in Arthur Scargill's village of Worsbrough, he turned into a great deal more than our researcher: he was also a thoughtful and knowledgeable guide to what it all meant. Dr Clare Beckett of Bradford University also brought her own knowledge and understanding to a research project she conducted for us on women in the strike.

Some fellow journalists were very generous with their knowledge, time and contacts. Jeff Apter, Paris stringer for newspapers and magazines throughout the English-speaking world, not only arranged our interview with French and international trade union leader Alain Simon and acted as interpreter during it, but also threw new light on the mechanics of the strike by describing to us his own role in getting French trade unionists' money into the hands of the National Union of Mineworkers.

Paul Routledge, at the time industrial correspondent of *The Times* and later Arthur Scargill's biographer, gave us full access to his papers, his contacts, his memories and his great store of knowledge. Nicholas Jones was the BBC's industrial correspondent, and he showed us how the battle for public opinion was won and lost. Geoffrey Goodman, then the industrial editor of the *Daily Mirror*, was not just a reporter but at one point a player, and he gave generously of his knowledge and understanding. David Seymour of the *Mirror* gave us important insights into the Maxwell era. Reporting on the strike for the *Mirror* was Terry Pattinson, and he too played his own part in the story; he helped us to piece together the incident in which he was involved, and offered his own interesting reflections.

We are also grateful to freelance photographer Peter Arkell; the *Guardian*'s Paul Brown; freelance Kevin Cahill; Mick Costello, former industrial editor of the *Morning Star* and industrial organizer of the Communist Party; freelance Barbara Fox; the *Guardian*'s Seumas Milne, author of a book about the tangled finances of the miners' union during the strike; Helen Hague; and Simon Pirani, formerly of *Newsline*.

Members of the Conservative government of the time gave us helpful, open interviews and clear insights into their thinking as the strike possessed. We want to thank in particular Peter Walker, the then Energy Secretary, and his then Parliamentary Under Secretary, the coal minister David Hunt; Norman Tebbit, then Trade and Industry Secretary; and Lord Wakeham, Chief Whip at the time and later Energy Secretary, for his help and political insight. Of course we would have liked to talk to Margaret Thatcher, but we understand she is too frail to give interviews.

Some of their civil servants gave us invaluable interviews, and we have to thank in particular Lord Turnbull, the former Cabinet Secretary, who, as Margaret Thatcher's private secretary in Downing Street during the strike, provided very useful insights and interpretation of some of the material the authors obtained under the Freedom of Information Act. Ivor Manley, Deputy Secretary at the Department of Energy, and Sir Tim Bell, who advised ministers on strategy and in particular communications strategy, were also very helpful.

Miners' leaders of the time were extremely helpful too, with one significant exception. We want to express our gratitude for useful and frank interviews given to us by Kevin Barron (now MP for Rother Valley), Trevor Bell, Ken Capstick, Dave Feickert, Eric Illsley (now MP for Barnsley Central) and Anne Scargill. The late Mick McGahey gave an interview to one of the authors for another book some years ago, and we have used it here. We also want to thank Roger Windsor for helping us, as far as he could, from his home in France, and Nell Myers for the brief but useful discussion we had with her at Arthur Scargill's door. We had some limited assistance from the architect who designed the NUM building, Malcolm Lister.

Neil Kinnock, Leader of the Opposition at the time, opened up his papers to us, and talked openly and honestly about everything he did during the strike, and what he thinks and feels about it now. Alain Simon, former leader of the miners' section of the Confédération Générale du Travail and a key player in international trade union politics, gave us an interesting interview.

Key players in British trade unions were central to our research, and we are grateful to them for the trouble they took and the candour with which they spoke to us. We are especially grateful to a trade union leader who was no longer alive while we were researching this book. Soon after his retirement, the late Bill Keys handed one of the authors his detailed thirty-page diary of the miners' strike, explaining his secret negotiations, and told us all about it. Keys, we reveal here, was the TUC's secret player, the man on whom its hopes for a settlement finally depended. His diary has enabled us to tell the full story of the last few months of the strike for the first time.

John Monks, the TUC's head of organization and industrial relations at the time and later its General Secretary, was one of the few people in the secret of the Keys initiative, and apart from confirming what is in

Keys' diary, he was a great source of help, information and advice. Paul Mackney, recently retired General Secretary of the University and College Union, turned up at the home of one of the authors carrying a holdall containing his huge and magnificent collection of books and pamphlets about the strike, which he loaned to us for the duration. The late John Lyons gave one of the authors an interview some years ago, which has been recycled here.

Other union leaders who gave us helpful interviews and information include Rodney Bickerstaffe, Ken Cameron, Cyril Cooper and John Edmonds.

Of course, the name missing from all this is Arthur Scargill. We would dearly have liked to talk to him. He was the central figure. We are sure that he will passionately disagree with some of our conclusions, and we would have wanted to give his view. He mounted a ferocious attack on two previous writers in which he wrote: 'Authority on this subject [the strike] can only come from the NUM itself – to be precise, from the Union's national officials who were at the very heart of the struggle, and who knew exactly what took place throughout.'[1] Of those three national officials, Mick McGahey is dead and Peter Heathfield is too frail to be interviewed – which leaves Scargill. So we shall not have much sympathy if Scargill denounces us, too, for failing to talk to the national officials.

We have done everything possible to ensure that Scargill's perspective is reflected here, interviewing his closest union collaborators, including Alain Simon (who says he is today perhaps Scargill's closest friend) and Ken Capstick, and putting to them all the questions we would have liked to put to Scargill. But occasionally, faced with the sometimes baffling question 'Why did Arthur do such-and-such?', even they, after a brave stab at an answer, had to say: 'I don't know. You'd have to ask Arthur.' We'd love to.

But we have done the best we can by Arthur, despite Arthur – which we suspect is something a large number of people could say truthfully. We do not know why he chooses not to defend his own record. We did everything we could to get an interview, working through his close friend, press officer and amanuensis Nell Myers, and our only insight into his reasons for refusing us comes from her.

We wrote to Scargill at both the union headquarters and his home address. When, after a month, we had had no reply, Francis Beckett and researcher Dan Johnson drove to his house and knocked on the door, unannounced. It was answered by Nell Myers.

Nell is tall and elegant, with an intelligent face and a thoughtful, literary style of speech. But this was not the grim, unsmiling Nell Myers we had known in the 1980s. She seemed more relaxed, easier in her own skin, happier, instinctively courteous. We could see Scargill through the window, sitting in the living room, reading a book.

Things did not get off to a good start. Beckett explained their mission, and reminded her that they had known each other in the 1980s when they were both trade union press officers. Myers, in a friendly way, said she remembered it all well, but then added: 'Then you wrote that dreadful book about the Communist Party.'

Leaving behind as fast as possible this apparently awkward topic, Beckett and Johnson moved the conversation on, and left with a promise that if they emailed Myers, they would not this time go without a reply. She was as good as her word, replying very quickly to Beckett's follow-up email to say that his earlier letters had not been received, and asking what the point was of another book on the strike. She made it clear that she thought the book might be a hatchet job on Scargill, and in his reply Beckett assured her that this was not the intention. The book could offer a historical perspective that was to be found in no previous work, he said. Myers then wrote to say that Arthur had turned us down – and that she herself had 'picked up a sense of foreboding when reading your second email. All these people perpetually lurking in some historical ether ready or so it seems to have a go at him; or perhaps you have a fresh tranche!' She felt, she told us, that Arthur's 'warnings of what would happen if the entire trade union movement didn't fight alongside the NUM have been proved correct.'

And that was that.

CHAPTER 1

THE SHADOW OF 1926

1920 TO 1945

The story of the 1984–5 miners' strike starts in 1926. Without the 1926 general strike, nothing that happened in the next six decades makes sense. And the foundations of the 1926 general strike were laid six years earlier, in 1920, when trade unions were more powerful than they had ever been before – as they were again in 1978, six years before the 'great strike for jobs'.

Unions in 1920 had real power, and a record 45 per cent of the workforce belonged to one. This percentage was not reached again until 1974, when the unions were again stronger than ever – and, again, were within a decade of their most decisive defeat. Six and a half million trade unionists were affiliated through their unions to the Trades Union Congress, a peak not reached again until after the Second World War.[1]

Many small craft unions had merged into big general unions that survived more or less intact until very recently – the Amalgamated Engineering Union, the Transport and General Workers' Union, the National Union of General and Municipal Workers, with a quarter of a million or so workers. There was another merger mania in the 1970s, in which dozens of smaller unions disappeared into these three already huge unions. But in 1920 even the biggest general unions were dwarfed by the 900,000-strong Miners' Federation of Great Britain (MFGB) – the aristocracy of organized labour.

There were reasons for that. Britain needed coal, and had needed it for more than a century. Getting it out of the ground was harsh, back-breaking and horrifyingly dangerous work, and the coal owners had a long record of exploiting the men, forcing them to work long hours for little pay, housing them in hovels and skimping on the expenditure necessary to provide safe working conditions. So the miners had built up a strong trade union tradition to protect themselves. When they went on strike, they all went, though they knew that after the strike the owners, if they emerged from the battle strong enough to do so, would victimize strike leaders and evict them from their homes. 'Scab' – strike-breaker – was the most offensive name you could call a miner.

Nineteen-twenty also saw the revival of the Triple Alliance – miners, dockers and railwaymen – and the threat of concerted action by all three, which had the potential to bring the country to a standstill. It saw too the strengthening of the central organization of the unions, the Trades Union Congress, with its own General Council and permanent General Secretary. The TUC had already, before the First World War, been the key player in the creation of the Labour Party, and up to the 1990s union leaders looked on the Labour Party as an errant younger brother, and on Labour politicians as grubby chaps who had occasional uses. The real work of the working class, they believed, was done in union offices.

There was a revolutionary spirit around in 1920, born of wild post-war optimism and a determination never to go back to the old, unfair prewar society. There were many – as there were again in the 1970s – who believed that trade unionism was far more than a means of pro-tecting wages, working conditions and jobs: it could be an instrument for the creation of a better and fairer society.

It was the year in which the Communist Party of Great Britain (CPGB) was founded. One day in the summer of 1920, 160 revolution-ary socialists from several previously warring little groups came together at the Cannon Street Hotel near St Paul's Cathedral.

Encouraged by emissaries and money from the father of world revolution himself, Vladimir Lenin, they agreed to bury their differences and join together to found the CPGB. The Labour-supporting *Daily Herald* commented: 'The founders of the new Party believe – as most competent observers are coming to believe – that the capitalist system is collapsing.'

It was two and a half years since the Russian revolution of 1917, and the mood of the times seemed to be with them. In a nation that had fought and won the most terrible and destructive war in history, limbless ex-servicemen were reduced to begging and selling matches on the streets of the cities. The Conservative-dominated government under David Lloyd George which had won the snap election after the war – the 'khaki election' – seemed only interested in returning to the old, unfair and class-ridden prewar society. When there is a strong mood for change, and there seems no hope of change in the democratic process, then revolutionary talk catches on. And the lives of the generation of 1920 were indelibly scarred by the war. Some had opposed it, had been assaulted daily by men and handed white feathers by women, and thrown into jail. Others had seen in the trenches things that no one should ever see, had lost nearly all their male friends, and had never quite got over the sense of guilt that they had somehow survived. It seemed a betrayal of their dead friends to accept the injustices they found when they returned. Had their friends died so that their wives and children should be starved and exploited?

The new political and industrial militancy, born out of the First World War, and the vast gap between conspicuous wealth and grinding poverty, which had been accepted as the natural order of things before the war, made a mix which many people believed meant revolution.

Support for the Russian revolution, as well as a determination to emulate it in Britain, was a key part of the new party's thinking, and it went well beyond CPGB members. The Party's influence, in 1920 as again in 1984, extended well beyond the relatively small number of people who were actually paid-up members. Thus it was that a young

3

Communist firebrand called Harry Pollitt, who was to become the CPGB's most important leader in its entire history, was able in 1920 to lead the London dockers, through their trade union, to refuse to load arms on to a ship, the *Jolly George*, because the arms were to be used against the Bolsheviks in Russia. And thus it was that, though its formal membership never amounted to much, the Communist Party was a key player in key events for the next sixty years – until the end of the great miners' strike of 1984–5.

Strikes were frequent in 1920, and frequently successful, because unions were well supported. Union leaders became national figures, another tradition that lasted until the 1984–5 miners' strike and then ceased abruptly. From 1920 to 1984, the great union leaders were household names ranking alongside top politicians: Ernest Bevin, Walter Citrine, Arthur Cook, Frank Cousins, Hugh Scanlon, Jack Jones, Lawrence Daly, Len Murray, Arthur Scargill.

Some of the harshest living and working conditions in the country were to be found in mining communities. They had poverty pay and tied housing that was often not fit for human habitation. Their tiny, basic terraced homes were packed into small spaces in areas where there was no alternative employment. They had outdoor lavatories: 'You had to go out the back, go up the steps and walk about fifteen or twenty yards and carry a bucket of water with you,' recalled one veteran, years later.[2]

These homes were normally rented from the mine owner, who would sometimes sell a miner his home, if the miner's wife was also working and they could raise the money. Aneurin Bevan, who, a quarter of a century later, was to be the creator of the National Health Service, was the son of a South Wales miner, and his parents bought their home from the mine owner. His mother was up before 5 a.m. to get her husband to the mine and her eight children out to school so that she could start work as a seamstress. By that means they scraped together the money to buy their tiny four-room terraced cottage, only to find that the pit underneath the cottage caused subsidence and they had to spend their evenings propping up the roof. Bevan said years later that the mine owner, Lord Tredegar, 'having taken out the kernel, the coal, wanted to sell the shell.'[3]

But coal was a vital resource, and employed nearly a million miners, who potentially had great industrial muscle. They believed that they did not need to live in squalor: they could fight for something better. That was what their union and their socialist faith told them. Anne Perkins writes: 'The importance of solidarity for survival in the pits, the shared danger at work and hardship at home, the stark division between labour and capital, and the lack of anything else to do made God and socialism popular and often overlapping sources of solace.'[4]

The mines, nationalized during the First World War, were de-nationalized immediately afterwards, much to the disappointment of the miners, who with some justice blamed the mine owners' greed and lack of enterprise for the unnecessary harshness of their lives. Renationalization was top of the list of demands put to the government by the MFGB, along with reductions in hours and an increase in pay.

But the Conservative-dominated government under David Lloyd George was determined to disentangle itself from its wartime involvement with mining. The coal owners saw their dividends shrinking as they failed to compete with foreign coal, and resorted to the simple formula of cutting the cost of production by cutting the miners' wages and increasing their hours. The Triple Alliance was invoked, and a dockers', miners' and railwaymen's strike called for 21 April 1921, but the dockers and railwaymen refused in the end to come out with the miners. They thought the MFGB should have negotiated a compromise.

So the miners went on strike alone. They held out until June and returned to work with pay not just reduced but, in many districts, halved. In the increased poverty and squalor in which they lived, they nursed a deep sense of grievance against the fellow trade unionists who they believed had betrayed them.

Industrial action having failed, for the moment, to produce the goods, they focused their hopes on political action through the Labour Party. They had some right to do so. The unions had created the Labour

Party. In fact, until 1918 the Labour Party did not even recruit individual members. You could only become a member by being in an affiliated trade union or a socialist society like the Fabians.

In January 1924 Labour's first-ever Prime Minister, Ramsay MacDonald, took office. That day, David Kirkwood, a newly elected left-wing Labour MP, told his cheering supporters as his London-bound train pulled out of Glasgow station: 'When we come back, all this will belong to the people.' But as he was speaking, MacDonald was apologizing to King George V for the behaviour of Labour supporters at their victory rally: 'They had got into the way of singing "The Red Flag" . . . By degrees he hoped to break down this habit.'[5]

Less than a year later, MacDonald's government fell. The Communist paper, *Workers Weekly*, published an 'Open Letter to the Fighting Forces' calling on soldiers to 'let it be known that, neither in the class war nor in a military war, will you turn your guns on your fellow workers'. The editor, Johnny Campbell, was charged with incitement to mutiny, but the charge was withdrawn by the Labour Attorney General, Sir Patrick Hastings, and the resulting row brought down the government – which did not have an overall parliamentary majority and could only survive with Liberal support. The Conservatives under Stanley Baldwin won the resulting general election by a landslide.

Labour had achieved virtually none of its aims. Left-wing Labour MP James Maxton said that the fall of the government would not be a tragedy; in fact 'the sooner they were out the better, as every day they were leading us further from socialism.'[6] So the baton passed back to the unions. Frank Hodges, the MFGB General Secretary who, three years earlier, had tried to do a deal with the government as the other unions wanted, and had been prevented by his National Executive, was voted out of office in 1924, edged aside by a young militant called Arthur Cook. The son of a soldier from Somerset, himself a Baptist preacher, Cook speedily became an iconic figure among the miners, who admired him and followed him.

By all the rules he should have been a poor speaker, for he had a high voice, and his speeches were not held together by a logical structure, but they were emotional, and had an evangelical rhythm, and he was saying what the miners wanted to hear. He would take off his jacket and intone passionately the views he wished his audience to adopt, and he was loved and admired in mining communities, much as Arthur Scargill was sixty years later. Scargill is said to have modelled himself on Arthur Cook, and there are superficial similarities, but the two men were fundamentally different characters.

Cook became General Secretary under a Labour government, but had to deal with its Conservative successor, whose huge majority – 419 seats to Labour's 159 – made it very powerful. One of its first actions was to return to the Gold Standard, a decision which was to store up much trouble for Labour later, but which the conventional economists of the time considered inevitable. It seemed to the less conventional economist John Maynard Keynes that it was done for the benefit of city financiers, at the expense of the workers – especially miners. For a time Winston Churchill, the Chancellor of the Exchequer, seemed to agree, with words that might years later have stood as a rebuke to Margaret Thatcher: 'I would rather see finance less proud and industry more content.'[7] But in the end he bowed to conventional advice.

The decision contributed to reduced profits in the mining industry, and in the summer of 1925 the coal owners announced their intention to cut miners' pay. They argued that they were now losing £1m a month; the miners retorted that in the previous four years the owners had made profits of £58.4m. If they had shown any inclination to share the proceeds of the fat years with their workers, their workers might have been more sympathetic when the lean years came.

Arthur Cook tramped the country with a slogan that was to become famous: 'Not a minute on the day, not a penny off the pay.' And the government capitulated. It set up an enquiry under Sir Herbert Samuel, and meanwhile mine owners would get a subsidy sufficient to pay the miners.

It was a great victory for the unions. But the subsidy was to run out on 1 May 1926. What would happen then? Scotland Yard's Special Branch predicted bloody revolution orchestrated from Moscow. There

7

were excitable voices in the unions and the Labour Party predicting not just victory for the miners but a better world. Ernest Bevin, General Secretary of the Transport and General Workers' Union and Britain's leading trade unionist, tried hard to insist that, if it came to a general strike, it would be solely an industrial matter, not a political one, but few people on either side believed him.

The Samuel Report, when it appeared, solved nothing – but it had bought the government a year in which to prepare for the general strike that most people now considered inevitable. Prime Minister Stanley Baldwin made it clear that the subsidy would not be extended, and the mine owners said that without the subsidy there would be pay cuts and longer hours. Baldwin's last-minute attempt at compromise was rejected by the Cabinet.

The day the subsidy ran out, a meeting of the executives of every trade union affiliated to the TUC voted almost unanimously to support the miners with a general strike, to begin at midnight on 3 May.

The Conservative Party saw the general strike as an attempt to overthrow the state, and was intent on a showdown which would put the working class in its place for a generation. This attitude was reflected in the government's newspaper for the strike, run by Churchill and called the *British Gazette*. Its attacks on the TUC were extreme and unrestrained, in keeping with Churchill's belief that the strike was an attempt at revolution. The TUC's answer was the *British Worker*. It had just four pages – the *Gazette* had nearly all the newsprint available – and was run with nothing like the same flair. Where the government was well prepared and well organized, the TUC was faltering and inefficient.

The TUC knew that abandoning the miners as they had done in 1921 would split the unions and the Labour Party, probably for ever, and destroy their political and industrial effectiveness. But TUC leaders feared the perception that this was a political struggle, not an industrial one, for most union leaders, then as now, were not at all revolutionary.

As it was to show again in 1984, the British government, when it feels the need, can operate efficiently to defeat a threat to the established order, even if it means adopting measures that in peaceable times it would consider dangerously socialistic. Churchill was allowed to confiscate newsprint in order to produce the *British Gazette*. The BBC was effectively commandeered as an instrument of the state: it refused to broadcast anything from the unions or the Labour Party. Churchill emphasized the supposed threat to the state by making the army highly visible. Army and navy leave was dramatically cancelled. Britain's leading Communists, including Harry Pollitt, were sent to prison for 'seditious libel and incitement to mutiny', probably because the government massively overestimated the organizing ability of the infant Communist Party and believed it capable of turning the general strike into a revolution.

TUC leaders, privately horrified, searched for a way out, and grabbed like drowning men at the chance of negotiations through the medium of the enquiry chairman, Sir Herbert Samuel. The return-to-work formula they agreed on 12 May, against the wishes of the miners' leadership, was effectively a capitulation. Cook made one last appeal to the TUC General Council: 'Gentlemen, I know the sacrifice you have made. You do not want to bring the miners down. Gentlemen, don't do it.' But they did.

The TUC capitulated on the basis of a vague assurance by Sir Herbert Samuel that, provided the general strike was called off, negotiations on miners' pay and conditions would resume – an assurance that was soon afterwards disowned by the Prime Minister. 'Surrender!' was the triumphant banner headline in the *British Gazette*.

Many trade unions were left on the edge of bankruptcy, and their membership plummeted. Employers took advantage of their weakness to cut wages, and high unemployment meant that workers had no choice but to accept those wages. Their leaders began openly to attack the MFGB leaders who they believed had brought these troubles upon them, and Cook in particular.

The miners stayed out for another seven months, resenting the other unions for abandoning them, bitterly angry with those miners who had worked – had 'scabbed' on the dispute – and impotently angry at the growing triumphalism of the mine owners, who extracted a terrible price from their defeated workforce. The government no longer felt under threat, and put through a Bill requiring the miners to work eight-hour shifts. Arthur Cook tried to get the railway unions not to handle coal, but was abruptly turned down.

Cook saw the way things were going and desperately sought a way out, in order to lessen the sacrifice he had to demand of his members. He met Prime Minister Stanley Baldwin on 31 May. This is one of the most startling differences between him and Scargill, who sometimes liked to consider himself Cook's natural successor: Scargill never contemplated such a course, and took care to distance himself from the TUC leaders who, at a similar stage in 1985, met Margaret Thatcher. No doubt Scargill wished to avoid being outflanked on the left, which is what happened to Cook.

Cook was not only attacked by his old friends in the Communist Party: he also faced the wrath of an angry young miners' activist from South Wales called Aneurin Bevan, who told him: 'We say there are possibilities and probabilities of more favourable terms in the near future.' But Cook knew there were not, and wrote in a press statement in June: 'Is it not time, I ask, to declare an armistice?' A settlement could be conducted after an end to the dispute had been declared: 'Such a scheme could be worked out, while the men are working, in a spirit of fair play.' So it could – but only if the government felt like showing magnanimity to a defeated opponent, and it did not.

Cook told a special MFGB conference on 30 July: 'I don't like the Samuel Report – I hate it – but it is not a question of likes and dislikes. It is a question of determining how strong we are to get what we want . . . Is it leadership to sit still and drift, drift to disaster?' Later he told miners in Porth: 'It is not cowardice to face the facts of a situation, and I say that a leader who leads men blindly when he knows different is not only a traitor to himself and his own conscience, but he is betraying the men he is leading.' Cook even entered into secret negotiations, which, when they were revealed two years later, got him into serious trouble with his union.[8]

The President of the MFGB, Herbert Smith, took a more intractable position, and may have made a settlement impossible. Cook was the miners' only full-time official and, unlike Arthur Scargill sixty years later, was not able to share out the work of detailed negotiation and presentation and leave himself free to fulfil the very heavy public speaking programme he took on. The huge rallies Cook addressed every day took a heavy toll on his voice and strength. He collapsed a couple of times, and seems never to have recovered his health fully. An anti-strike demonstrator kicked him in Chelmsford, causing an old mining injury to flare up, but he refused to stop work to get it treated, with the result that five years later, in 1931, the leg had to be amputated.

His health was not helped by his insistence on sharing his members' sacrifices. He refused to take his salary, accepting only the lockout pay that his members were getting. 'Part of his brain told Cook that the miners would be beaten,' writes his most recent biographer. 'The rest of his body, particularly his heart and guts, told him they must fight.'[9]

He created a newspaper, *The Miner*, which was an instant success in the coalfields, the first issue selling 60,000, the second 80,000 and the third 110,000. In the first issue he wrote: 'Shall the miners be beaten by starvation? . . . The weapon of the capitalists is starvation. Shall the cry of a child for food break the hearts of Britain's strongest men?'[10] But his union's funds were near exhaustion. The Soviet miners' union secretly sent huge sums of money, as they were to do in 1984–5 – about two thirds of all the money available to the MFGB – which, whatever evils are attributed to Moscow gold, undoubtedly saved the lives of many starving British children whose own government was prepared calmly to watch their suffering.

Another sombre precursor of the 1984–5 strike came in November. Nottinghamshire miners' leader George Spencer had been expelled from the MFGB for advocating surrender, and set up a breakaway union, the Nottinghamshire Miners' Industrial Union. Now Spencer began local negotiations for an end to the strike, and the drift back to work in Derbyshire, Nottinghamshire, Warwickshire and Staffordshire became a torrent. Only South Wales, Yorkshire and Durham stayed out, and they went back by the end of the month, on harsh conditions imposed by vengeful coal owners.

It was, as Cook feared, the near starvation of their wives and children that at last forced the miners back to work, on lower wages and with longer hours. By the time they went back, the rest of the country had started to forget. But miners never forgot. Thirty years later, in 1956, the members of the miners' club in Goldthorpe, South Yorkshire, voted by 90 votes to 36 not to re-admit men who had 'scabbed' on the 1926 strike.[11]

Cook knew that he had been defeated and had to rebuild his union, and put renewed activity into the Labour Party, ignoring as best he could the studied insults of Labour leader Ramsay MacDonald, and producing a manifesto together with James Maxton, the leader of the Independent Labour Party.

The most active union men were not allowed to go back to work. Their union could not protect them from this victimization, and, with high unemployment, their families starved, though again many of them were saved by Soviet gold. There was widespread destitution and malnutrition in pit villages. When starving men turned up in the union's London offices, and the union had nothing to offer them, Cook gave them money he could not afford from his own pocket.

At the 1929 general election, Baldwin's government went down to defeat and Ramsay MacDonald became Prime Minister for the second time, but still without an overall parliamentary majority. Cook now knew that a Labour government represented the only realistic way for him to get a better deal for his members. He had no more time for Ramsay MacDonald than did the Communist Party or the Independent Labour Party, which now formed the left-wing opposition to MacDonald in Parliament. He thought, as they did, that MacDonald was a weak, vain man, and the working class had little to hope for from him. But MacDonald headed a Labour government pledged to repeal the eight hours act, and getting action on that pledge was the only hope Cook could see. If the price was buttering up the hated MacDonald, it was a price he was prepared to pay. He even agreed to speak for the Labour leader against his Communist opponent Harry Pollitt in MacDonald's own constituency, forgetting all the sneers MacDonald had heaped on him. For his pains, Cook was branded a renegade by his old friends in the Communist Party. His reward for humbling himself was a Bill for a seven-and-a-half-hour day, which was almost completely wrecked by the House of Lords and never properly implemented, and the enmity of some of his oldest friends on the left. He died two years later.

But he was realistic and right. Not only had his union been decisively defeated, but unions are always in a poor bargaining position when there is high unemployment. New employment was located mostly in the south of England. In the old industrial heartlands of South Wales, the West of Scotland, Lancashire, Tyneside and West Yorkshire, unemployment never fell below a million in the 1920s and remained at between 40 per cent and 60 per cent, sometimes even 80 per cent, during the 1930s, made worse by the great crash that hit Wall Street in 1929 and arrived in London in force in 1931. This also produced a decline in trade union membership, from around six and a half million in 1920 to its lowest point in the interwar years of three and a quarter million in 1933, after which it started slowly to rise again.

The 1931 financial crisis brought down the Labour government, but MacDonald left the Labour Party to become Prime Minister of a National government which was, in effect, a Conservative government in which Conservative leader Stanley Baldwin was the key figure – and four years later Baldwin replaced MacDonald in Downing Street.

In September 1934, the Gresford pit in Denbighshire suffered an explosion which took the lives of 265 men and boys. As a result the MFGB was able to get a Royal Commission on mine safety, at a time when mine accidents were increasing fast: in the mid-1930s there were 134 deaths per 100,000 miners. The resulting discontent produced a huge vote for strike action in November 1935 which brought about some pay improvements.

The MFGB was strengthened by the discovery that wages were lowest in Nottinghamshire, heart of George Spencer's breakaway union, the only union now recognized in Nottinghamshire. In 1936 miners at Harworth colliery in Nottinghamshire who were members of the MFGB came out on strike for recognition. It lasted for six months and was one of the bitterest strikes in even the miners' bitter history, with furious clashes between miners and police. The MFGB Branch President, Mick Kane, was sentenced to two years' imprisonment with hard labour. Eleven miners and one miner's wife were given sentences ranging from four to fifteen months' jail with hard labour. But it weakened the hold of the Spencer union, which agreed to open negotiations on returning to the MFGB. At first, acrimony was so great that the deal was rejected in a ballot of MFGB members, but in 1937 the Spencer union returned to the fold. The merger terms allowed George Spencer to become President of the Nottinghamshire miners within the MFGB.

This might sound like a good thing for the miners' union, but that is not how the miners' union sees it today. There is now, once again, a breakaway union in Nottinghamshire, the legacy of the 1984–5 strike; and the union's own official account of its history blames the defeat of the 1984–5 miners' strike on the return to the fold of the Spencer union in 1937. It brought back, says the website, 'both the perspective and apparatus which had engineered disastrous division in 1926. The nature of Spencerism thus re-entered the body politic of the MFGB, where it would remain in later years as part of the National Union of Mineworkers.'

It sounds, as in its worst moments the miners' union often does, as though it has taken to heart the phrase often (wrongly) attributed to Lenin: 'Fewer but better Russians.' However, the NUM version of events as the Second World War started cannot seriously be challenged. 'The outbreak of war', they say, 'exposed the coal owners' callous treatment of the vital energy source under their control. Indiscriminate colliery closures, investment starvation, safety standards ignored – these were the hallmarks of private ownership. Consequently, when with the onset of war the Government needed a dramatic increase in coal production, the privately held industry had been ill-equipped to meet demand.'[12]

Miners were asked to strain every sinew to put this right for the war effort, and to teach the 'Bevin boys' – young men conscripted to work down the mines in the same way as other young men were conscripted as soldiers. They did what was asked of them, with very little disruption except for a strike in 1944 which obtained a national minimum wage; but they made it clear that they expected their reward to be nationalization after the war.

The same year as the strike, long and careful negotiations between the regions that made up the MFGB resulted in amalgamation of the autonomous unions into one national union. The founding conference of the National Union of Mineworkers was held, ironically perhaps, in Nottingham.

The NUM's first great victory was to ensure that the Labour Party went into the 1945 election pledged to nationalize the mines. The 1945–51 Labour government under Clement Attlee was the only great reforming government the Labour Party has ever produced, and every part of the Attlee settlement improved the lives of miners, despite the grim economic circumstances. It took its agenda from the 1942 Beveridge Report, in which Sir William Beveridge called for a serious assault on the 'five giants' – Want, Disease, Ignorance, Squalor and Idleness; and it believed in a strong public sector, with essential services like coal and rail in public ownership.

Aneurin Bevan, the son of a South Wales miner, the young man who had condemned Arthur Cook for preparing to settle in 1926, was the man Attlee chose to slay Disease and Squalor: the housing minister who built millions of council houses, and the health minister who created the National Health Service. Under the NHS, men and women from mining communities no longer had to dread being unable to pay for the medical care they needed when they fell ill.

The 1944 Education Act was implemented in full, so that every citizen had the right to free schooling until they were fifteen, which within a generation more or less eliminated illiteracy in mining communities. Under the National Insurance Act and the Industrial Injuries Act, both of them the responsibility of another minister from a Welsh mining family, Jim Griffiths, a man no longer had to fear actual starvation for his family if he lost his job or could not work because of injury. Nationalization of the mines was accompanied by nationalization of the railways, electricity, gas, inland waterways, steel and the Bank of England.

The Coal Industry Nationalization Act was one of the Attlee government's first acts. It was not easy to frame it and turn it into legislation, and a lesser government than Attlee's might have given up the struggle. Fuel and power minister Emanuel Shinwell complained that despite having talked about it for years, Labour had not given serious thought to how it was to be done. A scheme had to be devised from scratch, and Shinwell was given one of the brightest of the new generation of Labour MPs to help him, Hugh Gaitskell. It was Gaitskell who steered it through Parliament, with infinite care and patience, becoming the unlikely hero of nationalization.

On 1 January 1947, all the rights, assets and liabilities of the industry were transferred from the coal owners to the new National Coal Board. It was one of those gala days that mining communities did so well. Miners and their families marched behind banners and colliery bands to the pitheads, cheering, shouting, weeping. Plaques proclaimed: 'This colliery is now managed by the National Coal Board on behalf of the people.' They cheered and wept as the blue and white flag of the NCB was unfurled above them. They had waited a long time for this moment, and saw it as their time of liberation from a sort of slavery, and from domination of their industry by bosses whom they considered both greedy and lazy. Now they would be treated properly, and they would be happier in their work, for they knew they would be working for the common good. As though to reassure them that this would indeed happen, two trade union leaders were appointed to the NCB, Walter Citrine of the TUC and Ebby Edwards of the NUM.

Coal, as Peter Hennessy puts it, had 'never lost its symbolic, almost romantic place in the Labour movement as the industry where the excesses of capitalism had left blood in the seams.'[13] Its nationalization was, the miners believed, the dawn of a new world, freer, fresher, fairer; a world in which men would no longer have to fear that their pittance of a wage would not keep their families; where people, not profits, would matter.

The investment-starved industry saw new capital. The NCB's duty now was to provide Britain with adequate supplies of fuel, not to make higher profits than a competitor. For most miners, nationalization, at first at any rate, did what it said on the tin. Miners could start planning for all the things they had once only been able to dream of, and the NUM's Miners' Charter called for modernization, the sinking of new pits, training, safety laws, compensation payments for industrial injury and disease, a five-day week without loss of pay, pensions at the age of fifty-five, and construction of new towns and villages with good housing in mining areas.

They were living at last in a world where all these things seemed possible, and they started to get them. A 1947 agreement gave miners the five-day week they had sought for so long, and their wages began, at last, to go up steadily, until by 1950 they were at the top of the industrial wages league, giving miners' families for the first time a standard of living to match that of other industrial workers.

There were those in the NUM who regretted that the managers in the NCB were often the same people who had managed the privately owned mines; who complained that private ownership had been replaced by state rather than common ownership; and who felt bitter that compensation had been paid to the former owners who had exploited the miners for decades. There were those, both in the NUM and the NCB, who felt that the government shackled the home-grown mining industry unfairly. Many miners felt the terms of nationalization left the NCB competing with one hand tied behind its back. They complained that the profitable ancillary industries – distribution, the manufacture and supply of equipment and machinery – were left in private hands.

But in the immediate aftermath of nationalization, these voices were lost in the general euphoria. The NUM even agreed – as it would never have done for the private coal owners – that, with the country desperate for coal, miners would work a sixth shift voluntarily on a Saturday, even though a five-day week had been agreed. There was unhappiness among the miners about it, but, as Britain went into the freezing winter of 1947 with a looming economic crisis, they could see the need for it. Shinwell and food minister John Strachey were the targets of a popular Conservative slogan that year: 'Starve with Strachey and shiver with Shinwell.'

Nationalization had been so long hoped for that it was unlikely to bear the weight of expectation it aroused. And as oil from the Middle East started to become a realistic alternative energy source, and nuclear energy started to look like a long-term possibility, the government initiated pit closure programmes, and the miners' goodwill began to dissipate. In the ten years after nationalization there were several local strikes, and unease grew through the 1950s as the nation, for the first time, started to become less reliant on coal; the Conservative government under Winston Churchill which displaced Attlee's government in 1951 talked increasingly of moving away from coal and towards oil and nuclear power. By 1956, to its cost, the government was relying heavily on oil from the Middle East. Scotland, South Wales, Northumberland and Durham all lost about a third of their pits.

Still, the miners were better paid than their fathers had been, and governments of both political parties carefully cultivated their leaders. The return of Churchill as Prime Minister revived memories of the harsh Home Secretary in 1910 who had ordered the army to fire on striking miners, and the authoritarian Chancellor in 1926 who had run the *British Gazette*, but Churchill in 1951 was in no mood to seek confrontation with the unions. 'I've settled with the miners,' he once told his

Chancellor, R.A. Butler. 'Really, Prime Minister?' said Butler. 'On whose terms?' 'Theirs, of course,' replied Churchill. 'Dammit, one must have electric light.'

So the battle with the government, predicted by Arthur Horner, the NUM's Communist General Secretary until 1959, never materialized. Instead the miners' President, Sir William Lawther, knighted by Attlee and a far more emollient figure than Horner, outraged his members by attending Churchill's birthday celebrations and denouncing industrial action for political ends as 'a great evil'.

In the Harold Macmillan years, from 1957 until 1964, 264 collieries closed and the number of miners in Britain fell by nearly a third, while their wages gradually slipped behind inflation. This caused far less trouble than might have been expected, partly because the Macmillan government took care to ensure that redundancy was achieved with some care for the lives of the men whose jobs were lost, and in close consultation with the union. With a Thatcher in Downing Street and a Scargill at the head of the NUM, things might have been very different, but, like Churchill before him, Macmillan had no desire to fall out with the unions, which he thought a valid component of a democratic state, even if in practice he looked down on them in a patrician and rather snobbish way. He confided with amusement to his diary that, when they came to see him, TUC leaders 'all behaved beautifully and were so respectable, with their dark blue suits and bowlers, that they looked like a lot of undertakers'. He 'distributed various "secret" documents to them – which they seemed to like'. He sent them away happy, presumably patting them kindly on their heads and giving them each a shiny new sixpence.

The arrival of a Labour government under Harold Wilson in 1964, after thirteen Conservative years, did little to slow down the programme. This was a major disappointment to the NUM, which thought it had a deal with the Labour Party, entered into when the Party was in opposition, to expand the industry as part of its fuel policy. Three hundred more pits were closed by Harold Wilson's Labour government, and the workforce slumped from more than 750,000 in the late 1950s to 320,000 by 1968. Just before the general strike, the MFGB had had 900,000 members.

That, according to the militants in the NUM, was when miners should have gone on strike to stop pit closures. But they did not. Pit closures forced miners to move from coalfield to coalfield in search of secure jobs. The NUM opposed the policy with lobbies and campaigns. It said repeatedly that depending on imported energy from the Middle East was economic madness; but there was no strike action until the late 1960s.

The move back to militancy mirrored what was going on in the rest of the unions, for, where the sixties were not swinging, they were insurrectionary instead. On 5 August 1967, in Sheffield, left-wing militants in the NUM met together for the first time, calling themselves the left caucus, to co-ordinate tactics throughout the country in order to ensure that another left-winger was elected General Secretary when Will Paynter retired at the end of 1968. They were concerned that the job, occupied for so long by one of their own – for Paynter had succeeded the left-winger Arthur Horner – might be captured by the right: the trade unionists who believed the road to improvement was the tortuous one of talking to government, not the direct one of fighting for justice industrially. One of the Yorkshire representatives on the left caucus was the youthful Arthur Scargill, whose career was already being carefully nurtured by the Communist Party, determined to wrest control of the Yorkshire coalfield from the right and the compromisers.

The caucus chose as its candidate Lawrence Daly, one of the most attractive and colourful characters the trade unions ever produced. He was a former miner from Fife and, like many mining union leaders, a self-taught intellectual who knew reams of poetry by heart – not just Rabbie Burns, though that was his favourite – and could recite it with passion and feeling, especially when he was drunk. (One of the authors treasures the memory of standing with Daly on Euston station at midnight, some time in the early seventies, after a long session in the pub, and reciting the whole of Act 1, Scene 2, of *Julius Caesar*. First Daly played Brutus, then they changed parts and he played Cassius.) Short, thick-set, naturally intelligent, entertaining, Daly was also an inspiring orator, and a militant trade unionist who used to say: 'We only get what we are strong enough to take.'

By that time the NUM had achieved a common wage agreement, so that all miners everywhere were paid the same for doing the same job. Now, instead of a series of local disputes about local wage rates, came the threat of national strike action over the hours that surface workers had to put in. At the union's national conference in October 1969, Arthur Scargill had proposed a strike – and, against the opposition of the National Executive, the proposal was carried overwhelmingly. The strike was unofficial, but thousands of miners came out. The strike saw the first use of flying pickets, and in some areas, notably Yorkshire, no mining took place at all for the whole of the two weeks that it lasted.

Judged by its avowed aims, it was not a success. The eight-hour day for surface workers, its ostensible objective, was not achieved. But the union's left wing had a deeper purpose. What they were interested in was who was to run the union in the future, and the strike immeasurably strengthened their position inside the NUM. So the face-saving return-to-work deal put together by TUC General Secretary Vic Feather as the strike began to collapse is still presented, in the official NUM history, as a victory for militancy and Arthur Scargill. 'It was clear that the union was never, ever, going to be the same again,' he said afterwards.[14] The right wing in the union, Paul Routledge writes, 'were being outflanked and outmanoeuvred by younger, smarter, more politically committed miners'.[15] The same thing was happening in other trade unions, but the miners were leading the way.

Daly's victory ensured that the left had the general secretaryship, and in 1971 came the chance to capture the presidency as well – the job that included being the union's chief negotiator. The left candidate was probably the most liked and respected Communist in Britain, Mick McGahey. McGahey had a voice that sounded as though it was filtered through thick, dense layers of coal dust, tobacco and scotch whisky, which it was, for to a hard youth in the pit he added a lifetime of chain-smoking and whisky drinking. He was clever, sociable and emotional, and never looked entirely happy in the union official's uniform of dark suit, white shirt and tie, though he always wore it – the tie never quite done up, the glasses perched just above their rightful place on his ears.

Joe Gormley, the candidate proposed by the right wing in the union, shared McGahey's sociability but little else. He was a clever negotiator from Lancashire, chubby, cheerful, likeable and cunning. The right, still smarting from their defeat at the hands of Daly and aware that they were less well organized than the left, put everything they had into Gormley's campaign. Helped by a fear that the union would be run by two left-wing Scots, Gormley won a massive victory.

Harold Wilson's Labour government was unexpectedly beaten in the 1970 election, and a Conservative government under Edward Heath faced the growing unrest and militancy in the coalfields. The 1971 NUM conference demanded substantial pay rises and called for strike action if they were not conceded. It also took a decision that was to have momentous consequences: it lowered the percentage in the ballot required for calling an official national strike from two thirds to 55 per cent.

Its demands were not conceded, and for the first time since 1926 a national coal strike was called. It went to a ballot, and the vote only just made the new ballot margin – the percentage was just 58.8: before the 1971 conference they could not have called the strike. But this time the NUM faced a government far less well prepared than in 1926, and far more vulnerable, and it started its strike in the depth of winter, on 9 January 1972, so that the lack of coal bit quickly. The strike looked like a winner from the start. There was enough coal to last eight weeks, but solidarity action from other unions stopped it being moved, encouraged by NUM flying pickets who went to power stations, docks, ports and wharves all over Britain. The mines themselves did not require pickets, for, despite the narrowness of the strike ballot, not a single miner broke the strike. No one ever shouted 'scab', for there was no one to shout it at.

Joe Gormley, having opposed the strike, was determined once it was called to win it. Lawrence Daly's Scottish charm was set to work on the middle classes. Lord Lambton had just resigned from the government in disgrace after revelations about his association with prostitutes, and Daly told his audiences that the miners' pay claim was rather less than 'government ministers are willing to pay to ladies of easy virtue, for what I understand is considerably less than an eight-hour shift.'

Exactly a month after the start of the strike, Heath was forced to declare a state of emergency, as voltage had to be reduced across the national grid; a few days later he agreed to set up a public inquiry into miners' wages. He tried to persuade the miners to go back to work while it was sitting, but memories are long in the mining community, and just saying the words 'Samuel Commission, 1926' was enough to persuade the miners that they were not going to go back without a satisfactory settlement.

So Lord Wilberforce, the enquiry chairman, was told to work at breakneck speed, and he did: his report was completed in just two days. He was also under pressure to find a way to pay the miners enough to get them back to work, and he managed that too. The day after the settlement, miners carried Lawrence Daly shoulder-high through Mansfield in Nottinghamshire.

The strike had another effect, of even longer-term significance than the NUM victory. Before it, no one outside Yorkshire and delegates to NUM conferences had heard of Arthur Scargill. By the end of it he was on the way to being a household name. He was credited (wrongly) with having invented flying pickets. Journalists loved him: he was dashing, fluent and quotable, and happy to talk up his own role.

'We took the view that we were in a class war,' he told *New Left Review*. 'We were not playing cricket on the village green, like they did in '26.' He told the *Observer* Colour Supplement that in Barnsley he ran a 'strike operations room' like a military headquarters, with a map showing ports, power stations, steelworks and mines, and from there he despatched pickets 'like shock troops'.[16]

But what really made his name was what became known as the Battle of Saltley Gates. On 7 February Scargill heard that police were allowing lorries to take coke from a depot in Saltley, Birmingham. He led 400 Yorkshire miners to the gates of the depot. The battle between police and miners raged for three days, while television cameras recorded every twist and turn and Scargill directed his men through a mega-phone. After three days, the lorries were still moving coke, 100 pickets were in jail and fifty were in hospital. So with the help of his old friend and mentor Frank Watters, now the Communist Party's man in Birmingham, he persuaded local unions in the city to call a one-day strike. Thousands more miners came, from all over the country. The Chief Constable took an instant decision: he closed the gates, as Scargill wanted.

That was the day the government appointed a Court of Enquiry, which is the basis of the myth that Scargill and Saltley won the strike for the NUM. In fact, though Saltley's symbolic importance was enormous, its practical importance was not that great, and the course of the strike was probably not much affected. The coke heap in Saltley, which was a fraction of the size Scargill claimed, would have been used up in a fort-night.[17] It was not, as Scargill seems to believe, the turning point of the strike, but it was the turning point of his career. It may also have been the moment in which he began to believe in his own invincibility. 'All I ever hoped for, in unionism and solidarity, all I've dreamed of, came true on February 10 at Saltley in Birmingham. I cried that day.'[18]

After it he was elected to his first full-time union job, as Yorkshire's compensation agent: the person who assembles a case to show that a miner's illness is due to an industrial disease like pneumoconiosis, and he is therefore entitled to compensation. He was very good at it. Whatever else he did or didn't do with his life, a lot of miners in Yorkshire owe their relative comfort in illness to Scargill's skill, fluent advocacy, determination and hard work.

Soon afterwards he was elected to the National Executive, and in 1973 became President of the Yorkshire miners, just as another strike was in the offing. The value of what they had won looked like being eroded by the government's incomes policy. This time there was an added pressure on the government: the Yom Kippur war in the Middle East, which drove up oil prices. Gormley and Edward Heath met secretly to try to work out a formula for a settlement, and Gormley used all his considerable negotiating skills to extract enough to avoid conflict.

Of all the executive members, Scargill was the most ferociously determined to take the dispute to a strike, and to scupper the efforts of his President to avert one. The TUC tried to broker a deal, but a strike ballot was set for 1 February, returning the largest majority for a strike in the union's history: 81 per cent. The strike was called for 9 February, and before it began Heath called a general election for 28 February.

Heath stood on the platform 'Who governs Britain?' A victory in the election would be interpreted by the government as a mandate to stand firm against the miners, and the voters knew it. He wrote to Joe Gormley, asking that the strike be suspended during the election campaign. If it had been just up to Gormley, this would have been agreed, for apart from sympathizing with the Prime Minister's point of view, Gormley was wise in the ways of public relations, and knew that refusing the Prime Minister's request would count against Labour in the election. But he was overturned by his National Executive.

This time Heath declared a state of emergency straightaway, and limited industry to a three-day week. Shops and offices could not use electricity into the evening, and television channels had to close down no later than 10.30 p.m.

Labour's election victory was desperately narrow. The miners came close to disaster in 1974. But Labour's victory made possible a swift conclusion to negotiations with Wilson's new Secretary of State for Employment, Michael Foot. The new government, the NCB and the unions set about agreeing a long-term strategy for the industry: the Plan for Coal, which set both short-term (150m tonnes per year) and long-term (200m tonnes per year) production targets for the industry. The NUM was delighted. It was a plan for a booming, optimistic industry of the future, not the grimy old smokestack industry ready only for slow dismantlement, which was how they felt governments had seen it until then. During the 1970s new coalfields were opened such as Selby in Yorkshire, along with drift mines in various parts of Britain. For the first time in two decades, investment poured into the industry. And the miners' disease – the black dust, pneumoconiosis – was tackled on a large scale for the first time, with over £200m going into a scheme for its victims.

It was, however, the unions that at last brought Labour down in 1979. By then Wilson had resigned. His successor, James Callaghan, tried hard to make the deal with the unions over wage rises stick, but the huge public sector strikes of the winter of 1978–9 were fatal to his electoral prospects. Margaret Thatcher was elected at the head of a far more radical Conservative government than Britain had ever known.

CHAPTER 2

ENTER THATCHER, STAGE RIGHT, AND SCARGILL, STAGE LEFT

Margaret Thatcher, and the philosophy she stood for, did not spring on the world new-minted in the 1970s. Hers was a strand of thinking in the Conservative Party which can be traced back at least as far as 1957, the first year of Harold Macmillan's premiership, when Peter Thorneycroft resigned as Chancellor of the Exchequer along with his Financial Secretary Enoch Powell and his Economic Secretary Nigel Birch. These three men stood for a new brand of Conservatism, distinguished at first by their convictions that money supply had to be controlled and inflation kept down with low wage settlements, and the free market was the key to both prosperity and freedom itself. They had no patience with the patrician way in which Macmillan humoured and, in their eyes, appeased the unions and regarded them as having a legitimate voice in the state. In future years the battle lines lengthened to embrace the Atlantic alliance and the European Union.

Macmillan won that first battle, riding with seemingly effortless ease the storm that Thorneycroft, Powell and Birch hoped to whip up. But his protégé Edward Heath lost the last battle, ejected from the leadership of his Party by Margaret Thatcher in 1975, a year after losing the general election.

Like all politicians who actually change the world – such as that other great change-maker of the twentieth century, Clement Attlee –

the grocer's daughter from Grantham had very clear and precise ideas about how a country should be run. 'It is not government, but free enterprise, which is capable of creating wealth, providing jobs and raising living standards' – so away with the strong public sector of the Attlee settlement, and in particular away with nationalization. Talking of herself and Ronald Reagan, she said: 'Our belief in the virtues of hard work and enterprise led us to cut taxes. Our belief in private property led to the sale of state industries . . . Our belief in sound money led to the monetarist policies that attacked inflation . . .'[1] It could all hardly be clearer.

That is why Margaret Thatcher's victory in the 1979 election was a watershed. It marked the end of the Attlee settlement of Britain's affairs, which had endured for more than thirty years, and the start of a new and very different settlement that is still with us. No one under forty knows what it is like to live in a country where trade unions are a force in the land; where the public sector is a recognized and respected player in the economy; where the idea of a job for life is not meant as an insult; where heavy industry and those who work in it are considered vital to the British economy. That was Britain before the 1984–5 miners' strike, the moment when Clement Attlee's Britain turned into Margaret Thatcher's Britain: a Britain in which heavy industry – the smokestack industries, as they were called – gave way to service industries like call centres and distribution centres; in which the strong public sector of the Attlee settlement was humiliated and almost all its powers handed to businesses, charities and churches.

Thatcher's Britain was also one in which the extraordinary limitations on people's freedom of movement that were imposed during the strike brought Britain nearer to civil war than it has come for 400 years. The borders of one county, Nottinghamshire, were effectively closed. Before 1984, the idea of police stopping a coach-load of people for no other purpose than to prevent them attending a lawful demonstration would have seemed an appalling affront to free speech. Since then, it has become almost routine.

In 1979 it looked as though one aspect of Thatcher policy would be an attempt to gain revenge on the miners for their defeat of Edward Heath in 1974, *pour encourager les autres* – as a means of ensuring that the unions knew who the boss was. The outcome of the conflict, and whether it would be a skirmish or an out-and-out war, would depend largely on the nature of the leadership teams chosen by both sides, and on the preliminary skirmishing. Those fateful decisions were made between 1979 and 1983.

Sir Keith Joseph, who headed the right-wing Centre for Policy Studies, had been given the job of drawing up and researching fresh policies for the new government in Thatcher's Shadow Cabinet. He embraced the monetarist theories of Milton Friedman, which were to sweep away much of British industry in the 1980s, and he helped shape the Thatcher government's social Conservatism, attacking single parents for fecklessness in a way that would be anathema today to Tories like David Cameron.

Sir Keith was given a major role by Thatcher in the writing of the Conservative manifesto for the 1979 election. But the manifesto itself was a tepid affair with no hint of the radical revolution on the way. It reflected Thatcher's still weak position among the party's grandees and what were to be known as the 'wets': the Tories who followed Heath in backing the postwar consensus, like James Prior and Peter Walker.

While promising crackdowns on picketing, the closed shop and un-official strikes, the manifesto said that a 'strong and responsible trade union movement could play a big part in our economic recovery.' Its only reference to the coal industry was: 'We believe that a competitive and efficient coal industry has an important role in meeting energy demand, together with a proper contribution from nuclear power. All energy developments raise important environmental issues, and we shall ensure the fullest public participation in major new decisions.'

The manifesto ended with a passage that seemed designed to avoid frightening the horses – the Labour and Liberal Democrat voters who might be tempted, because of the winter of discontent, to vote Tory. 'We make no lavish promises. The repeated disappointment of rising expectations has led to a marked loss of faith in politicians' promises. Too much has gone wrong in Britain for us to hope to put it all right in a year or so. Many things will simply have to wait until the economy has been revived and we are once again creating the wealth on which so much else depends.'

Thatcher's first Cabinet reflected this moderation. Sir Keith got the Industry job so that he could start his work on bringing forward industries for privatization. But Heathite James Prior became Employment Secretary with responsibility for bringing in new trade union legislation. Other prominent wets in the Cabinet included Lord Carrington at the Foreign Office, Sir Geoffrey Howe as Chancellor, Francis Pym at Defence, Willie Whitelaw at the Home Office, Peter Walker at Agriculture, and Sir Ian Gilmour as Lord Privy Seal. The 'drys', the out-and-out Thatcherites, were few: they included John Biffen, Chief Secretary to the Treasury, Lord Young, minister without portfolio, and David Howell, the Energy Secretary.

Howell's immediate preoccupation was nuclear power. A memo from him to a Cabinet committee chaired by Thatcher on 23 October 1979 proposed a programme of new nuclear power stations, which, he told his colleagues, would have the advantage of removing a substantial proportion of electricity production from the danger of disruption by industrial action by miners or transport workers.[2] But that would only be a long-term solution. In the short term there were to be other plans.

Meanwhile at the Department of Industry Sir Keith was about to meet Ian MacGregor, who had been approached by the government to take over British Steel. MacGregor, already sixty-seven in 1979, was not sure who recommended him. He thought it could have been Jim Prior, whose son, David, worked alongside him at the US investment bank Lazard Frères in New York, or the Tory donor and biscuit king Sir Hector Laing. Perhaps, he thought, the idea came from Sir Keith himself.[3] The appointment in 1980 was highly controversial and led to a row in the Commons when it was revealed that the deal included paying Lazards some £875,000 compensation for the loss of his services, an astronomical sum in the early 1980s.[4]

MacGregor, though Scottish born, was seen as a highly controversial American figure. He had been appointed by Jim Callaghan in the previous Labour government as a part-time director of the ailing state giant British Leyland and became embroiled in a dispute with a shop steward whom the media dubbed 'Red Robbo'. He was no diplomat and sometimes rather crass in his dealings with people. He had a high opinion of himself and very strong views about streamlining loss-making companies by sacking staff; he was intolerant of anything smacking of organized labour. He seemed to represent everything that Thatcher stood for and admired.

His tenure at British Steel would deliver everything that Thatcher and Joseph wanted. When the Tories inherited the nationalized industry in 1979 it employed 166,000 staff and produced 14m tons of steel annually at a loss of £1.8 billion. MacGregor was remorseless in closing loss-making plants and creating large-scale redundancies. Most of the redundancies were voluntary but were made against a background of huge increases in unemployment, and they damaged many traditional steelworking communities. By 1983, there were only 71,000 staff, with losses cut to £256m.

The big trade union in the steel industry was the Iron and Steel Trades Confederation (ISTC), which did not have 100 per cent membership in the plants, and was led by the very moderate Bill Sirs. At the time of MacGregor's appointment the union was recovering from a thirteen-week strike which had got nowhere, and MacGregor went over the heads of the union by holding a ballot of the workforce, who agreed to his modernization plan, even though many were to lose their jobs.

Despite such industrial victories, the Thatcher government was by 1981 deeply unpopular. The opposition should have been making great headway, and would have done had Labour not been locked in internecine struggle. Unemployment was heading rapidly towards three million, inflation was rising (hitting 15 per cent that year) and the doubling of VAT had put even more upward pressure on prices following Geoffrey Howe's 1979 Budget. A statement from 364 distinguished economists said that Thatcher's new government had got everything wrong. At the beginning of 1981 it would have been an even bet to say Thatcher's experiment would not survive. But that year was to be the turning point. It is the key to how the Tories, against all odds in those dark winter days at the dawn of 1981, were to lay the ground for their fight against the miners.

David Howell, the Energy Secretary, finally admitted, after prevaricating throughout the life of the government, that the coal industry must face cuts. Despite high and rising unemployment, it must have seemed to the government that Ian MacGregor's success in forcing steelworkers to accept job losses and plant closures was a good omen for the coal industry. But at the NCB, instead of the brash US-trained MacGregor, the Chairman was a moderate figure with no love for making redundancies, Sir Derek Ezra. Howell's objective was to force Ezra's hand by cutting the cash limits within which the NCB had to operate. This left Sir Derek no option but to propose closures.

The number of closures, never officially published at the time, was to be twenty-three collieries; but the NUM's President, Joe Gormley, raised fury among his members by overestimating the total, talking of forty to fifty closures. The government in February 1981 had calculated that the union would hesitate to organize a walk-out, following the failed steelworkers' strike. But the NUM was not the ISTC and the collective memories of victory against the Heath government in the 1970s were embedded in the coal mining communities. Instead the NUM executive gave the NCB a week to withdraw the cuts and get the government to hand over extra cash. Joe Gormley warned some of the most militant miners in South Wales that they should not walk out without a strike ballot because the NCB could go to the courts and claim damages. But nobody listened. Within days, without a ballot or conference vote, half the miners were on strike, some of them in traditionally moderate areas such as Nottinghamshire and the West Midlands.

Ministers were genuinely shocked, particularly as they found coal stocks were low in the middle of winter, and they were in no position to fight the miners' demands. So they backed off. In February a hastily arranged meeting between Joe Gormley, some members of the NUM executive, the NCB and David Howell led to withdrawal of the plans and a promise to put any future plans for pit closures through a normal colliery review procedure. Thatcher let it be known, using the Parliamentary press lobby, that she had no wish to have a fight with the miners. It was nothing less than a Tory U-turn.

Kevin Barron, then a Yorkshire NUM militant, who was to campaign for Arthur Scargill to be the new NUM President, remembers the astonishment and the cheers in his local miners' club as they saw the announcement on television that the government had backed down in the face of unilateral and illegal action by the NUM. 'I couldn't believe what I was seeing on the TV screens,' he said.

His view was probably the dominant one among the miners but other, more sceptical leaders of the union were suspicious of what it might mean for the future. Mick McGahey, the Communist Vice-President of the NUM, saw it for what it was, a body swerve. Like many left-wing miners' leaders, McGahey had a great sense of history, and he compared it to the infamous Red Friday in 1925 when the government appeared to back down from a fight with the miners, only to regroup once it had gained a breathing space to take on the industry, and defeat it in the 1926 general strike. He guessed, correctly, that the need to back down in 1981 helped convince both Thatcher and Joseph that they must ultimately take on the miners and defeat them.

But first there had to be two other big changes that would help Thatcher gain the upper hand in dealing with the dispute. The first was outside her control but it was very helpful. On 26 March the Labour Party split when what became known as the 'Gang of Four' – former Labour Cabinet ministers Roy Jenkins, Shirley Williams, David Owen and Bill Rodgers – left to form the Social Democratic Party. The schism had been a long time coming, as under the leadership of Michael Foot Labour had become much more left-wing in response to the Thatcher government. Bitterness, backbiting and general viciousness between more right-wing members like the Manifesto Group and the left led by Tony Benn had become intolerable.

For Thatcher a divided opposition was a golden opportunity, and instead of trimming her policies, as many of the wet members of her Cabinet hoped, she took the opportunity to expand and entrench her allies, strengthening her wing of the Cabinet in a September reshuffle. There had already been a reshuffle in January which saw Pym removed from Defence and Leon Brittan brought into the Cabinet as Chief Secretary to the Treasury; the losers were clearly the wets, but this was the first major declaration of intent. Now three ministers disappeared: Sir Ian Gilmour, Lord Soames and Mark Carlisle. Others were demoted or moved from key posts, notably Jim Prior, who left his key post at Employment to go into semi-exile in Northern Ireland. He was replaced by the tougher Thatcherite Norman Tebbit. Nigel Lawson replaced David Howell at Energy and John Biffen took over Industry from Sir Keith Joseph, who went to Education.

With a new, reinvigorated team, Thatcher prepared for a potential miners' strike. A secret Cabinet committee was set up to organize how this would be done, and Peter Gregson, a Cabinet Office official with responsibility for industry, was asked to chair it. The Cabinet Office has confirmed that the committee code-named MISC57 was set up for this purpose but has refused to release its contents under the Freedom of Information Act. What is known is that Gregson was to become a trusted aide of the PM whose advice was freely given and sought during the dispute that was to follow.

Gregson is said by fellow civil servants Ivor Manley, Deputy Secretary at the Department of Energy at the time, and Andrew Turnbull, Thatcher's private secretary at Number Ten (who went on to be Cabinet Secretary under Tony Blair), to have been a devoted and professional civil servant who lived for his job. He was not married. He lived in South East London and worked long hours on any task that he was given. He was a tactician, able to see what was needed and give ministers valuable options when they needed them. Under instructions from Thatcher, Sir Keith Joseph, Nigel Lawson and Leon Brittan, he did a thorough job in helping the government prepare for an expected confrontation.

Ministers and civil servants put together a three-pronged approach. First, a decision was made to ensure that the government would never be caught out again with a shortfall of coal. More money was allowed (the opposite of the government cuts imposed on the NCB to encourage the first pit closures) to stockpile coal in advance of any action. There was also co-ordination over the delivery of supplies, with the Central Electricity Generating Board brought into the discussion to ensure that power stations would not be deprived of coal. The figures for coal stocks speak for themselves. In 1981 there were 39.34m tonnes; in 1984 at the time of the strike the figure had risen to 48.7m tonnes.

The same committee also examined the prospect of expanding dual oil- and coal-fired power stations to ensure security of supply, even though oil was more expensive and the cost of converting power stations was enormous.

The second prong was the need for tough policing. The government was acutely aware of how the young miners' leader Arthur Scargill, then a rising star in Yorkshire, had helped break the government during the picketing over Saltley coke depot. So preparations were drawn up for the revival of the Scotland Yard National Reporting Centre, with talks with the Association of Chief Police Officers (ACPO), which was to be critical during the strike. The aim was swift and effective co-ordination of police forces to handle any flying pickets, a tactic that was to prove invaluable.

Finally there was a strengthening of anti-strike laws, begun by Jim Prior and carried on by Norman Tebbit. This would give the government enormous powers to handle secondary picketing. In the event, the new laws were not used as much during the dispute as the government had expected. Scargill's decision to refuse a ballot and the internal divisions inside the NUM in 1984 made it unnecessary to apply the full force of new laws, not all of which were in place at the time of the dispute.

Still, none of this was going to be any use to them if the Conservatives lost the next general election. It was not until March 1982 that the tide changed for Thatcher, and the change was not of her making. On

19 March 1982 Argentina seized South Georgia, followed swiftly by the Falkland Islands themselves. The action proved a huge test for the Thatcher government which could have gone dreadfully wrong. She could have been blamed for sending the wrong signals the previous year by withdrawing Britain's last patrol vessel in the South Atlantic, HMS *Endurance*, and would certainly have suffered politically if military action did not produce swift results.

But her luck held. Thatcher took the extremely risky decision to reclaim the Falklands by sending a task force of military ships to the South Atlantic. During the resulting war the British lost a destroyer, HMS *Sheffield*, and British forces made a controversial decision to sink the Argentine Navy's pride, the battleship *Belgrano*. Britain retook the islands on 14 June. It all transformed Thatcher's fortunes. From being one of the most unpopular prime ministers in history, she became a plucky war heroine who had risked all to restore British pride.

The retaking of the Falklands, added to Labour's internal troubles, paved the way for a landslide political victory for the Tories the following year, and the scene was set for a triumphant Thatcher to dominate politics for the next decade.

For the coal miners the transformation of her position was bad news. Thatcher had discovered that taking risks paid off. It looks certain that by the autumn of 1982 the government had decided they must act over the coal mining industry. Certainly Scargill thought a dispute was inevitable once the NUM obtained a leaked report that had been prepared for the Monopolies and Mergers Commission, which clearly showed that between seventy-five and ninety-five pits had been earmarked for closure over the next ten years. The famous pit closure list became a matter of dispute between the union, the NCB and the government, which, of course, denied that it was a plan. The list was crucial to setting the scene for the strike, in making miners believe their industry was next for the Thatcherite chop.

The government also moved in other ways in 1982 to prepare the ground. They decided to ask Ian MacGregor, after his success at the British Steel Corporation, to take over the chairmanship of the NCB.

With Sir Derek Ezra standing down and his deputy, Sir Norman Siddall, not keen to take up the reins, the idea was first put to MacGregor by Nigel Lawson, the Energy Secretary, at the Garrick Club in November. MacGregor claims to have been reluctant, telling Thatcher before Christmas that 'my advice is to get someone younger on whom you can depend.'[5]

Perhaps he did say that. But he was also busy negotiating a fresh deal for large sums of cash to be paid to his US company, Lazards, in compensation for the loss of his services. Lawson despatched his Deputy Secretary Ivor Manley to see MacGregor. Manley recalls: 'I just thought he was asking for far too much money and we shouldn't go ahead and pay him all this. I can't remember the sums but it was a lot of money.' The Inland Revenue had also raised private doubts about the huge cost of the deal and whether it broke British tax rules by paying cash to a US firm. But Lawson was insistent, ordering Manley to continue the talks and give MacGregor what he wanted.

When MacGregor's appointment was announced the next year, it caused waves of anger not only in the NUM but among fellow directors in the NCB, and even within the least militant union of the lot, the British Association of Colliery Management. The BACM were to continue sniping and complaining privately about the way the NCB was run, as minutes of a meeting between them and the Board in November 1983 (released under the Freedom of Information Act) show. They were also privately appalled at the appointment of MacGregor and his way of doing business without always informing them, which was described at one stage as the Americanization of the Board.

Thatcher's landslide election victory on 9 June 1983 gave her fresh impetus for another big reshuffle. She promoted Nigel Lawson to Chancellor and Leon Brittan to Home Secretary. Cecil Parkinson became Trade and Industry Secretary. Tebbit stayed as Employment Secretary and Peter Walker was promoted to Energy Secretary. This was the Cabinet that was to confront the miners' strike, except for one face, which was to disappear. A crisis blew up at the Tory Party conference the following September when Cecil Parkinson had to admit he had fathered a child with his secretary, Sarah Keays. The furore that followed forced him to leave the government and led to Tebbit taking over his Trade and Industry job, with Tom King becoming Employment Secretary.

The big surprise in all this was the appointment and promotion of Walker to the Energy brief. He was known to be a wet, yet he now had the job of supervising huge nationalized industries which Tebbit was to describe later that year as 'a drain on the taxpayer'. But Thatcher knew what she was doing. Walker was to prove the most cool-headed of the lot when the dispute began. He knew that if he was to prove to Thatcher that he could be trusted he would have to take the initiative and show he was in control. From the outset he steeped himself in the detail of the industry and made sure he met the main players, including Scargill and MacGregor. He was going to be a friend of neither the coal chairman nor the miners' leader. In fact, according to Manley, neither was a clubbable sort: Scargill stood back from participating with the other energy unions when they met the new Secretary of State, while MacGregor wanted little to do with other nationalized industry bosses and as little to do with Walker as possible. MacGregor was furious at Walker's appointment. He felt he had been let down and the two men never hit it off.

MacGregor's natural allies were Tebbit and Lawson, as well as the later public relations guru and Thatcherite Tim Bell and the wealthy Tory right-wing eccentric David Hart. He was not naturally likely to warm to Peter Walker and successive coal ministers Giles Shaw and David Hunt. So if Walker was going to be successful he had to woo Thatcher and neutralize Tebbit, who hated him, and make sure he was in charge. With help from Ivor Manley he was able to do it, by being on top of the job and with the aid of a very efficient Whitehall machine. But he also did it by getting rid of the mantle of being a wet. He succeeded in implementing a redundancy scheme for miners that was the most generous of its time, and he looked for new markets and uses for British coal, which probably put him in the wet tradition. But he was ruthless and as tough as nails in fighting the dispute that was to come, and that is why he gained the increasing confidence of Thatcher as the drama enfolded.

Meanwhile Arthur Scargill was working his way to the top of the NUM. While the monetarists were grouping around Peter Thorneycroft, Enoch Powell and Nigel Birch in the late 1950s, aiming to shift the balance in the Conservative Party, the Communist Party began working quietly in Yorkshire to shift the balance of power in the NUM. But in the 1960s and the 1970s, the Communist Party found itself outflanked on the left, which was taken over by a new generation.

The unions had grown used to power. In the 1970s, Jack Jones and Hugh Scanlon, leaders of the two biggest unions, were considered to be two of the most powerful people in Britain, and the NUM President Joe Gormley was a considerable figure too. But Jones and Scanlon were experienced political animals who knew the difference between appearance and reality, and the limitations of their power. Their successors, as they retired at the end of the 1970s, were not always so wise.

It often seemed to trade union activists that the question was not how they should keep and consolidate the unions' power, but what use they should make of it. Power in the unions was on its way down through the ranks, away from general secretaries and towards shop stewards. The unions had power and influence they had never before enjoyed. But they were not as powerful as their activists, or their enemies, thought they were. The 1977 Grunwick strike portrayed the sad reality: that when unions had to protect workers against really bad employers, as often as not they failed. The long-running dispute broke out after the North London film processing firm sacked workers for joining a union. Mass pickets, often hundreds of them, descended on the firm's premises each morning to try to stop workers from being bussed in, leading to clashes with police. Arthur Scargill, then the Yorkshire NUM President, already a household name and one of the two or three best-known trade unionists in the country, led coach-loads of Yorkshire miners to join the pickets. He was arrested. He saw it as a triumph. But the strike was lost. The workers stayed sacked.

Nonetheless, Grunwick and Scargill's arrest there had a huge place in the folklore of the left. A new, sharp-toothed left wing had grown up – young men and women who were born in the late 1940s and early 1950s and saw their politics through the distorting mirror of 1968. For them, New Jerusalem was just around the corner, its arrival impeded only by cautious, reactionary, elderly trade union leaders, with their fatal addiction to compromise. For them, the Labour Party had failed and betrayed them, and so had the Communist Party – for Communist union leaders like NUM Vice-President Mick McGahey seemed not to be manning any barricades. In many unions there was a 'rank and file' organization, which claimed to be the voice of the ordinary member and was actually the voice of the Socialist Workers Party.

As the new left mobilized to take control, the old guard mobilized against them. Elections to top union posts were hard-fought and divisive. The best-known newspaper columnist of the time, Bernard Levin, frequently used his column in *The Times* to campaign for his candidates for fairly minor posts in his union, the National Union of Journalists, and no one thought this was disproportionate. Power struggles in smoke-filled rooms seemed to matter dreadfully. Few stopped to ask whether, when the smoke cleared, the power might be seen to have gone with it.

Of course, in the end far less separated the two sides in the trade union movement than they both imagined. Both sides thought the collective voice of employees, which is what unions really are, was a key protection against exploitation and ought to be strengthened; and, thinking this, weakened it to destruction. For it seemed to both sides that the real battles, and the real victories, were to be had inside the unions. Gaining control of the organization and bending it to their will was the first objective, and often the only one. The internal victory was all that mattered; the outside world could take care of itself.

The new left needed heroes who would defeat not the Conservative government but the compromisers within – not the Thatchers but the Joe Gormleys. The heroes had to be young, and attractive, and fluent, and charismatic, and preferably romantic, but most of all they had to be impossible to outflank on the left. There had to be no issue on which someone else could take a view that was identifiably more radical than theirs. Those were the days of what Neil Kinnock called impossibilism.

Militants put forward demands they knew were unachievable, so that they could condemn 'union bureaucrats' for failing to achieve them. 'I've got you double the wages, and you only work Fridays,' a triumphant union official is said to have reported, and the man selling *Socialist Worker* called out: 'What, every bloody Friday?'

Scargill fitted the bill perfectly. Briefly a Communist when young, he had been trained, and his career nurtured, by Bert Ramelson, first Yorkshire district secretary and then industrial organizer for the Communist Party and, for a time in the 1970s, a surprisingly significant figure with great influence in the unions and, through them, in the Labour Party. Scargill's other mentor was Frank Watters, the Party's area secretary in the South Yorkshire coalfield. But Ramelson and Watters were orthodox communists, willing to be bound by Party discipline, and Scargill was not, so he could outflank the Communist Party on the left, a key requirement for a left-wing hero in the late 1970s and early 1980s.

Relatively young – he was forty-four when he became NUM President – Scargill was a riveting platform presence, he did not seem to know the meaning of compromise, he always wanted to go one step further than anyone else thought wise, he had absolute certainty, and at meetings of the left caucus on the miners' executive 'he always seemed to want to appear further left than anyone else,' according to South Wales executive member Terry Thomas.[6]

Vice-President Mick McGahey was the leader of the left on the NUM National Executive, and by end of the 1970s he and Scargill were barely on speaking terms, for they had so long been rivals for the left nomination for President when Joe Gormley retired. McGahey saw Scargill as the sort of ultra-left adventurer that disciplined Communists rather despise.

Scargill was effectively running for the top job from 1977, when he was arrested at Grunwick, and founded the *Yorkshire Miner* as a rival to the Union's national paper *The Miner*. His first editor was a young left-wing local journalist, Maurice Jones. One of Jones's first outings with his new boss was to the Grunwick picket line, where he too was arrested.

Apparently thinking the police were making veiled threats to his daughter, Jones dramatically rushed to East Germany and asked for political asylum. Scargill sent a colleague to East Germany to calm his editor down and bring him home.

Scargill took the traditional trade union leader's view that real power rested in the unions, not with politicians. In the late 1970s, playwright John Mortimer interviewed him. Scargill, reported Mortimer, was quite offended to be asked if he would like to be in Parliament. 'I was asking King Arthur if he'd care for a post as a corporal. He has been offered four Labour seats, but why should he forsake the reality of union rule for the pallid pretensions of Westminster?'

Joe Gormley was determined that the presidency would remain in right-wing hands after he went, so much so that he deliberately delayed his retirement until Mick McGahey was too old under the union's rules to stand for the job. The tactic might have seemed clever at the time, but Gormley miscalculated badly. He thought the right could beat Scargill. He was wrong. In November 1981 Arthur Scargill was elected President of the NUM with over 70 per cent of the vote. The man who had led the militants in the defeat of Heath was now leading the miners. The message to the government could not be clearer. It is no wonder that at the same time confidential memos were sent out by the NCB to its regions telling them to start stockpiling coal, implementing the first stage of the MISC57 plan.

Scargill was a new sort of union leader. There was a razzmatazz about him that was entirely different to the grey, elderly men in grey suits muttering 'I 'ave to consult my executive committee' who mostly led the unions. He was new, exciting, he had carefully coiffured hair and neat suits and apparently an ocean of self-confidence. He sat for a portrait of himself, and hung it in his office. He said he supported extra-parliamentary action to defeat Norman Tebbit's labour law reforms; he attacked Labour leader Michael Foot for not being left-wing enough; he called the split in the Labour ranks which led to Roy Jenkins and the others leaving to form the Social Democratic Party 'the best thing that has happened to the Labour Party. It has provided a siphon to take out of the party those elements that were poisoning it, because of their non-belief in socialism.' He announced that all the elements that caused Heath's downfall were now present.

His first strike call, over pay, was rejected in a ballot of the membership after Joe Gormley argued against it in an article in the *Daily Express*. Scargill accused Gormley of 'an act of betrayal without parallel in the history of the NUM' and 'collaborationist use of the capitalist press' and tried unsuccessfully to persuade the executive to condemn Gormley. He also made himself deeply unpopular with the union's staff, demanding a level of day-to-day control that the relaxed Gormley had never wanted, taking away the small Christmas bonus they had received since 1956, demanding that the names of all incoming telephone callers were recorded on a central log, and eventually moving the union's headquarters from its fine London building to Sheffield, to bring it closer to the coalfields, or so the President claimed. 'London is a place where you can very easily get sucked into the system and I have no intention of allowing that to happen,' he said.[7] Sheffield, as it happens, is close to the village of Worsborough, just outside Barnsley, where Scargill has lived all his life. Only a tiny handful of the original staff went to Sheffield, and the rest were made redundant.

The Labour Party was having the same battles as the trade unions – unsurprisingly, because at that time the link between the two was, as it had always been, very close, and they saw themselves as the two branches of what was then collectively called the labour movement. Union leaders were still the key power brokers in Labour Party politics. Scargill was a crucial figure in the Labour Party's early 1980s internal warfare, fighting alongside Tony Benn for the soul of the Party, helping to make Michael Foot leader rather than Dennis Healey, then in 1981 throwing himself into the campaign to get Tony Benn rather than Healey elected to the meaningless post of deputy leader.

Foot had hoped for a little respite from perpetual warfare, and a respite in 1981 meant electing Healey unopposed. But the spirit of the times was against him, and the new machinery for electing Labour leaders and deputy leaders, which placed the unions centre stage, cranked into motion. The six-month campaign hinged on how the big unions were going to vote, and by the end of it the Party was looking like exactly what Margaret Thatcher said it was – the plaything of the unions. It was, though few of the union leaders seemed to see it at the time, the worst possible introduction to what would be, in 1984–5, a life or death struggle for the unions.

Labour went down by a landslide in the 1983 general election, Foot resigned and, even before the contest for the succession had properly begun, two Welsh trade union leaders, whose unions were affiliated to the Labour Party, announced they were supporting Neil Kinnock, which effectively ensured that Kinnock got the job. The two leaders were the TGWU's Moss Evans and Clive Jenkins of the white-collar union ASTMS; they were collectively known as the Taffia. Neither of them saw any reason to hide the enormous power they wielded, and both of them rather enjoyed the fact that they had effectively chosen the next Labour leader and probably the next Prime Minister. A year later, as the miners took on the government, the unions started to realize what harm their hubris might do to them.

Of course the new NUM President's core business was not fighting for Tony Benn but fighting pit closures. In November 1983 the union ordered an overtime ban. This was successful in cutting production by between 25 and 30 per cent over the next few months and became a worry for NCB officials who were secretly committed to creating a stockpile of coal. The worry is shown by the meticulous weekly figures kept by the NCB on coal production. But, unfortunately for the union, it was too late to dent significantly the stockpile that been built up since November 1981.

Under MacGregor the NCB refused to agree a pay deal unless the miners agreed to job losses and pit closures. The NUM refused to agree and there was still a dispute when the miners began their strike in 1984.

Meanwhile a dispute between one of the print unions, the National Graphical Association, and a local newspaper proprietor spiralled out of control. The NGA refused to obey Norman Tebbit's new union laws about mass picketing and was first fined £675,000, then had the whole of its £11m assets sequestrated – confiscated by the state. Scargill watched, fulminated against the TUC for its refusal to support the NGA and defy the law, and started secretly to make preparations for the day when this would happen to the NUM.

There was one last key change to be made. NUM General Secretary Lawrence Daly was persuaded to take early retirement, and Scargill's nominee Peter Heathfield, secretary of the Derbyshire miners, was elected in his place. Heathfield had a reputation for integrity and quiet, solid competence, and assured everyone that he was ready to stand up to Scargill. Within two years all this was to be tested to destruction.

CHAPTER 3

THE GREAT STRIKE

6 MARCH TO 31 MARCH, 1984

The great strike for jobs started by accident. Of course no one admitted it at the time. Both sides had gone far too far to admit that they didn't really mean it. Only years later did it emerge that when, on 1 March 1985, George Hayes, the South Yorkshire Coal Board director, told Yorkshire union leaders that Cortonwood would close in five weeks' time, on 6 April 1984, he had misunderstood his instructions and jumped the gun.

The Cortonwood announcement derailed government plans, and overshadowed the national challenge the NCB intended to throw down. It was not until 6 March, six days after Hayes' announcement, that NCB Chairman Ian MacGregor told the unions nationally of plans to cut four million tonnes of capacity and make 20,000 men redundant. He expected this to lead to a strike ballot, which he hoped the NUM executive would lose, and he thought that would be an end to resistance. He did not realize that it was too late for such tactical considerations. The strike, bottled up for months, was already under way.

And it was all a mistake. The NCB never intended to include Cortonwood in the list of pits to be closed at that time. An internal report says: 'In procedural terms the Area Director was wrong to announce closure at a General Review Meeting . . . Closure has not yet been confirmed by the Board . . .' No proper closure procedure had begun at the very pit which started the strike; it had all been wrongly handled from the beginning. It was a little like the famous spoof headline: 'Archduke Ferdinand alive – First World War fought by mistake.' Only this time it was no spoof.

It was very quickly too late for either side to admit such a mistake, and the memo has remained secret until now. It concluded: 'This is one we cannot "back off", and I would suggest that the matter be put back to Area for further discussion within the review Procedure as required.'

Cortonwood was the spark that ignited the strike. But it started the strike only in the sense that the assassination of Archduke Ferdinand at Sarajevo in 1914 started the First World War. European politics and the rhetoric of their leaders caused the war, and after Arthur Scargill and Margaret Thatcher had been squaring up to each other for months, the strike only needed a spark. This is, as we shall see, just one of many ways in which 'the great strike for jobs' resembled the First World War.

For the 839 miners who worked at Cortonwood, Hayes' announcement came as a shock and felt like a betrayal. Every indication until that morning was that the NCB planned to keep the pit open. Several months earlier eighty men had been transferred there from Elsecar pit and promised a secure future for at least five years. Just a year previously, George Hayes had told the NUM and NACODS (the National Association of Colliery Overmen, Deputies and Shotfirers, the small union representing the managers in the mines) that the pit would remain open until the last coalface ran out in 1989. During the summer the NCB had spent £1m to improve the washery at the colliery and installed a new generating plant at a cost of £100,000; by Christmas it completed a £40,000 modernization of the pithead baths.

Hayes' meeting was with the Yorkshire NUM President, Jack Taylor, and General Secretary Owen Briscoe, as well as NACODS President Ken Sampey, at the NCB offices near Manver colliery. There he gave them the bad news he thought he had been authorized to give. He said that South Yorkshire had been told to cut output by 500,000 tonnes a year –

and Cortonwood provided 280,000 tonnes. He argued that as it had to close in five years, it was better to do it now so young men could find new jobs elsewhere. That was an argument which the union leaders knew was going to sound hollow to the eighty men who had recently transferred there because they were told that Cortonwood had a secure future.

Jenny Evans's husband worked at Cortonwood, and she knew there was no other source of employment for her village of Brampton Blerlow. 'I thought, that can't be right, there must be some mistake,' she said twenty years later. 'When it had sunk in we realized we had no choice but to fight. I believed totally in the strike.' It was the start of a year of hardship for the Evans family, and thousands of other families.[1]

This was the first pit ordered to close by the NCB without the approval of the NUM, so it was more than a local tragedy: it was a national challenge.

Just four days after Hayes' announcement, on the following Sunday, 4 March, at a meeting of the Cortonwood NUM branch at Brampton parish hall, 500 miners voted to fight the closure. The next day 300 of them picketed the NUM Yorkshire offices in Barnsley where the Yorkshire area council was meeting. In a splendid panelled room in the period building, with a wooden desk for each delegate, the delegate for Cortonwood, Mick Carter, told the area council about being called into the manager's office to be told that the pit was to close in five weeks, and he asked for support from the union. He pointed out that in 1981 the Yorkshire miners had decided they would take strike action to prevent any pit in Yorkshire being closed on grounds other than proven seam exhaustion.

'So what could we do?' says Ken Capstick, a Yorkshire executive member who still works for the NUM today and is close to Arthur Scargill, as he has always been. 'We had a ballot decision which was something like 80 per cent or more in favour [to strike to prevent pit closures], in Yorkshire, and we had a delegate in the council chamber asking us what we're going to do because his pit is going to close. So we voted unanimously to take strike action and we embarked on a strike in Yorkshire.'

Capstick adds this, twenty-five years on: 'If I could go right back to 1984 and I was in that council chamber and I was watching Mick Carter making his speech, what would I do, knowing what I know now? I'd vote for strike action – even knowing everything I know that happened – because it was right. It was right. That's what I believe. Because it was right and I believe in it and I'd still do the same again. That represents a victory of some kind. It's got to do. I can't see how it can't. Do you follow my logic or not?'

After the meeting Jack Taylor announced that the Yorkshire executive had called an all-out stoppage of the area's 56,000 miners from 9 March. The strike had begun.

The Yorkshire NUM council had acted without taking a ballot, a decision that would come back to haunt them. The question of ballots was to divide the miners' union for the next twelve months and bring it more grief than almost anything else. To add to their troubles, it was the worst possible time to start a strike, from the NUM's point of view. There was the whole summer to get through before the shortage of coal was going to bite. The NCB may have been in a mess, having triggered the strike more or less by accident, but the NUM was in no better shape, for at least some of the delegates must have known perfectly well that they really needed to find an excuse to hold off until autumn, and call a strike when winter was approaching.

Still, they were sure they had no choice. 'It was like the gauntlet being thrown down by the government.' With Yorkshire's man Arthur Scargill now installed as national President, they felt sure of national backing. Neither Scargill nor Thatcher could ignore anything that looked like a gauntlet being thrown down.

Just three days after the Yorkshire area council had called a strike over Cortonwood, the NUM National Executive, meeting at the union's head office in Sheffield on 8 March, made strikes in Yorkshire and Scotland official – which meant that no NUM member who cared about his friends or his neighbours would go into work there and risk being labelled a 'scab' – and called for support for them from the rest of the country.

The strike vote at the NUM executive was overwhelming, but it was not unanimous. The executive voted by 21 to 3 for the action, the three objectors being right-wing members calling for a national strike ballot. The division over whether to have a ballot grew with every passing day, and became bitter and toxic. Afterwards, one of the three who voted for a national ballot, Trevor Bell, who had stood against Scargill for President in 1981 and represented white-collar workers on the NUM executive, wondered how the once powerful right wing had been so decisively defeated. Perhaps, he thought, some right-wingers believed local strikes might not affect their more moderate areas.

There was, however, a serious constitutional problem. The strike was called under Rule 41 of the NUM rule book, which said that local strikes can be made official by the National Executive without a ballot. But Rule 43 said that a national strike can only be called if there is a ballot. Was this national or local? The right wing argued that this was turning into a national strike and required a ballot – and that in any case, what-ever the rule book said, they needed a ballot to get a united and effective strike. Many on the left, like Kent miners' leader Jack Collins, argued against a ballot on the grounds that it meant one man having the right to vote another man out of work.

Right from the start, this division threatened to explode into violent confrontation. Early in the strike, Trevor Bell spoke at Sheffield City Hall and advocated a national ballot. He said that, if the union wanted the support of people like the Labour Party leader Neil Kinnock, it had to prove that the strike had been called democratically. 'That didn't go down well with a lot of them,' he says.

As he left the meeting, a policeman quietly asked Bell to accompany him through a side door. Outside, 'there were three policemen and an inspector waiting, and they said, "Where's your car?" and I said, "It's in the multi-storey car park down near the NUM office." And they said, "We just think we ought to take you to your car." And they took me to my car and I went towards it with my key in my hand and the inspector said, "Wait," took the key and looked under the car and he opened the car. He opened the car door and then said, "All right,

Mr Bell, you can go."' It was, he was told, the result of information the police had received.[2]

The left would certainly reply that this was either the police being mischievous or bogus threats made by *agents provocateurs*. Given the way the strike swiftly began being fought, this is at least as plausible an explanation as that real threats were made on Bell's life by striking miners. Spies and *agents provocateurs* are an inevitable feature of war.

Whatever the truth, after that meeting, NCB industrial relations chief Ned Smith asked for the registration number of Bell's car. 'I didn't know why he was bothered,' says Bell. 'But then I noticed that as I went down the motorway, there'd be a police motorcyclist behind me until I turned off to go into Sheffield.'

Following the 8 March executive decision, Yorkshire miners from Doncaster began to picket Nottinghamshire pits, in order to get the vast and productive Nottinghamshire coalfield out on strike. They travelled to Harworth, the most northerly of the Nottinghamshire collieries. The Nottinghamshire miners had not been called out on strike, and the Yorkshire region had agreed to keep pickets out of Nottinghamshire until the Notts area council strike ballot, which was to take place four days later.

The Nottinghamshire executive was recommending a 'yes' vote and feared that pickets before the ballot would only alienate their members and make a 'yes' vote harder to obtain. Notts General Secretary Henry Richardson said the pickets 'set the men against the strike'. He said prophetically: 'Calling us scabs will not help. If Notts are scabs before we start, Notts will become scabs.'[3] So the union asked the pickets to go home – but some of them kept coming back to Nottinghamshire, in defiance of the union. The Yorkshire area council sanctioned the flying pickets, but the Nottinghamshire leaders still wanted them to stay away.[4] Here were the seeds of great trouble and bitterness in the future, not only in Nottinghamshire but in neighbouring Derbyshire and other areas too.

On 9 March the miners of Durham and Kent, two of the more militant coalfields in the country, agreed to support the strike. But the

Nottinghamshire leaders were still calling for a pithead ballot. Positions were starting to harden, with Nottinghamshire leading one side and Yorkshire the other.

By Monday, 12 March, the national strike was taking shape, but even then only half the 184,000 miners were on strike. The strike was solid, or almost solid, in Yorkshire, Kent, South Wales and Scotland, while mining villages in Nottinghamshire, Derbyshire, Leicestershire, Staffordshire and parts of the North West refused to join in the action.

How could they be brought into the strike? If giving them a ballot was ruled out, there was only one way to get them in: to make use of the loyalty to their union that was second nature in all mining communities. If you sent large numbers of men to picket the mines where work was still going on, surely miners would be ashamed to cross the picket line. That was how it had always worked. 'Scab' was still the most offensive thing you could say to a miner. If proof were needed, surely the crucial picketing of Saltley in 1972 provided it.

So miners started to travel from Yorkshire, South Wales, Scotland and Kent to the areas where support was thin or non-existent, to try to persuade working miners to join the strike.

Scargill and those round him seem to have thought that Nottinghamshire would come out, and that, if a push was needed, the flying pickets would provide it. Today Ken Capstick admits that perhaps they should have anticipated the problem, because of the history of the Nottinghamshire NUM. The spectre of Spencerism, he now thinks, was still alive and well in the Nottinghamshire leadership, and that was what caused the trouble.

'I knew very early on in the strike – I'm talking about the first week or two – that we had a problem because there was some pits that clearly were not going to come out on strike,' says Capstick. 'Normally when miners go to picket a pit they come out on strike with you. They might disagree with you – there might be arguments, but those arguments usually take place whilst you are on strike. Normally my experience has been that when you go, they come out on strike and they'll disagree with you at the meetings that are held.'

But Capstick – as good a guide as we have to Scargill's thinking at the start of the strike – believes that 'the die had been cast somehow. We'd sent the pickets into Nottinghamshire and into Lancashire and there had been resistance to it, there were problems there that were difficult to turn around.'

The government and the NCB may have been caught out by the timing, but they had prepared well, and knew just what they were going to do about it. Their strategy depended absolutely on the one thing Capstick did not count on: miners crossing picket lines to go to work. The NUM was to be surprised at the speed and ruthlessness with which the NCB acted.

A special meeting was convened at the Edwinstowe headquarters of the North Notts Mining Board by area director J.E. Wood to plan and co-ordinate action against the pickets. The meeting was to be the first of the daily briefings held until the strike ended a year later. The military precision at local and national level to deal with picketing made the NUM look positively amateurish.

Initially, the North Notts management received a rebuff from Nottinghamshire Constabulary. Minutes of the first meeting on 13 March record the then Assistant Chief Constable telling the local board that it could not intervene against the pickets. The minutes note: 'The area director had spoken to the Assistant Chief Constable (Notts). He was told, "Unless there has been proven violence it was a matter for the Board to take action through the civil courts."'

The moment NCB headquarters at Hobart House was informed of this, MacGregor decided to seek an injunction from the High Court to stop Yorkshire miners picketing outside their area. He sent his lawyers up to Nottinghamshire that evening. There was no hesitation, no indecision: plans had been laid for just this contingency. Lawyers and NCB officials worked through the night preparing affidavits and at six the next morning colliery managers were summoned to Edwinstowe to sign them. By that evening they were in London so they could be used in the High Court to gain a speedy injunction. The minutes recall managers 'swore an oath on holy writ'.[5]

The NCB had their injunction by 14 March, just six days after the NUM executive had declared the strike official and two weeks after the announcement that Cortonwood was to close. The junior brief was Charlie Falconer, the future Lord Chancellor and already a close friend of Tony Blair. Falconer was later to play a much bigger role in the dispute, and to make a significant contribution to the miners' defeat.

This injunction set the scene for the bitter confrontations which made the miners' strike the most violent industrial dispute Britain has ever seen – for how could such an injunction ever be enforced, except by deploying the police as though it were an army, and sending it in to stop the miners by force?

The next day, 15 March, with pickets coming from Yorkshire and a legal threat to their union, Nottinghamshire leaders called out their members on strike, before they had held an area ballot. Their own leaders and those of the NCB had forced their hand. It was a decision they stumbled into; it was not part of a plan.

The contrast between the efficiency, ruthlessness and determination of the NCB and the amateurishness of the NUM leadership was shown by events over the same days in Barnsley. Eric Illsley, then a young Yorkshire NUM official and now Labour MP for Barnsley Central, remembers Yorkshire NUM officials retrieving a huge 6 ft x 4 ft map from the attic of their Barnsley HQ – a map that had last been used by Scargill during the 1974 miners' strike. It showed the location of every pit and power station in the UK and was the manual for organizing the flying pickets that were so successful in that strike.

Unfortunately, things had changed since 1974. The map was ten years out of date and some of the power stations had closed. But Yorkshire pickets relied on it to organize action, with the result that pickets spent hours standing outside closed pits and power stations wondering why it was deathly quiet. Illsley recalls: 'Many a time I can remember a call in the dead of night from some pickets in Wales or somewhere else – saying, "We've got here but there's nought but broken windows."' The NUM updated their map as the strike progressed.

The NUM headquarters' picture of how the strike was going was haphazard and vague; the NCB's was precise and organized. Twice a day, industrial relations director Ned Smith produced for his colleagues an exact description of how things were in every region: precise numbers of miners working and amounts of coal produced. He had been doing it throughout the overtime ban, and simply carried on when the strike started.

Those around Arthur Scargill seemed at first to be able to compensate for the union's administrative failings by their belief in victory. Divided and poorly organized the miners might be, especially compared with the employers, but they were brimming with optimism and confidence. The government, despite its preparations and its brave public stance, was not confident at all.

Many people, including most trade union leaders, thought Scargill had been outmanoeuvred into calling a strike in March, and he would struggle to sustain the strike all through the summer before it started to bite in the cold days of winter when a lot of fuel would be needed. Privately, ministers knew that Cortonwood was not a clever piece of outmanoeuvring but a mistake, and that taking on Scargill was going to be an expensive and difficult business.

None knew better than Peter Gregson, then head of the economic secretariat at the Cabinet Office, who chaired MISC57, the secret Cabinet Committee set up in 1981 to prepare for strike. He was to become a key figure, one of the few people during the strike to whom the Prime Minister listened. On 13 March, the day after the strike went national, Gregson sent a secret memo[6] to Mrs Thatcher to prepare her for a meeting with Ian MacGregor the next day.

Gregson saw the dangers ahead where perhaps Margaret Thatcher did not. His memo was blind copied to Sir Robert Armstrong, the Cabinet Secretary, and to an interesting shadowy figure, Brigadier Budd, a member of the Civil Contingencies Secretariat of the Cabinet Office who, in the 1990s, would become very keen on setting up a National Alert and Information System in government.

Gregson's memo showed that the government had no grounds for complacency. The figures were blunt. Current assessment of 'endurance' – the phrase used to describe how long the government could hold out – suggested months and weeks, not a year. Power stations could last for another six months, 'assuming build up to maximum oil burn over four weeks'. Large-scale industry like steel that relied on coal had only six weeks, while the privately owned cement industry had fourteen to eighteen weeks' supply for its furnaces. Domestic stocks ran to six weeks, which in the middle of March was probably not going to be such a problem.

The memo went on to specify the scale of the problem facing power stations. To keep the power stations going for six months, the amount of oil needed was going to have to jump from 60,000 tonnes a week to 350,000 tonnes. No easy solution there either.

Gregson warned: 'It will not be possible to build up to maximum oil burn . . . in less than four weeks without running into logistical difficulties and precipitating a major disturbance in the oil market.' Nor was the CEGB, despite being ordered by the government to draw up contingency plans, keen to order a sixfold increase in oil deliveries. 'They will be . . . reluctant to enter into firm commitments until they are reasonably certain that they have to increase oil burn, and they will not wish to start extra oil burn (net additional cost of maximum oil burn is £20m a week) until a national strike seems inevitable.' Thatcher was advised to steer the CEGB in that direction. She did. The CEGB came into line and was seen as a staunch government ally throughout.

Gregson also described how the government was already acting to contain picketing. The Home Office and the Scottish Office were meeting with chief police officers in areas where picketing had begun and 'mutual aid' plans, involving sending police from other trouble spots, were being prepared.

At that very early stage the government was already thinking about how to break the strike using the employment laws. According to the memo, the official public stance was that it was for the NCB and other parties to decide whether to bring a civil case against the NUM. Gregson's assessment was that the government's best hopes lay in the internal opposition within the NUM. So it might be best not to use the Employment Acts, since this might cause a backlash. He conceded that this might change, prophetically warning: 'There is in any case the possibility of action by some businessman in the private sector and the government would have no way of preventing that even if it wished to do so.'

Gregson advised Thatcher to seek MacGregor's assessment of how the situation would develop, find out what further steps the NCB had in mind to influence the rank-and-file miners against strike action, and ask him how he thought the government could best help.

The Thatcher–MacGregor meeting was not about the miners' strike, but another issue altogether, the Channel Tunnel rail and road link. MacGregor – on the very day the NCB was in court obtaining an injunction against the NUM for illegal picketing – had requested the meeting with the PM to get her support for Euroroute, a combined road and rail link. The note of the meeting made by Andrew Turnbull later that day[7] revealed that MacGregor opened the meeting with a strong defence of the feasibility of the project. Mindful of the power of the unions, MacGregor began by insisting the new Channel link must carry road traffic. He argued that 'The rail-only tunnels would perpetuate and even enhance the monopoly powers of rail unions on both sides of the Channel.'

MacGregor then said: 'Prime Minister, are you are aware that we are facing a very serious situation in the pits?'[8] But Thatcher knew much more than her NCB Chairman realized, because she had read Gregson's brief. Like Gregson, MacGregor saw grounds for hope that the strike might be quite short. He told Peter Walker, the Energy Secretary, that the strike would be certain to be over by May when the deduction of benefits hit miners and their families came into play.[9] But MacGregor went on: 'You have got to do something, because you are dealing with a well-rehearsed and organized rebellion here . . . You know, from what Scargill has said, that he is out to topple the government. If it goes on, I fear he will succeed.'[10]

The Prime Minister, who had already reached this conclusion for herself, immediately picked up the phone and called Leon Brittan, the Home Secretary. Her request was simple and she wanted an immediate response. She told him to get on to the Association of Chief Police Officers (ACPO) and organize a national centre to co-ordinate action to stop the picketing. This was done that very day – and the result was to activate the National Reporting Centre (NRC), which was to play a huge role in containing the dispute and give enormous power to the Centre to direct operations.

The NRC, based at New Scotland Yard, had come into existence during the 1972 miners' strike, and was activated when police forces in more than one area judged they were likely to need reinforcements to deal with threats to public order. It maintained full details of police availability throughout England and Wales. It deployed Police Support Units consisting of twenty-three officers. By mid-March the NRC was making daily deployments of up to 8,000 officers, who often travelled hundreds of miles a day.

Civil liberties groups were concerned that, with officers being deployed nationally, how they policed a particular situation could easily become subject to national political direction, and the police could become a bludgeon with which to beat the strikers – as indeed they did. There was close liaison between the NRC and the Home Secretary, which made it possible for the government to influence the way in which the strike was policed. The NRC also acted as a clearing-house for information on the strike. Journalist Nick Davies, in the second week of the strike, reported an officer passing on pickets' coach registration numbers to a Midland force being mobilized by the NRC, and instructing that the coach be monitored until it reached the Nottinghamshire border, then turned back there.[11] The scene was set for one of the most co-ordinated and brutal police operations in British history.

The next day, 15 March, in a statement to Parliament about the unrest and picketing, the Home Secretary told MPs: 'A major co-ordinated police response, involving police officers from throughout the country, has been deployed to ensure that any miner who wishes to work at any pit may do so.' The police, he said, already had extensive powers under the common law. They could stop coaches, cars and people on foot who clearly intended to join a mass picket, if the picket was intimidating or if they thought there was a risk of violence, or even just because of the sheer numbers involved.

Meanwhile the Energy Secretary, Peter Walker, was working along different lines. His job at that stage, as he saw it, was to make sure the miners rejected a strike in a ballot, for he was sure that the union would be true to its history and not maintain a strike without a ballot. He says he had already put together 'the most generous package miners have ever been offered in terms of a pay deal, incredibly gener-ous payments for moving collieries and voluntary redundancy at an early age; the total package was enormous and the Treasury weren't terribly amused.'

Now, as the strike began, Walker moved to make it even more attractive for the miners to leave the industry, by increasing redun-dancy payments to £1,000 for each year of service for all miners between twenty-one and fifty. He was terrified that the proposals would leak before the announcement. 'I never circulated this around all ministers but just sent it to those on a need-to-know basis.' He also feared that his department – which had strong links with the miners' union – would leak his every move in advance. Walker did not trust his civil servants.

One civil servant was alleged to be victimized because he was a known Labour supporter, and he was kept out of the loop to such an extent that his career was at risk. In an interview with the authors Walker could not recall the incident but said that there was a worry about leaks getting back to the unions. Only the intervention of Brian Hayes, then Permanent Secretary at the Department of Industry, saved the mandarin's job; Hayes persuaded his boss, Norman Tebbit, of the injustice of the case. The civil servant was transferred to Tebbit's depart-ment after assurances that he was not a far leftie or Scargillite. When he was summoned to meet his new boss, he was asked: 'Do you know why you are here?'

'No.'

'It's because your Secretary of State is such a shit,' Tebbit told him.

On 15 March, two days after Gregson's memo, and the day that Nottinghamshire miners' leaders called their members out, one of the flying pickets, 24-year-old David Jones, was killed at Ollerton colliery in Nottinghamshire during violent scenes between the pickets and working miners. The cause of death was later confirmed at an inquest as a severe blow to the chest from a brick, and to this day no one knows for certain who threw it. The police had stopped the bus carrying David and other miners to picket in the south of Nottinghamshire, so they were forced to get off the bus and walk to picket at the nearest pit, Ollerton. His family are full of bitterness that the police should have stopped the coach on lawful business; if they had not, David Jones would be alive today. Stopping coaches like that was to become one of the most controversial police activities for the duration of the strike.

David Jones' death was dismissed in one sentence in the minutes of the Directors of the North Notts Mining Board of 15 March. 'A flying picket died of natural causes during the fighting with other pickets, it is alleged he had been wounded by a brick' is the only reference. Next to it is a call for more affidavits from managers to stop the picketing. There was little or no publicity.

For striking miners, this added to their growing resentment and sense of alienation from society. They had watched newspapers manufacture public indignation against them over attacks on, and intimidation of, working miners, and they had listened to the government's emphasis on the threats made by Scargill to law and order. In all this they saw no reference at all to David Jones.

David's father, Mark Jones, wrote a book about the son he had lost. It is an artless but heart-rending account of how his grief turned during the strike into the blackest pit of anger and bitterness. 'If someone had to die why could they not take me instead of him? The years I have left I would gladly have given for him,' he writes, and then: 'Every trade unionist should look into his or her heart and stand up and be counted on the miners' side in this struggle.'

Mark Jones took comfort from Arthur Scargill coming back to the family home after the funeral. The family tried to cheer up David's mother 'by saying she had done one thing that Margaret Thatcher would never do, and that was to have Arthur Scargill on his knees, as he knelt down when she was sitting in a chair to offer her comfort and solace. This was a joke that went through the house for weeks after.'

In Mark Jones' account of learning of his son's death, you can hear the powerless rage that was overtaking him and many people in mining communities. His loathing of the press is only exceeded by his loathing of the police. 'They covered up what really happened. If it had been a policeman, they would have found out everything. They even found a woman who threw an egg at a lorry in Wales because she was a picket's wife, but they couldn't find out who threw a brick and killed my son . . . The police are a paramilitary force now.'[12]

How could Mark Jones and his wife not have been bitter? They saw their fit, strong, enterprising and energetic son go out to picket one day, and come back in a coffin because some thug threw a brick at him, and the media and the authorities seemed not to give a damn. Almost no effort was made to find the brick-thrower. Yet a few months later, when a man was killed driving a strikebreaker to work, they watched the media whip itself up into a state of fury, saw a huge police manhunt and long prison sentences handed down. How could they fail to draw the lesson that whether your death mattered depended entirely on whether the establishment approved of your political views? How could they fail to go for solace to what seemed to them like the most extreme political group they could find?

For after David's death, Mr and Mrs Jones joined the Workers Revolutionary Party, the most extreme and centralist of the tiny, warring Trotskyist groups. It was the WRP that published Mark Jones' book.

Perhaps Arthur Scargill also influenced their choice, for he is thought to have become close to the WRP, whose paper *Newsline* was the only one he was prepared to help. The WRP did reasonably well out of the strike, making many new members – unlike the Communist Party, which gained only about seventy additional members in the whole twelve months. The Joneses offer a good illustration of why.

Despite the NCB's High Court injunction demanding the withdrawal of the Yorkshire flying pickets, it was very quickly clear that they were not going to be withdrawn. So the Board went back to court on 16 March and got leave to bring a contempt action against the Yorkshire miners. The Board wanted to have the union fined and a writ of sequestration, which would ensure that it could not use any of its money or assets. But when the court came to consider it on 19 March the hearing was adjourned indefinitely by Mr Justice Caulfield because miners were already returning to work in Nottinghamshire following an area ballot.

The same day, striking miners suffered a significant defeat when area ballots in the Midlands, North East and North West coalfields revealed a heavy vote against a national strike. Arthur Scargill was forced to concede that he did not have full national support for a strike. 'I am prepared to consider what my membership wants,' he said; but he still opposed a ballot.

On the other hand, the embattled Nottinghamshire leader, Henry Richardson, with half his members still at work, felt he had no alternative but to go for a national ballot. 'If we don't hold a ballot we are never going to get out of this mess,' he said. But there was no ballot, and no let-up in the activities of the flying pickets.

In the intervening twenty-five years, Scargill has not changed his view about the ballot. Today Ken Capstick still insists, as Scargill did at the time, that having a ballot only mattered to the media, the government and the NCB, and points out that the miners who were striking did not want a ballot. Here's how Capstick sees the question. 'If you have two armies opposing each other, would you ballot one of the armies because the other army was screaming at them to do it? No. We were out on strike. We had voted with our feet. The strike was on, it was effective. Why on earth would we? Tactically, the pits were stood, there was no coal coming out. Why on earth would we go and ballot the members in that circumstance?' He does not believe a ballot would have brought Nottinghamshire into the strike.

On 16 March, the day after the death of David Jones and the decision by Nottinghamshire leaders to call their members out, and a week and a day into the strike, the NUM finally got round to informing the TUC officially that there was a dispute. Scargill, who encouraged the NUM to remember the TUC's betrayal of 1926 as well as the repeated betrayals of the Nottinghamshire miners, wanted to keep the TUC at arm's length – though, as we shall see, this started to change when the outlook became grim. According to the TUC General Council's laconic report to the 1984 Congress, 'On March 16, 1984, the NUM, in accordance with Rule 11(a), informed the TUC that the union's National Executive Committee had endorsed strike action in the Yorkshire and Scottish areas of the union. The NUM also said that it would endorse similar action taken by any of the union's other areas. The NUM indicated that they were not requesting the intervention or the assistance of the TUC and said that should such be required, they would contact the TUC again.'

Two days later, on 18 March, it began to become clear that the police were to be used as a weapon to break the strike. Three thousand police were sent into Nottinghamshire – it later rose to 8,000 – and pickets from Kent were turned back hundreds of miles from their destination, at the Dartford tunnel. The forty-two pits still open in the Midlands were dependent on a huge police presence.

By the end of the month a Labour MP was accusing the police of questioning nineteen pickets on their political beliefs and what they thought of Arthur Scargill – which police continued to do throughout the strike. The police denied that they were acting outside the law, or that they were creating a police state. David Hall, President of the ACPO and controller of the NRC, insisted on 20 March: 'There is nothing paramilitary about our operation.'

This was not true. The build-up of an efficient police operation to co-ordinate action against aggressive picketing by strikers was one of the planks of Thatcher's planning for the eventuality of a strike. The scale of the operation in Nottinghamshire can be seen in the meticulous records maintained by the North Notts Mining Board during this period.[13] They kept a daily tally of the number of pickets and police in the area. After a week when they had been able to produce only 82,000 tonnes of coal and deliver only 46,000 tonnes by rail, collating details of picketing was essential – and it was even more essential to ensure a big police presence. The following week it became clear that the strategy to contain picketing by a mass police presence was working. On Monday, 19 March, 430 pickets came to the area, rising to 550 on Tuesday. But by Tuesday a mass picket of Thoresby colliery by 300 pickets was out-numbered by 800 police. On Wednesday, 435 pickets were facing 1,300 police. By Thursday, 1,350 pickets had come to North Nottinghamshire, but they were still outnumbered by 1,880 police officers. On Friday, picketing had fallen to 727 but there were 1,135 police. This pattern was to continue throughout the strike, the picketing miners very rarely getting the upper hand.

Despite this North Notts was losing coal orders, with supplies to Northern Ireland being the first hit. On Monday, 26 March, a terse note in the North Notts Mining Board's records reads: 'orders lost to Poland and other foreign powers.'

As the police stepped up their action, so did the pickets. A lorry blockade of the M1, inspired by similar blockades in France, took place in South Yorkshire on 27 March, and picketing of other pits intensified. The police had some effect because only 171 pickets got through to North Notts, surrounded by 546 police.

On that day, Ned Smith's report to his colleagues included the infor-mation that in Staffordshire, four men were 'sitting in' on the surface at Hem Heath colliery, demanding to see an NUM official other than those at their pit, so they could present their demand for a ballot. And, the same day, it had a bit of a gloat. 'Picketing at Cadley Hill much lighter,' Smith reported. 'Only 150 pickets, many of whom arrived too late for the afternoon shift, having been made to leave their buses and walk from Coalville (11 miles).'[14]

The next day pickets and police at Cresswell colliery were evenly matched, the strikers having found ways to get to Nottinghamshire through Derbyshire. Reaction from the North Notts Mining Board executive was swift and efficient. A request went to Derbyshire police for roadblocks and the next day they were in place.

In the meantime the role of the rest of the trade union movement was being tested. The right-wing-led power workers' union made it clear it would not support the miners, by advising its members that they could cross NUM picket lines. But the leaders of the more left-wing rail and transport unions, and even the moderate steel union, were prepared on 29 March to agree to a blockade of coal, though Bill Sirs, leader of the ISTC, later warned Scargill: 'I am not here to see the steel industry crucified on someone else's altar.'

The reason the unions were so divided was, again, that the NUM had taken a decision not to hold a ballot of all miners. As Geoffrey Goodman points out: 'The . . . problem with the tactics employed by the NUM was that those unions who most actively wanted to give support to the miners – the NUR, ASLEF [the two rail unions], the National Union of Seamen, TGWU and NUPE [National Union of Public Employees] – invariably found that their own members were at best lukewarm in support of the NUM. The rank-and-file reaction among other unions was that they wanted to see full support for the strike from all NUM members before they committed their support.'[15] Instead they saw, by 27 March, a divided union: leaders in the eight areas which had voted in ballots against the strike were telling their members to work normally, while the areas with the biggest support, in Yorkshire, South Wales and Kent, were determined to press their comrades to stop working.

The irony, as shown by a National Opinion Poll published on 31 March, is that Scargill might well have got a majority for a national strike. It revealed that 51 per cent of miners would vote for a strike with

34 per cent opposing the action. But this was never tested because by the end of March events had moved on too far, and neither side could be seen to be backing down. The absence of a ballot was, however, a crucial factor in the battle for public opinion and for support from other trade unions.

Another factor was the NUM's failure to make a proper play for public opinion. One thing the government and the NCB did have, and the NUM did not, was a clear understanding that public opinion was going to matter dreadfully. Crucial to this would be the industrial correspondents of the major Fleet Street papers and the major broadcasters.

Both sides seemed to have started out thinking that the industrial and labour correspondents were their enemy. Peter Walker told us: 'The problem if you are a politician involved in an industrial dispute is that you have to deal with the industrial relations correspondents who are close to the unions.' But NUM press officer Nell Myers wrote immediately after the dispute: 'The industrial correspondents, along with broadcasting technicians, are basically our enemies' front-line troops.'[16]

At one level it is perhaps a professional tribute to the industrial correspondents. But things are more complicated than that. Walker was nearer the truth than Myers. Groups of specialist journalists often take on something of the outward character of the people they report on: religious correspondents are often ardent churchgoers, royal correspondents are frequently tweedy and a tad snobbish, and so on. In the 1980s the industrial correspondents tended unconsciously to ape trade union officials, drinking hard and talking tough. They liked the company of union officials, whom they considered important people, and whose words and actions they always reported, which is why unions were so high-profile.

After the miners' strike, trade unions declined, as we shall see, quickly and sharply, and the industrial correspondents declined with them. A Fleet Street elite in 1984, within a decade they became an endangered species, and the unions miss them dreadfully, for union affairs are now covered, when they are covered at all, by business reporters, who are much less sympathetic. The decline of the industrial and labour correspondents has both mirrored and helped cause the decline of the unions themselves.

Myers was quite wrong about the industrial correspondents. There was a great deal of sympathy among them for the miners, which Myers could have tapped, if only she had thought it worthwhile. One of them, *The Times*'s Paul Routledge, quietly gave £5,000 towards the miners' cause while he was reporting the strike – something his employers would have found most disturbing, if they had known about it.

Routledge had, in fact, offered to leave *The Times* when Scargill became NUM President, to edit *The Miner* in place of Bob Houston. At that time – it turned to bitterness later on – Scargill and Routledge were close. Routledge would have been an asset to Scargill, and might also have acted as a bridge between Scargill and the industrial correspondents. But the message he got back was that Scargill did not want someone from Fleet Street. The idea of employing Routledge was well outside Scargill's comfort zone. Routledge would certainly have taken the view that he knew more about editing magazines than did the national President, which is not a view that would have commended itself to Scargill.

The only paper that is thought to have had some preferential treatment was *Newsline*, the tiny-circulation publication produced by the WRP. Theirs were the only reporters who sometimes got behind the picket lines. But even *Newsline* people were not safe. 'A group of pickets thought I was from the Tory press,' remembers Peter Arkell, at that time a *Newsline* photographer. 'They were very threatening, it was very frightening.' They demanded he hand over his film and, wisely, he did so.

But he says he gave the names of those who threatened him to the strike committee, and they said they had no record of pickets with those names. 'So perhaps they were *agents provocateurs*.' Perhaps they were. In war, you never know for certain.

If even Arkell was not safe behind the picket lines, you can be certain that the BBC's Nicholas Jones would not have been. 'That was the last time any union thought it could win without the media,' wrote Jones.

'Never again will a union fighting a strike seek to alienate the journalists assigned to the story. A few years later, when firefighters were on strike, journalists joined them by the brazier behind the picket line, and we were able to see a disciplined union making its case.'[17]

Ms Myers and her boss were not short of colleagues from other unions to beg her to change her stance towards the industrial correspondents. Since Margaret Thatcher's election victory in 1979, trade unions had belatedly realized that industrial muscle was not enough: they needed public opinion on their side. They started doing what companies had done for years, adopting professional public relations techniques and hiring media officers. But, since Scargill's election, the NUM had put this process in reverse.

Under Joe Gormley, *The Miner* was edited by Bob Houston, a large, noisy but able and experienced Scottish journalist who also helped Gormley with media relations. Houston was particularly close to his fellow hard-drinking Scot Lawrence Daly. When Scargill became President, he and Houston seem to have taken one look at each other and decided the relationship would not work. Houston was too much of a journalist, and not enough of a Scargillite.

As press officer Scargill appointed Houston's secretary, Nell Myers, who knew less about journalism than Houston and, according to Nicholas Jones, 'worshipped the ground Scargill stood on'. Scargill's conception of the job can be judged from the fact that she combined it with being his personal assistant.

Myers was the daughter of American communists who kept the faith with great courage when communism was illegal in the USA. She had been in the American Communist Party in the early and mid sixties, and joined the CPGB when she came to England. Thin and tense, in those days she wore a permanently fierce expression.

Myers refused to talk to journalists, whom she clearly loathed. She hardly ever returned their telephone calls. She sent out NUM policy papers with no embargo. That might sound like a small technical matter, but any journalist or press officer knew that it meant they would probably get no coverage, because journalists tend to assume that such documents are either out of date or have already been published or broadcast elsewhere.[18]

Her one guiding principle was utter and uncritical loyalty to Scargill. Seumas Milne of the *Guardian*, probably the only journalist whom Scargill trusts, told us that if the NUM president was looking for someone to do the job of a traditional trade union press officer, Nell was a bad appointment. Scargill, however, wasn't looking for that, he was looking for something different. But no one has been able to tell us what it was that Scargill was looking for.

Myers wrote after the strike: 'We discovered a long time ago than no amount of "access" for industrial correspondents from trade union officials stands a chance against similar briefings between respective employers.'[19] So, while Peter Walker thought the industrial correspondents were the enemy and went out of his way to win them over, Myers and Scargill thought they were the enemy and saw no point in doing anything at all to court them.

Yet at the same time Scargill was obsessed by the media and his image in it. Nicholas Jones has provided a remarkable description of his style as the strike began. Scargill, he writes, was responsible for issuing press statements, writing almost all of them himself, and then presided at every news conference. Myers had to get his guidance before dealing with even the simplest query, and other staff were told to direct all queries to Myers, who lived in London and often worked from home, away from the NUM's Sheffield headquarters. The NUM switchboard operator was instructed to log all calls and say who the caller was asking for, thus ensuring that no one could step out of line and help a journalist.

Jones writes: 'Mr Scargill enjoyed relying on his own judgement when making statements to the press. His skill as a communicator seemed entirely self-taught, acquired through observation; he was held in awe by his staff, many of whom he had selected or recommended for appointment following the union's move to Sheffield.' At press conferences, 'before the journalists crowded in to hear Mr Scargill, some members of his staff would try to reserve seats for themselves, later looking on with obvious admiration at the way the President handled those reporters who asked difficult questions.'[20]

Scargill was playing to an audience of appreciative staff, and what went down well with them was not always the most useful thing to say to the press.

None of this stopped him from telling a miners' rally in the Jubilee Gardens, when the strike was three months' old: 'Throughout this dispute, day after day, television, radio and the press have consistently put over the views of the coal board and government even when they have been exposed of being guilty of duplicity and guilty of telling lies . . . This bunch of piranha fish will always go on supporting Mrs Thatcher.' (Cheers.)

But the way in which Scargill chose to handle the media should not disguise the fact that he had a point. There really was a media campaign of lies and distortions waged against him and the miners. When he made that speech, he had just seen a picture in the *Sun* of himself at a rally, raising his arm in greeting. The picture was grabbed at just the right moment to present it as though it were a Nazi salute, under the headline MINE FUHRER. It was true that the miners' case never got a fair hearing, and only a part of the brutally unfair coverage they got can be put down to the ineptness of their media relations. Some of the coverage was twisted by snobbery and class hatred. Take this, from one Frank Musgrove in the *Sunday Times* of 12 August:

> There has been a massive haemorrhage of talent from the mining communities . . . which have drained away the most enterprising men . . . It is the diluted human residues that remain, especially in Yorkshire and Durham . . . Five years in the E-stream of a comprehensive school is an excellent training in sheer bloody-mindedness.

The trouble was that Scargill so effectively poisoned his activists' minds against journalists – all journalists without discrimination – that no journalist was safe on the pickets' side of the lines. 'Reporters were simply not welcome in the pit villages,' writes Nicholas Jones, a reporter whose instincts were with the miners.

To edit *The Miner* instead of Bob Houston, Scargill brought Maurice Jones from the *Yorkshire Miner*, and, says Nicholas Jones, 'the paper was entirely controlled by Scargill. No editorial judgements were made by Maurice Jones.'[21] Jones and Myers vied for the President's ear. Jones disliked his boss's growing reliance on Myers, resented the fact that she was asked to produce an issue of *The Miner* while he was away, objected to Scargill making her deputy editor of the paper, and according to Seumas Milne even became convinced she was a CIA plant.[22]

By the end of March 1984, after just three weeks of industrial action, every important aspect of the strike had emerged. The NCB had taken the public relations initiative, and never lost it. The divisions inside the union – which were eventually to lead to the creation of the breakaway Union of Democratic Mineworkers – were already there, and grew with each passing week. So did the emphasis in the media, particularly on TV, on the violent nature of the picketing and the growing hatred between strikers and working miners, and between pickets and police.

The pro-active role of the police, which came to dominate the dispute as thousands of officers were drafted into Nottinghamshire from all over the country, and the paramilitary nature of their actions could be seen in their efforts to stop pickets getting within 100 miles of their destination.

The determination of the government to break the strike, with the help of the security services and the police, was already evident. And the legal battle that would end with the sequestration of the NUM's accounts was already taking embryonic form, in the alacrity with which the NCB under Ian MacGregor went to the courts to stop the pickets.

The start of the strike may have been an accident, but it did not catch the government unprepared. MacGregor was clear from the start about two things, and they were to prove the only two things that mattered. First, 'the key to the whole strike was Nottinghamshire and its 31,000 miners. If we could keep this vast and prosperous coalfield going, then I was convinced, however long it took, we could succeed.' So far the

NUM had rather played into his hands, with its refusal to hold a ballot or even to court public opinion. The second was that, if he was to keep Nottinghamshire open, he needed tough policing to counter the picketing. Understated British-style policing was no good to him. He was, he told Thatcher on 14 March, 'wishing I had a bunch of good untidy American cops out there.'[23] American cops get stuck in, especially with striking trade unionists. He told her that, to get Nottinghamshire, he needed aggressive policing. She gave it to him. He used it ruthlessly to deliver victory, and the first and bloodiest battlefield on which he used it was Orgreave in Yorkshire.

CHAPTER 4

THE BATTLE OF ORGREAVE

1 APRIL TO 21 JUNE

The issue of whether to hold a national ballot had lost none of its power to divide the miners and their natural supporters in other unions. While Scargill was sure flying pickets would bring miners out – and was soon to put this to its ultimate test in the pitched battles between miners and police that became known as the Battle of Orgreave – Labour leader Neil Kinnock contacted him and begged him to change his mind and agree to a ballot. The two spoke on the telephone on 9 April, and Kinnock had a transcript made of the conversation because he did not trust the miners' leader.

Kinnock came from a mining family and a mining community. An emotional man with a strong sense of family and community, he was distressed to see internecine warfare among the miners – and of course the absence of a ballot was a dreadful political millstone round his neck as well.

Scargill said the Tories were panicking, but Kinnock did not see it like that: 'Well, what I think they want most – and this is how cynical they are – what they want most here is no ballot, and they think there is enormous political profit for them if they can use the taunt of no ballot. And they are not going into the nuances or the rectitude of the

NUM constitution, that's my feeling. I don't think it's the product of any nervousness they've got, I think it's much more to do with political profit they think they can secure.'

Kinnock added: 'We want the national ballot . . . Now I've said to everyone that only you can take that decision – the NEC of the NUM, that is – and I've resisted all the taunts, all the pressure about national ballot this, national ballot that.'

He said his South Wales miners were worried: 'They are guys now who have been absolutely to the forefront but they are now extremely – well, not querulous, that's not fair to them – but they are bewildered and they are wondering what kind of strategy they can depend on and how long they can last out.' He said he feared Scargill was splitting the union.[1]

Failing to achieve anything with Scargill, Kinnock went public the next day, calling for a ballot in careful words designed to ensure that he could not be accused of attacking the miners. He said he feared a division in the NUM 'which could be cataclysmic'.

Today, more than two decades on, Kinnock wishes he had gone further. He says: 'I still curse myself for not taking the chance and saying, to a miners' meeting – I would not have said it to anyone else – you will not get sympathetic action without a ballot, and coal stocks are piled up.'

Three days later, on 12 April, at the NUM National Executive meeting, right-wing executive members decided to make a stand on the issue, convinced that running a national strike without a ballot was disastrous. They were supported by a prominent left-winger, the Nottinghamshire miners' General Secretary, Henry Richardson. He was watching the men he led being divided acrimoniously from their fellow miners in Yorkshire, Kent and elsewhere. He told the executive prophetically: 'The longer we go on the bigger the split. Our men who are striking are getting nothing . . . The majority of Notts miners are saying, "We shall not move without a ballot . . ." We are destroying trade unionism in Nottinghamshire.'

Nottinghamshire's Ray Chadburn described what he had seen in the Notts coalfields: 'Miner is against miner and father against son, family against family.' Striking miners had been picketing his home, shouting, 'Come out here, you bastard.'

Mick McGahey spoke against a ballot: 'It is the media who have got "ballotitis". It was war from the moment MacGregor was appointed.' McGahey seemed, however, in his often unexpectedly subtle way, to open a door for a ballot when he proposed a special conference instead: 'Nobody here is against ballots, in fact a special conference should consider a ballot vote. You can express an opinion there. We need a conference to unify us.' The truth was that McGahey, the most respected Communist in Britain, had had to work hard to get the Communist Party to endorse Arthur Scargill's 'no ballot' position, and the Party later regretted its endorsement. This lack of wholesale support for his tactics widened the growing gulf between Scargill and the party under whose tutelage he had first learned his politics. Within days of the end of the strike, the Party's new industrial organizer Pete Carter wrote an analysis of Scargill's tactics which concluded that mass picketing was a mistake and there ought to have been a ballot. 'The Communist Party is ready to settle,' remarked the NCB Deputy Chairman Jim Cowan two months later, and he had it pretty nearly right.[2]

It is almost certain that, in his heart, McGahey knew the 'no ballot' policy was a mistake, but kept his own counsel because he was sure a split between himself and Scargill would damage the union and the strike even more. His proposal that the question of a ballot should go to the conference did not satisfy the right-wingers on the executive. They knew that such a conference would be dominated by left-wing areas, and the ballot proposal would stand no chance. So they demanded an immediate ballot, in the knowledge that several executive members had been mandated to vote in favour of having one. They thought they had enough votes to swing it. They probably did, and Scargill probably knew it, because he scuppered the ballot with a procedural manoeuvre.

Scargill made a presidential ruling from the chair that the ballot proposal could not be put: it could only be put at the special delegate conference which he proposed should be called on 19 April. His ruling was upheld by 13 votes to 8.[3] Several executive members who had been mandated to vote for a ballot but wanted to vote against one were able to vote as they wished without breaking their mandate, because they were simply able to support the Chairman's ruling.[4]

There was never any realistic chance that the conference would insist on a ballot against the President's opposition, and it did not. It voted to spread the strike. Now the NUM leadership's task was to convince members that they were going to win – which at that stage, despite the problems with Nottinghamshire and ballots, looked perfectly likely. Morale was high. If commitment and energy and confidence were enough to win, the miners had it sewn up.

The NUM paper *The Miner* tried hard from the first to make coal stocks into a heartening story for the striking miners. THE COAL BOARD'S GREAT STOCKS BUBBLE HAS BURST was its lead headline at the start of April. The story began: 'Repeated claims that there is no immediate threat to supplies have proven untrue.' But they had not been proved untrue. The claims were still to be tested, and Neil Kinnock for one felt fairly sure that the Board had sufficient stocks to sit out a longer strike than the miners could stage.

He tried to tell Scargill so in that 9 April telephone conversation: 'The other thing I'm interested in is this stocks position. Obviously the CEGB are increasing their oil – that doesn't cause them any problems, does it? And what time would it cost them? It still means, as you say, seven or eight weeks. I mean, what is the strategy over that period? Because you know they are in no trouble, MacGregor or the government, over such a period because that takes us then into May, June, the end of June . . .'[5]

The same issue of *The Miner* ran a stop press item: 'In a magnificent display of solidarity with the country's miners, six key unions are to black the transport of all coal.'[6] The National Union of Railwaymen had voted not to move coal. 'All coal is black,' read one deadpan miner's placard.

Nonetheless, some coal was still moving, and the steelworkers' union ISTC refused to follow the NUR's example. ISTC leader Bill Sirs found himself under furious attack from Mick McGahey at the TUC General Council meeting on 22 May for failing to support the miners. The miners had supported the steelworkers when they were in dispute, McGahey told Sirs.[7]

John Lyons, leader of the Engineers and Managers Association, received a letter from Peter Heathfield telling him that miners would picket power stations where Lyons's members worked, and that they should be deemed to be picketing even if they were not there. Lyons did not, even for an instant, consider instructing his members along these lines.[8]

Mick McGahey once told one of the authors: 'Other union leaders who wanted to help us had to face the question from their members: why should we sacrifice our jobs when 20 per cent of the miners are producing coal?' He added: 'When you're in a class battle with the full offensive of the enemy against you and the bullets flying around, it's a luxury to sit back and analyse.' But it was the reason why the ban on coal movements imposed by the transport unions was not very effective, and many transport workers continued to move coal out of the areas where it was still being mined.

The language used by other union leaders seemed to betray the sense of foreboding they felt for the whole movement. Moss Evans, General Secretary of the TGWU, Britain's biggest union, called for financial support so that the miners should not be 'starved into submission'.[9] The powerful print union SOGAT, like many others, gave money – £15,000 to start with – after hearing from its General Secretary Bill Keys that, while one might dispute the miners' tactics, other unions could not stand by and watch them being defeated.

Bill Keys also used his extensive media contacts, and his union's considerable muscle in the newspaper industry, to try to do something about the daily condemnation of the miners that appeared in the press. He got Arthur Scargill a right of reply to one particularly vitriolic piece in the *Daily Express* (and was disappointed that the miners' leader, he felt, used it to pay off old scores instead of setting out his case). He was a vital figure in a secret group of left-wing union leaders who met regularly to decide how best they could help the miners. He was their liaison with the miners – and, significantly, they decided he should work through McGahey, not Scargill.

At his own union's conference, Keys took the opportunity of meeting two South Wales miners' leaders, Terry Thomas and Emlyn Jenkins, who had appealed for support and understanding, and of pressing the case for a ballot. 'They took the attitude, well, how can you invite a scab in Notts to partake in a ballot. To which my reply was, well, you could have had the ballot before these people became scabs. They remained loyal, but I could not help but get the impression that they agreed with me.'[10] This was the beginning of a secret mission, never before revealed, which almost secured the miners something that could have been dressed up to look like a partial victory.

The NUM Nottinghamshire leaders called on their members to join in the action and not cross picket lines set up in the county by Yorkshire miners, a call the members rejected in a ballot at the start of April. The pickets came anyway. If those picket lines could be broken, MacGregor was confident that enough Nottinghamshire miners would allow themselves to be escorted through by the police. There were even reports of teams of men being paid to go into Nottinghamshire and persuade miners to go back to work. Their paymaster was David Hart, a wealthy Old Etonian (he had inherited a fortune from his father) of very right-wing views, who was keen to break the strike to teach the unions a lesson. He was close to MacGregor and had once, in *The Times*, welcomed high unemployment as a stage in emancipating the working class from wage slavery. During the strike he co-ordinated, financed and encouraged the groups who were breaking it. He was sure the NUM must be defeated at all costs. MacGregor, apparently with affection, called him 'Stalin'.[11] *The Times* industrial correspondent Paul Routledge complained bitterly to his editor, William Rees-Mogg, that Hart should not be allowed to comment in the newspaper in the guise of an independent freelance journalist, when in reality he was funding the return-to-work campaign.

Hart was described in the press as an adviser to Thatcher over the strike. Andrew (now Lord) Turnbull, who was Thatcher's private secretary at the time, believes his connections to Thatcher were overblown. He recalls considerable anger in Downing Street over the suggestion that Hart was an adviser to Thatcher. He recalled few occasions when Hart managed to see her. When he did, he was shabbily dressed in jeans and a sweater, or sometimes a not too well-fitting check jacket. Hart's main interest in seeing her was to rubbish Walker, whom he perceived as a wet only too ready to get a settlement. But any effort he might make to influence the Prime Minister would be quickly overturned by Walker's more regular appearances at Downing Street, sharing the day's developments in the strike over a late-night glass of whisky with the PM. David Hunt, later the coal minister, and Ivor Manley, Walker's Deputy Secretary, both said Walker made a point of keeping Thatcher regularly briefed, so he could control events and keep his lines into Number Ten open. Turnbull observed: 'Peter Walker came out of this extremely well.'

Tim (now Lord) Bell describes Hart as an eccentric figure who later, like MacGregor, became emotionally attached to the working miners in Nottinghamshire. According to Bell, Hart and MacGregor built up quite a rapport with the UDM's working miners and drank with them in pubs. Bell said: 'David Hart had a habit of taking snuff and used to go down to the local pub and share his snuff with the miners.'

To complement Hart's efforts, MacGregor needed strong-arm tactics to make the pickets ineffective. Riot police were used from the start. The National and Local Government Officers Association (NALGO, now called Unison) condemned this at the start of April in curiously ambiguous language: 'Whatever the rights and wrongs of mass picketing, it is clearly a disturbing and dangerous development for Continental-style riot police to be unleashed on trade unionists in an industrial dispute.'[12] On 9 April, 100 pickets were arrested outside mines in Nottinghamshire and Derbyshire, and many people were injured, both miners and police. By 12 April more than 1,000 miners had been arrested on picket lines.

After the first couple of weeks, all over the country, the police attitude towards strikers was cranked up. Strikers suddenly found themselves being treated as enemies of the state, and the friendly bobby turned into a ferocious figure with a horse and a lethal truncheon.

The tiny Kent mining workforce was among the first to notice the difference. They had been allocated the ports to picket, and told to try to persuade dockers not to unload foreign coal. A few Kent miners picketed the Wivenhoe port in Essex peacefully for several days; the manager even gave them a brazier beside which to warm themselves. But on 10 April, two days before the special miners' conference that rejected a ballot, everything changed suddenly. A convoy of police vans and nearly 100 police arrived and told the men they had no right to picket. 'They came across to us and said we were not pickets, we were demonstrators. They said it was secondary picketing – we were breaking the law and we shouldn't even be in the county.' And from then on, as elsewhere in the country, the picket line was hobbled by the police presence. Roadblocks were set up, and pickets routinely beaten up by police. The manager took back his brazier.

The confrontations at Wivenhoe followed a pattern that became sadly common throughout the country. Every picket you speak to has bitter stories about the police. 'They generally try to have digs at you on the line by saying, "I hope the strike goes on longer as I'm on £500 a week." They ask us how we spend our £3 a day picketing money – things like that. They make remarks about getting three holidays a year and living off the backs of the miners . . . They come out with comments about your wife or girlfriend you've left behind at home. They say: "Who's giving it one at home, like."'[13]

The National Council for Civil Liberties (NCCL) reported disturbing allegations about how miners and their wives were treated when arrested. Police were questioning them about their political views, including such matters as their views about Arthur Scargill and how they voted at the last general election. Since the strike, far too many such allegations have emerged for them all to be mistaken or mischievous. It happened, quite often.

Another routine practice identified by the NCCL was for officers to conceal their numbers by covering up their shoulders, thus making it impossible for pickets to lodge complaints against any individual officer.

Police determination to keep Nottinghamshire working is well illustrated by Anne Scargill's experiences. Anne, wife of Arthur and the inspiration behind the organization which became nationally known as Women Against Pit Closures, was a regular and encouraging presence on picket lines. In April she led a group of women to picket peacefully in Nottinghamshire, and they met with some Nottinghamshire women in a supermarket car park.

At the pithead, the twenty women saw only about eight police. 'They didn't know how to handle women, did they? We weren't violent but we gave them [the working miners] some stick.' They had some success: two of the men turned back, first for some reason throwing their sandwiches to the women, who ate them. A few others abused them, but it never looked like getting ugly: 'We didn't swear or anything but we did give them some back. It was a lively picket but nobody had overstepped the mark. It was really light-hearted.' The small group of policemen seemed to join in the spirit of the occasion.

But then police reinforcements arrived, and the women knew there was going to be trouble, because as they got out of the bus they adjusted their chinstraps. Suddenly the atmosphere was very different. Everyone went quiet. There was a sense of menace.

Quite how it started, Anne Scargill does not know, but suddenly they grabbed one of the women and bundled her into a police van. Her friend tried to get her from the police, and they took her too. Another woman made a comment about it, and into the van she went. Then Anne, who still had the residual respect for the police that she had learned as a child, approached the inspector quietly and said: 'Excuse me, can you tell me why you've arrested her when she's done nothing wrong?' He said: 'Take her as well.'

The van drove off with the four women in the back and a policeman in the front. Anne, who found the silence unnerving, asked the young policeman with them where he came from. He was from Somerset, and a very long way from home. One of the women – rather unhelpfully, Anne thought – said she hoped every man in Somerset was making free with his wife.

They got to the police station, the van was unlocked, and Anne got down the steps and started to run – she needed the toilet. But the policeman must have thought she was trying to escape, because he grabbed her hair.

They were taken to the desk sergeant, who asked her name. She said: 'You tell me what I've done wrong and I'll tell you what I'm called.' He asked again. She tried to lighten the atmosphere. 'Why, are going to take me on a date?' she said. 'You look quite attractive when you smile.' The sergeant does not appear to have been a man with a lively sense of humour.

They were put in a dog compound. 'It was raining and it was full of dog muck. We were in there for about an hour and Lynn wanted to go to the toilet and they wouldn't come so I started punching the door and shouting.' A policewoman took her to a room with a bath. She too asked Anne's name, and Anne said she would give it as soon as she had been told what she had done wrong. The policewoman told her to get undressed.

'I said, "What for, I'm not mucky, I got bathed this morning." She said, "Just get undressed." She said, "I'm looking for offensive weapons and drugs." I said, "I'm old enough to be your mother." She said, "I'm only doing my job." I said, "Yeah, that's what they said in Nazi Germany when they were taking the Jews to be slaughtered, only doing their job."'

Off came her clothes, she turned round for the policewoman's inspection, and then she put her clothes back on. But they kept her shoes. 'I said, "I'm not walking on this scruffy floor without shoes, even if I have to stop here all day." I said, "I don't walk round at home without shoes and it's a lot cleaner than it is here."' So they took out the shoelaces and gave her back her shoes.

The four women were given a filthy cell and left there for hours, until Anne was separated from the others and shown to a room where sat a man in a suit who offered her a cup of tea and asked her name. Anne gave the same reply she had always given: tell me what I've done wrong and I'll tell you what they call me. He said they could not do that yet because they did not know what they were going to charge her with.

He wanted to know which newspaper she read. She asked him which he read, and he said, the *Daily Mail*. 'Now I know why you're so biased,' said Anne, still trying to keep it light-hearted. He told her that she could have one phone call, so she called her office at the Co-op and said: 'I can't come into work today, Nottinghamshire Police won't let me.' And her colleague said: 'I know, it's all over the telly.' The man in the suit said: 'Are you Arthur Scargill's wife?' Anne Scargill persisted: 'Tell me what I've done wrong and I'll tell you who I am.'

The man was apparently fending off dozens of reporters, all saying he had Arthur Scargill's wife in his cells. Anne said: 'I'm not being funny, but I'm getting tired of this and if you don't charge me I'm not saying anything.' They took her away and put her in a cell by herself.

Anne Scargill was bound over until October and was not allowed to go picketing again in Nottingham until then. In October the magistrate stopped the case and pronounced the four women not guilty. There was a press pack outside, and she refused to leave to face them. The police just wanted to be rid of her, but she told them they would have to throw her out. 'You've got me into this situation for nothing, you can help me out.' With the worst possible grace, they agreed to show her a back exit, where a friend could pick her up.

Here is the lesson that Anne Scargill – an ordinary working-class Yorkshirewoman, even if she was married to one of the most famous men in Britain – learned from that day. It was a lesson many other women learned too. 'I was forty-four years old. I'd read in the papers that this had been done to ethnic people by the police and I thought they must have done something wrong for the police to take them. But that day taught me a real lesson about the police. It frightened me actually.'

While they were banned from Nottinghamshire, they picketed in Lancashire. The police, she says, 'were horrible to us.' One night they were singing after they left the picket line, and one of the police officers said loudly, so they could hear: 'The cows are in good voice this morning.' Anne says: 'We were singing often because we were frightened, and somebody said, "At least singing is better than crying."'

The government was prepared to use police as a battering ram, but it was less keen on paying for it. It tried to get Nottingham ratepayers to foot the bill, and partly succeeded. Papers released by the Home Office under the Freedom of Information Act show that the row went on for the first six months of the strike, despite pleas from Tory MPs, council leaders and Chief Constables.

The government appeared to be displaying generosity towards local authorities by promising not to penalize them for overspending caused by the strike. But ministers were determined not to pay all the bills. In March, Michael Spungin, leader of the Tory group on Nottinghamshire County Council, complained to Douglas Hurd, then a Home Office minister: 'It would be impossible for any Conservative in the county to defend a government decision to operate in that way on what is certainly a national problem which happens to be being fought out on the territory of Nottinghamshire by others.'

Home Secretary Leon Brittan appeared to concede, and on 11 May committed himself to paying half the extra cost up to the product of a 1p rate and 90 per cent afterwards. But this did not satisfy the police authorities, who became increasingly angry behind the scenes, as Home Office documents released under FOI reveal. Nottinghamshire was spending £2m a week, including £1.8m on police overtime and £20,000 a week to the Ministry of Defence to rent barracks for the police.

In May, Jim Lester, Conservative MP for Broxtowe, told the Prime Minister of the 'strong feeling of disappointment' in Nottinghamshire because the government was not providing enough financial support. The Prime Minister acknowledged that Nottinghamshire's police force had the largest bill – estimated at £25m – in a crucial battleground of the dispute. Exchanges between Andrew Turnbull, Thatcher's private secretary, and Leon Brittan's aides show that Brittan thought, 'It would be wrong in principle for central government to pay the full costs: policing is essentially a local matter.'

It was not until June that Brittan changed his mind. In a letter dated 6 June to Peter Rees, Chief Secretary to the Treasury, he admitted that Nottinghamshire was in trouble because of the cost of policing the picketing. The Chief Constable had stopped recruiting staff and frozen computer projects. A letter from the Home Office's F3 division two days earlier revealed that Nottinghamshire had set a date of 1 October to quit the regional crime squad and criminal intelligence unit. Derbyshire and South Yorkshire were expected to follow.[14] So Brittan had little choice. He announced extra funding at the Tory conference in October.

Another major cost for the government was where to billet all these extra police officers. Internal Home Office documents reveal the ministry was desperate to find suitable accommodation to house all the police, so they could be at the picket lines early in the morning. Morton Hospital, a closed NHS hospital at Clay Cross, was used because the spare capacity in every military base in the Midlands was full to overflowing and the MoD could not release any more space because 'it had been earmarked for a major military training programme'.

The hospital was needed urgently as police from Devon and Cornwall, Cambridgeshire, Lancashire and Cheshire had all been drafted to Derbyshire and could not travel there every day. Derbyshire County Council had refused to find or offer any accommodation for them and had objected on planning grounds to the use of the hospital. But a 'strictly confidential' letter from the head of the North Derbyshire Health Authority to the police showed he was only too happy to co-operate at £250 a week for rent, plus another £325 a week if they wished to use the Ashgate Maternity Home. His helpful advice included the useful information that, as the hospital was technically on Crown land, no planning application was required.

Such were the private deals made to aid the police and probably repeated up and down the country. We can now trace the story from the internal official note prepared in order to answer a question two months later, in June, from Dennis Skinner, MP for Bolsover, about the use of Morton Hospital to billet police.

MacGregor was talking loosely about bringing the army in, but the next day he struggled to distance himself from this, no doubt after a sharp rebuke from sources close to the Prime Minister. But it was starting to look and sound like warfare. Mick McGahey told the Scottish TUC: 'We are fighting for this country and we are telling this country we will not be bought off by your filthy money. We will keep our jobs and our dignity.'[15] He was rewarded with a resolution for mass secondary picketing to take place for one day in support of the striking miners.

As May began, Nottinghamshire was still producing coal. All its pits were working, and the split in the NUM was starting to become ugly. TUC leaders looked at the increasingly divided miners' union and could do little except fret. At this time, Scargill was asking them for nothing; it was not until later, with the strike crumbling around him, that he condemned them for not coming to his aid.

On 2 May, 6,000 Nottinghamshire miners, some with banners saying 'Adolph Scargill', staged a 'right to work' demonstration at the NUM area office in Mansfield. Scargill replied with a demonstration in Mansfield on 14 May, when striking miners sang 'There's only one Arthur Scargill' to the tune of 'Guantanamera'. The internal Home Office records sent to Peter Walker record that 12,000 people participated. The rally ended in violence when demonstrators fought with the 1,035 police, some of them mounted. Eighty-seven arrests were made, eighty-eight police officers injured and fifty-seven people charged.

Yet despite the NUM's problems, the strike was having a serious effect, and the government was far from certain of victory. The same day as Scargill's Nottinghamshire demonstration, 14 May, Peter Gregson at the Department of Energy sat down to write another of his remarkably blunt memos to the Prime Minister. The occasion this time was a private meeting between Thatcher, Walker and Nigel Lawson, the

Chancellor. The meeting had been requested by Walker after receiving some startling figures of the costs facing the taxpayer, even if the strike was brought speedily to an end.

Gregson was less sure than MacGregor that there was no threat to coal stocks. The NCB could deliver only 1.85m tonnes of coal a week to power stations. There would be huge costs to the taxpayer to keep the power stations going. Gregson's memo revealed that even if the strike was called off at the end of May, the oil – 350,000 tonnes a week – would have to continue to be delivered until mid-September to keep all power stations open. If it ended in June, huge oil deliveries would be needed until December, while if it continued until July, oil deliveries could be not reduced until March 1985.

The memo concluded: 'This has serious implications for costs, bearing in mind that the net extra cost of burning oil rather than coal is £20m a week and that, during the recovery period, the CEGB would be buying the oil in addition [underlined] to buying coal, so that the relevant figure would be the gross cost of £50m a week.'

Gregson told Thatcher secretly that he was not quite clear what his boss Peter Walker made of this, but he suggested that Nigel Lawson might want to put up electricity prices to pay for it. He warned: 'This might however give Scargill a useful propaganda advantage, although it has to be conceded that, as the weekend press showed, the cost of extra oilburn is already becoming an issue and the government may have to make its position clear on where the cost is to fall before long.' If only Scargill knew.

There were more negotiations in May, but it's likely that neither of the principals really wanted a resolution. MacGregor scented victory, and was more interested in what he could do to encourage the drift back to work, especially in Nottinghamshire. Scargill also believed in victory, and, in any case, negotiating was never what Scargill was best at, as the NCB's director of industrial relations, Ned Smith, told Paul Routledge: 'He could put a case across very well indeed. But once his brief was finished, if the answer was "no", Arthur was buggered because he wasn't a negotiator. What he said was right and had to be accepted.'[16]

Scargill told MacGregor that the closure list must be withdrawn before he would talk. The NCB offered to extend the timeframe for closures, but said it would still reduce capacity by 4m tonnes and cut 20,000 jobs. Scargill would not talk about it: 'As far as I'm concerned, pit closures and job losses are not negotiable.'

The talks collapsed, but not before Scargill had secretly assured Neil Kinnock that the NCB was about to cave in. On 1 June he spoke to Kinnock's adviser Dick Clements. He wanted Clements to tell Kinnock that the Board was now saying their closure plan could be withdrawn. Kinnock was not to tell anyone; he was, said Scargill, the first person to be told this.

'We are now negotiating,' Scargill told Clements. The Board had even told him 'that they would not talk with non-accredited miners' representatives', meaning the leaders of breakaway groups in Nottinghamshire. Scargill saw this as a clear statement that the Board was not going to exploit the union's divisions in Nottinghamshire, and that it would provide no aid or comfort to people who formed breakaway organizations from the NUM.

Clements realized this must be rubbish. Of course the board was going to exploit the divisions in Nottinghamshire. MacGregor and Thatcher had fomented that division precisely so that they could exploit it. Clements put the best light he could on it, writing to Kinnock: 'Scargill's enthusiasm for the Board's statement on this subject does indicate that he realizes the weakest link in his negotiating position.'[17]

Whether Scargill was trying to fool Kinnock or succeeding in fooling himself, we will probably never know. Either way, within a week the optimism was gone. On 7 June, a week after his talk with Clements, he and McGahey addressed a meeting of the national and regional officials of the TGWU. Scargill, says someone who was there, 'treated us to one of his rants and said: "I'm not asking you for support, I'm demanding it."' McGahey, more emollient throughout, asked for money: 'Money isn't everything, but when you haven't got any it's useful.'

By then Scargill and MacGregor seem to have jettisoned jaw-jaw for war-war, and the next decision taken by the generals was a crucial one. There was to be a pitched battle.

MacGregor and Scargill both wanted the pitched battle, but it was MacGregor who chose the battlefield. MacGregor wanted it a long way away from Nottinghamshire, where the real action was taking place. For him the main aim was to get Scargill's forces out of that county. He chose the Orgreave coke works, just south of Sheffield.

The Battle of Orgreave, as it would be known, has become a heroic defeat in miners' mythology. But to MacGregor it was nothing but a vast, and successful, diversionary tactic. MacGregor cared little what happened at Orgreave. But if he could have miners tied up with battling the police in irrelevant Orgreave, they would not be travelling south to picket in vital Nottinghamshire. Afterwards he gloated: 'All you had to do was make it known that you were going to get men back at a particular pit and all the pickets from that area would disappear from Nottingham or the other areas to cope with it.' Orgreave was, 'of all these efforts to divert Arthur Scargill's firepower, the most spectacular and the most successful . . . We were quite encouraged that [Scargill] thought it so important and did everything we could to help him continue to think so, but the truth was it mattered hardly a jot to us – beyond the fact that it kept him away from Nottingham.'[18]

There was another reason to redirect the battle to Orgreave. Its terrain favoured the police. It was not like Saltley, scene of Scargill's mythic victory, a city site, hemmed in by streets. Orgreave is in open country. No intelligent general on the miners' side would have chosen Orgreave for his battlefield.

At the start of the strike, pickets were not troubling much about Orgreave. Even after train drivers refused to take Orgreave's coke to the British Steel Corporation's works in Scunthorpe, forty miles away, at the start of May, and it had to go by lorry, there was just a small six-strong picket at Orgreave, and they did not prevent the British Steel employees who worked there from going into work. They talked peacefully to the lorry drivers, and at first even used the cokemen's canteen and lavatories, until these were locked and private security men hired to deny them access.[19]

The police drew more pickets to Orgreave by more or less putting a cordon round Nottinghamshire to prevent pickets' coaches getting into the county, and leaving the routes from the Nottinghamshire borders to Orgreave relatively clear. A Yorkshire striking miner who was arrested at Orgreave provides an unconscious hint of what was going on. Although he did not realize how little Orgreave mattered, he did see that Nottinghamshire mattered more, and that was where he really wanted to be that day. But it was getting harder and harder to get into the county, past the police roadblocks. 'We had to go further and further south on side roads before turning back up towards the Nottinghamshire coalfields, approaching them from the south, a direction from which we were not expected to come.' At last it became impossible to get to Nottinghamshire. 'We set off as normal for Nottinghamshire, Leicestershire and Derbyshire, with Orgreave as the fallback point if we weren't able to get through. Roadblocks were everywhere and by 7.30 a.m. we were at Orgreave having failed to get into Nottinghamshire.'[20] Orgreave became the fallback destination for pickets who could not get into Nottinghamshire.

Kevan Hunt, the NCB's deputy director of industrial relations, telephoned Scargill and said: 'Arthur, we need more tonnage out of Orgreave.' Would Scargill help him relieve this pressure point by allowing more coke from the plant?[21] Scargill at once called for a huge blockade to stop coke being sent by lorry. Both sides prepared for a pitched battle.

The three-week-long battle began early on 29 May. Pickets in Yorkshire were told to be there at 7.45 a.m., and well over 1,000 of them arrived, to find themselves facing mounted police and Alsatians. Thirty-five lorries, protected by wire mesh, arrived at Orgreave to load up and were met by a barrage of bottles, stones and broken fencing. Mounted police, supported by officers wearing riot gear and carrying shields, moved in; there were eighty-two arrests and 132 people were injured. A succession of baton charges were made against the pickets. Police on horseback laid about them with truncheons, and dogs were turned on the pickets.

The Home Office estimated that 6,000 pickets turned up facing 2,500 police. The coke lorries got through. Not that MacGregor cared much, but Scargill did. 'We did it at Grunwick and we can do it here,' he said afterwards, and called on his members and 'the whole trade union movement' to 'come here in their thousands in order that we can make aware to everybody that we're not prepared to see this kind of brutality inflicted against working men and women . . . What you have now in South Yorkshire is an actual police state tantamount to something you are used to seeing in Chile or Bolivia.'

Scargill promised to be back the next day, and the next. He called up every picket he could muster to this front line. Nonetheless, numbers declined, and most days after that pickets were outnumbered by police. Home Office figures confirm that the men were losing heart, with 3,000 pickets showing up on 30 May, and only 2,000 the following day. They came, they fought, they inflicted injuries and they were themselves injured. On 30 May Scargill himself was arrested at Orgreave and charged with obstruction as he led a column of pickets towards the plant.

Three days later *The Miner* offered its first full analysis of Orgreave, as always at once furiously angry and relentlessly upbeat. The splash headline was: BRITAIN'S MINERS ARE ON THE ROAD TO A CRUSHING VICTORY. Much of the front page was taken up with a picture of police horses over the caption: 'Mounted madmen deliberately trying to trample miners at British Steel's Orgreave plant. Coke is being shifted to Scunthorpe in defiance of an agreement with the Yorkshire NUM. A little known fact is that Ian MacGregor still remains on the board of British Steel.'

A double-page spread of shocking Orgreave pictures, many of them taken by pickets, was accompanied by a plea for more such pictures: 'The police are greatly concerned at the gathering photographic evidence of their brutality and have developed a new tactic. They yell "camera" to alert their colleagues engaged in violence. It is of the utmost importance that as many cameras as possible are taken on picket lines and arrangements made to get the film away safely.' This was not at all easy, because police had taken to seizing cameras and exposing the film.[22]

By these means, a couple of weeks later on 15 June, *The Miner* was able to show that troops were being used on the picket line. It printed a picture, taken by Yorkshire miner Tony Lowe, of a police van being driven by a man in soldier's uniform, with Lowe's dramatic story: 'The Sergeant yelled at police nearby, "Nick that bastard . . . get the camera" . . . Tony, knowing that the film would be lost if he were caught, dodged between two vans as the police gave chase. It gained him a few precious seconds to wind the film on. He carried on running, got among a group of other miners and threw the film to one, shouting to him to guard it with his life. With the police breathing down his neck he told the other miners to surround him as he feverishly put another film in his camera. A fight between one of the miners and a chasing policeman gave Tony a few more seconds before the police got to him. In full view of the public and at least four NUM witnesses, the police demanded the camera, opened the back and exposed the film to the light. Only now they will be aware they got the wrong film.'[23]

Being a peaceable picket did you no good. 'A big lad came along and told us to stop bricking [throwing bricks],' said one picket. 'He stood in front of the cops so that if we chucked any more bricks we'd hit him. Suddenly the wall of riot shields opened up and he was dragged in. We could see him on the ground with boots and truncheons going into him.'[24]

None of this hit the newspapers at the time – partly from bias, but partly because Scargill's explicit policy was to treat all journalists as enemies, and he had made sure they were not safe among the pickets. For self-protection, journalists congregated behind the police lines.

But it was generally true that newspapers covered violence against the police relentlessly, and ignored the many well-attested instances of police violence. Hence, as a Campaign for Press and Broadcasting

Freedom (CPBF) booklet reported during the strike, only one of Britain's seventeen national newspapers printed the photograph of a young woman being attacked with a truncheon by a mounted policeman at Orgreave.

The CPBF booklet also described how a Derbyshire miner's car was set on fire and the word 'Revenge' spray-painted on his house. Quickly Fleet Street's finest rushed to the scene, thinking that Peter Neilan was a working miner being targeted by strikers. But he was a striking miner, and one of those arrested was a working miner. Never has a press pack dissolved so quickly. 'Everyone seemed terribly disappointed,' said Mr Neilan.[25]

At Orgreave the BBC, whether deliberately or not, gave the entirely false impression that police did no more than respond to violence from the miners. On 18 June, the *Nine O'Clock News* screened film showing mounted police charging a large group of striking miners, and a group of miners throwing stones at police. But according to left-wing journalist Simon Pirani, 'by reversing the order, and showing the stone-throwing first, the editors of the programme gave the impression that the police charge had been provoked by violence from the mineworkers' side. This was the reverse of the truth.' The BBC claimed it was 'a mistake made in the haste of putting the news together'. Nicholas Jones, the BBC's then industrial correspondent, who has shown he is willing to challenge his old employers if he thinks they are wrong, insists: 'There was no BBC conspiracy to show the mineworkers in the worst possible light. If . . . shots of baton-wielding police and picket line strikers were in the wrong order, I am convinced it was an entirely innocent mistake.'[26]

The government set the stage for the final Battle of Orgreave. A secret letter (one of six numbered copies) sent to Andrew Turnbull, Thatcher's private secretary, on 5 June showed a strategy had been agreed between Leon Brittan, Norman Tebbit and Peter Walker with Ian MacGregor and Bob Haslam, the Chairman of British Steel.[27]

A memo from Michael Reidy, private secretary to Peter Walker, said that the combined efforts of the police and the British Steel workforce in keeping Orgreave open 'represented a considerable triumph in the face of mass picketing and intimidation'. Nonetheless, stocks were declining, and that fact would have to be treated with care and discretion, to stop the NUM claiming it as a victory. How could this best be done? With a slow rundown at 2,000 tonnes a week, or by transferring the rest of the 17,000 tonnes to Scunthorpe steelworks as fast as possible?

A slow rundown was ruled out because 'this would expose the Orgreave workforce to prolonged picketing and intimidation.' Anyway, the coke was needed now. Supplies of the right blend to fire Scunthorpe steelworks would run out significantly on 18 June and production was unlikely to be restarted, so imports would have to fill the gap after that. That meant a rapid transfer. Reidy said that British Steel must immediately write to the Chief Constable of South Yorkshire to tell him of plans to empty the Orgreave site. The scene was set for the full-scale Battle of Orgreave.

The chosen day was 18 June, the day when the miners finally and decisively lost the Battle of Orgreave. More than 4,000 police, with twenty-four dog handlers and forty-two mounted police, battled for ten hours with a similar number of pickets. The police knew that the NUM was going to pull out all the stops that day, bringing thousands of miners from as far away as Scotland, Kent and South Wales. By 9 a.m. the streets of Sheffield were blocked by an estimated 10,000 men walking to Orgreave.

There were ninety-three arrests and hundreds of people (there is no agreed figure) were injured, including Scargill himself. Quite how it happened, no one knows. One miner who was near said he saw some policemen giving the miners' President 'a good leathering' and Scargill claimed he was knocked down by a policeman. Police chiefs, unsurprisingly, saw a completely different incident in which Scargill tripped and banged his head on a railway sleeper. Scargill was badly concussed, had injuries on his arms and body and spent a night in hospital, but was back in action the next day.

Around him, there were dreadful scenes. Picket Bernard Jackson remembers how it started. After the usual push against the police lines, which had happened every day as the lorries left, 'the long riot shields parted and out rode fourteen mounted police straight into the pickets. As they did, police in the line beat on their riot shields with truncheons, creating a wall of noise which was meant to intimidate and frighten. It was more than simply a noise, it was a declaration that we were facing an army which had declared war on us.'

More and more cavalry charges followed. 'It made no difference if pickets stood still, raised their hands or ran away; truncheons were used on arms and legs, trunks and shoulders, and particularly on heads and faces. Men lay around unconscious or semi-conscious with vicious wounds on their bodies, more often than not with bloody gashes on the backs of their heads . . . When you've got half a ton of horse being ridden at you, you don't hang about.'

Police claimed that half-bricks, spikes, ball bearings and pieces of wood with spikes driven through them were used as missiles.

Jackson's account of his arrest, which to most people who were there sounds not only credible but normal, is that he saw police in riot gear running towards him as he was standing by a wall and not even attempting to speak to the lorry drivers. He says that an arm grabbed him round the neck from behind and he was smashed in the face with a riot shield. The policeman then put both arms round Jackson's neck, took his truncheon in both hands, and squeezed.

'Get bloody off, what's wrong with thee?' shouted Jackson, and the reply came from somewhere close to his ear: 'Shut your fucking mouth or I'll break your fucking neck.' The policeman dragged the miner through the field, every so often giving the truncheon round his neck a pull and shouting abuse into his ear. As they passed through the cordon, other policeman lashed out at him with their truncheons, and he heard shouts of 'Bastard miner' and 'Fucking Yorkie miner'.

Jackson spent a week in the grim Armley prison in Leeds and was charged with rioting. A year later he was acquitted of the charge. His verdict was this: 'We weren't victims of an industrial dispute, we were prisoners of war.'[28]

Reporter Malcolm Pithers described in the *Guardian* what he saw:

> The frustration on both sides spilled over into sickening scenes of miners being batoned and of police being attacked with bricks, slivers of glass as well as the containers of fuel. Although the police lines eventually held, officers did react violently. Truncheons were drawn and used on individuals by snatch squads.
>
> The day produced unreal, pitiful scenes. Cars were rolled downhill towards policemen and ignited to make a flaming barricade.
>
> At one point I heard a policeman yell at a photographer to take photographs of a hero. He was pointing to a mounted police officer whose arm was bleeding badly. An ambulanceman was holding the wound to stem the flow of blood. It was equally sickening to hear policemen clapping and cheering as a picket, bleeding heavily from a head wound, was helped into an ambulance . . .
>
> The barrage of rocks, bricks, and glass was kept up for hours. For most of this time policemen stood with riot shields to fend off the missiles. Charges were also made against the pickets with policemen lashing out with truncheons.[29]

Tony Clement, South Yorkshire's Assistant Chief Constable, put the trouble down to Scargill personally. He told reporters that the pickets only became violent when their President was there.[30] Clement may or may not have been right, but it is clearly true that the police lost control of themselves and behaved with violence of a sort which we like to think only happens in countries without Britain's liberal democratic traditions. MacGregor's wish for 'a bunch of good untidy American cops' seemed to have been fulfilled.

Ken Capstick, then an NUM branch delegate and now the editor of *The Miner*, remembers: 'It is frightening, a horse bearing down on you with a policeman on top and six to ten of them coming at you. You run.

I remember running up that hill like mad. We got to the top of the field and turned but they were still coming so we went on into the village. We were charged into the supermarket but the horses couldn't get in or they would have. Remember police went into people's houses when they opened their doors to give shelter to the miners.'

Naturally, while all this was going on, there were very few pickets in Nottinghamshire, and production continued there.

At Orgreave, all the loathing that had developed between striking miners and the police came to the surface. Bernard Jackson is only one of many witnesses to the way in which the police taunted striking miners with their huge overtime payments, while strikers and their families were starving. The story he tells is repeated by far too many other people for there to be any doubt of its truth:

> We'd had our noses rubbed in it before by police holding up £10 and
> £20 notes to the windows of their transits as they drove past. We knew
> the overtime they were earning and they knew we had nothing and
> this was just a nasty little bit of psychological warfare. But in the
> motorway service stations the real difference in our situations was
> brought home to us . . . As we scraped around between us for the
> price of a cup of tea and perhaps a sandwich, a seemingly endless line
> of blue uniforms filed past the serving area ordering double
> breakfasts, mountains of toast and mugs of tea. The last man paid the
> bill – often between £200 and £300.[31]

The police won the Battle of Orgreave for MacGregor. Not that it mattered – MacGregor did not care much if they lost – but it was a blow to the miners' morale that the vastly better equipped (and better fed) police ground them down, chasing proud miners who had fled for their lives up hill and down dale, until they hid from their tormentors.

To the Socialist Workers Party, then an important element of the left which had put great store on the Battle of Orgreave, the defeat was yet another sign that trade union leaders had betrayed the miners and the working class. Their analysis is that if only the TUC had had the courage to instruct every trade union member in the country to come to Orgreave, then the workers united would have been victorious.

They believed, and still believe, that those who let down the struggle include not just TUC leaders but also Yorkshire miners' leaders, notably President Jack Taylor, who did not carry within them the pure Scargillite flame. If they had, more men, both miners and non-miners, would have gone to Orgreave and the Battle of Orgreave would have been won.[32] This view is not widely shared, but it matters because the SWP cite Scargill as supporting it, and it seems almost certain that he did, and still does.

Orgreave knocked the stuffing out of mass picketing, and perhaps out of the whole dispute. It gave the police a psychological advantage which lasted for the rest of the strike. Increasingly miners were only able to picket their own pits, and they were penned in and peremptorily ordered about by the police. As the picket lines retreated out of Nottinghamshire and into Yorkshire, the police followed them, very much like a victorious army.

Orgreave served another tactical purpose for Thatcher. It tightened the noose round the neck of the Labour leadership, as Neil Kinnock balanced precariously between the media waiting for him to condemn the Orgreave pickets, and his party demanding that he condemn the police and turn up at Orgreave to show solidarity.

Orgreave and the scale of mass picketing did leave one unexpected headache for Thatcher. The courts could not cope with the number of miners arrested. Soon it became a matter of considerable concern in Number Ten. Twice Thatcher commissioned a report from one of her most venerable and longstanding allies, Lord Hailsham, the Lord Chancellor, on the progress of prosecutions. It made grim reading.

A confidential letter from Lord Hailsham to the PM on 21 June, three days after the Battle of Orgreave, explained that by pleading not guilty, the striking miners clogged up the judicial system. In Nottingham there were 114 cases outstanding, 42 in Newark, 113 in the outer suburbs of the county town, 252 in Worksop, and 518 in Mansfield. In Derbyshire, there were 200 outstanding cases in Chesterfield; in South Yorkshire there were 251 outstanding cases in Rotherham. Only in Sheffield and Staffordshire was progress made, with just under half of 118 cases concluded in Sheffield and 155 out of 187 in Staffordshire.

Hailsham had to consider emergency measures, such as appointing acting stipendiary magistrates and bringing in private solicitors to prosecute people, to cope. They did cope, just. Hailsham records that, after all that, many of the cases ended up being dismissed. Arresting hundreds of innocent men and almost bringing the courts to a halt was one very small part of the price of this almost worthless victory. The price was also heavy in terms of social cohesion and the welfare of thousands of families. But that was not a price Ian MacGregor had to pay.

CHAPTER 5

THATCHER AND THE ENEMY WITHIN, SCARGILL AND GENERAL WINTER

21 JUNE TO 2 OCTOBER

The dramatic defeat of the miners at Orgreave demonstrated to the Labour Party and TUC leadership that there was only one avenue open for the miners: to start negotiations with the NCB on how the strike could be ended. The government's official line, however absurd it might look, was still that they had nothing to do with the dispute and it was a matter that had to be resolved by the NUM and the NCB.

Ministers were still privately hoping that it might be resolved, as the secret memos written by Peter Gregson to the PM reveal. So no negotiating initiative could be expected from the government, even though they were fearful of the coming of winter, with the huge energy drain it would certainly bring. Like Scargill, they thought General Winter might thrust victory into the NUM's hands.

As for the NCB, Ian MacGregor sounded like a man who thought he only had to sit back and wait for victory. On the final day of the Battle of Orgreave, 21 July, he wrote triumphantly to all the members of the NUM saying that they could never win, and predicting that, if they stayed out, the strike could drag on until 1985.

How could Labour politicians help? Was any attempt doomed to be crushed between the iron egos of Arthur Scargill and Margaret

Thatcher, and by the distrust that had built up between Labour's leadership and Scargill?

Neil Kinnock began having regular Saturday morning breakfasts with the South Wales miners' research officer Kim Howells, once an NUM militant and Scargill supporter who now believed the President was leading the union to disaster. 'He was telling me what was going on on the inside; we wanted to try to save something,' says Kinnock. Labour leaders were thinking hard about how to minimize the damage and get the miners out of the hole they believed Scargill had dug for his members. Kinnock now regrets that he did not try to set up a direct line with Mick McGahey as well. 'We got on well for years, a great guy, I wish I'd had the sense to say, "Mick, this is my home phone number, we may never use it but just in case."' He is sure McGahey felt the same regret.

Meanwhile Kinnock encouraged his industry spokesman, Stan Orme, to see if he could do some freelance mediation. Orme's initiative, however, was sparked in the end by a parliamentary exchange. Across the dispatch box, Energy Minister Peter Walker said to his Labour shadow: 'Why don't you intervene?' For Walker it was simply one of many ways of reminding voters than the Labour Party had close links with the NUM. But Orme was one of those Labour MPs who had come up through the unions, in his case the engineers' union. He knew his way round labour disputes. He recorded in his diary: 'I found this extraordinary, coming from the Secretary of State for Energy. However, that evening I went home, slept on the challenge, and early next morning rang Arthur Scargill at the NUM HQ in Sheffield and suggested we had a meeting.' Scargill agreed to one. Orme told Scargill that he would also contact MacGregor.

Orme was an unusual sort of politician. Short and stout, with a high voice, a throwaway style of speaking, and crumpled suits, he did not have any of the charisma often considered vital for political success. But he was honest and thoughtful, and about as good a potential mediator as the political world could supply. And he had some sort of rapport with Scargill, which is more than could be said for either Kinnock or TUC General Secretary Len Murray.

The idea initially seemed to bear fruit. Orme provided the first links between the NUM and ACAS, the Advisory, Conciliation and Arbitration Service. Pat Lowry, then Chairman of ACAS, organized the first private meeting between the NUM and ACAS at a hotel near Northampton in July. But neither Peter Walker for the government nor Ian MacGregor at the NCB had any real interest in an intervention from ACAS. The NCB would not even meet ACAS; the board was not interested in an 'outside intervention' at this time.

Orme had more success with his attempt to get MacGregor and Scargill together. MacGregor and Orme seemed to warm to each other, despite the vast ideological gulf between them, and by the end of June the relationship, now on first-name terms, led to a proposal for a private meeting at MacGregor's Scottish cottage. The NCB Chairman called Orme to say the NUM should 'bring their tooth-brushes and pyjamas' to Scotland 'and we should stick it out until we got a solution.'[1]

This prepared the way for talks between the NUM and the NCB at the Rubens Hotel in London in July. But a lot was to happen before these talks could take place, much of it weakening the NUM position.

The steelworkers, under their General Secretary Bill Sirs, agreed to accept coal from any source to keep plants going so they could avoid layoffs. A twenty-four-hour NUR strike had had limited impact. In Nottinghamshire, working miners had taken over the executive on 2 July, a move that was to have lasting effects. The same day, Walker met MacGregor to discuss the situation, and the next day both of them had a private meeting with Thatcher.

By then MacGregor had seen the latest of the regular, detailed reports on opinion among the miners from Opinion Research and Communications (ORC), delivered the same day, 2 July. The NCB was providing itself with all the information it needed to fight a war. Such data was a very great deal more useful than what the NUM leadership had to guide them about the mood among the men, which essentially was Scargill's gut instincts as he stood in front of cheering meetings.

The practical difference between the leaders was that the NCB was willing to be told unpleasant truths. And ORC had unpleasant truths to give them. On 2 July Tommy Thompson of ORC told his client that almost no miner his team had interviewed thought the NCB would win, and many thought the NUM would win. Many of them believed the strike would achieve a lot. 'Six out of ten Durham miners and 49 per cent of Northumberland miners thought that they themselves would benefit from the strike,' wrote Thompson. And in both these areas, eight out of ten miners said they were certain not to go back to work in the next few weeks. 'These are the attitudes which have to be changed if the strike is to crumble in the north east,' wrote Thompson.[2]

The government's thinking at that time is revealed in a remarkably frank memo[3] written by Peter Gregson to Mrs Thatcher on the eve of the 3 July meeting with Walker and MacGregor. It contained a rare and revealing piece of advice from a mandarin to Mrs Thatcher on how to handle the American coal boss: 'When you see Mr MacGregor, I suggest that it will be very desirable to try and get him to do as much talking as possible at the beginning. As he is so laconic, it is all too easy to put words into his mouth and it would be much better for you to hear from him at the outset how he thinks the battle is going and how it can best be brought to a satisfactory conclusion.' No one ever found a more tactful way of telling Mrs Thatcher not to talk too much.

The six-page memo began with a description of the meeting between Walker and MacGregor that morning. It warned the Prime Minister that, although some miners had gone back to work, no consistent pattern had emerged, and none would emerge until the end of the holidays in August. It provided an insight into how co-ordinated ministers were in ensuring that the police were especially diligent in enforcing the right of miners to defy the strike unimpeded. 'Protection from intimidation is the main contribution which the government can make,' wrote Gregson. Where MacGregor was not satisfied with the police performance, he could secure immediate action from ministers.

The memo singled out North Derbyshire, where MacGregor had apparently found 'long standing difficulties with the left wing police authority resulting in the recent suspension of the Chief Constable'. Gregson assured Thatcher that Walker was contacting Leon Brittan, the Home Secretary, to make 'police effort in that area more effective'.

Gregson revealed MacGregor's take on the NUM delegate conference that was due on 11–12 July. He warned, 'The militants will be in control,' but added: 'There is just the possibility that Scargill might seek agreement at the conference for a snap ballot.' MacGregor thought that Scargill would strengthen his central authority and 'stifle dissent' and the government must be ready to counter him. He recorded MacGregor as saying: 'It will be necessary to exploit this fully in the media in the hope of alienating Scargill from the rank and file miners and from public sympathy generally.'

The memo reveals that, contrary to what they said at the time and for years afterwards, Walker and Thatcher knew about, and were interested in, the moves to set up a breakaway union, which became the Union of Democratic Miners. Gregson wrote: 'The NCB's attitude is that it cannot be seen to be assisting or encouraging such moves.' In fact we now know that the NCB took advice from top lawyers, including the future Lord Falconer, to advise them how to do precisely that, legally and secretly. But at this stage the advantage of the breakaway union was seen as marginal – a negotiating ploy with the NUM, should talks start.

The secret memo shows that MacGregor already knew that fifty-five pits were requiring continual observation for geological reasons. But the NCB did not think it could exploit this. Gregson thought the NUM, who were well informed locally, would always be able to argue that production could be resumed, if enough money was spent. Anyway, many of the pits where problems could arise were ones that the NCB wanted to keep open.

The NCB had already received applications for redundancy from miners, wrote Gregson, but from the wrong people: those with skills it still desperately needed. Nevertheless MacGregor was working on plans to close some pits while the strike was in full swing. This idea seems to have come from Walker and Thatcher. 'The advantage of doing so would be to demonstrate that the closure programme, which the dispute is all about, can be and is being achieved by consent and without hardship,' Gregson recorded. He cited MacGregor as saying: 'The NUM would no doubt argue even so that that the miners involved were traitors in selling the jobs of their grandchildren.' And there was a danger of losing miners who might vote against a strike should there be a ballot. There was, he wrote, a 'substantial downside' to going along that path.

The memo shows that at first MacGregor saw some hope in Stan Orme's initiative, but Scargill had dashed it in a speech in Rotherham by reviving his pre-condition that the closure programme must be withdrawn. 'The NCB must therefore tread the difficult path of being willing to resume talks, without actively seeking them,' wrote Gregson. But 'unless the NUM position is crumbling fast, the prospect of winter will give Scargill a major psychological advantage.'

The government had no magic bullet, said Gregson, but there were three things it could do. First, it must do everything in its power to get more miners back to work. Second, the public relations battle must be fought intelligently and inexorably: showing the government was reasonable, 'drawing attention relentlessly to Scargill as an anti-democratic bully with ulterior motives', making it clear that the issues at stake were so vital that a few easy concessions would not solve the problem. Third, 'taking discreet steps to prolong endurance into 1985'. If this was not producing results by September, Gregson thought they would have to take radical measures, like going ahead with closures and trying to get imported coal into the power stations.

Finally Gregson told the PM that the NCB aimed to increase coal deliveries to power stations from 420,000 tonnes a week to 570,000 tonnes during July – without giving 'Scargill and his friends in the rail and transport unions a new rallying point'. 'The main trial of strength' was at Llanwern and Ravenscraig, 'where pickets are blocking coal deliveries. Victory there would be a major boost for Scargill; failure a substantial but not a decisive blow against him.'

For the diehards on either side, these two great steelworks acquired a totemic importance. As we shall see in the next chapter, Neil Kinnock was involved in efforts to find a compromise over Llanwern which would not break the strike, but would not destroy the steelworks either. In Scotland, Mick McGahey was quietly involved in a similar exercise over Ravenscraig. He got an agreement to allow 18,000 tonnes of coal into Ravenscraig each week. The *Socialist Worker* historians of the strike regard this as proof that the pure faith of revolutionary fervour did not really burn in McGahey. Scratch him, and he turns out to be a traitor to the working class too, just like Kinnock. John Monks says that McGahey had to be very careful to avoid being branded as the man who sold out the miners. 'The Communist Party could not afford to be seen as class collaborators,' he said.

Whether or not McGahey knew it, the steel bosses were genuinely alarmed at the prospect of the closure of Ravenscraig. They feared it would destroy their business. His deal was one that allowed British coal in and kept the steelworks open – but it was not enough: the steel bosses wanted foreign coal too. When a giant ore carrier, the *Ostia*, docked at Hunterson with fresh supplies of coal, the dockers, members of the TGWU and sympathetic to the miners, refused to unload her.

A British Steel delegation went to see Norman Tebbit to urge him to intervene personally and raise it in the Cabinet. He saw them and kept them waiting all afternoon while a Cabinet committee deliberated. Then he came back to the delegation, and, according to his account, just said to them: 'Carry on your business.' They said: 'Is that all?' He replied: 'Yes.'

So they made their arrangements and ensured that other dockers would unload them, under the eye of a non-TGWU supervisor. This was absolutely forbidden by the Dock Labour Scheme, which had been devised to give the union sufficient power to defend its members in the docks; breaking those rules was one of the many body-blows to union power suffered during the strike. At any other time, the contravention of the Dock Labour Scheme would have been a major story, but in the middle of the miners' strike it passed practically unnoticed.

Tebbit regards this moment as a key turning point in the strike. 'If the dockers had come out and called a national strike, we would have lost.'

When talks began on 5 July, Labour leaders and the TUC still saw a compromise as a realistic thing to hope for. By 9 July there was talk of movement on both sides; then talks were adjourned for a few days. Unfortunately, just at that moment the NUM executive was preoccupied with internal revenge. It proposed to change the rules in order to discipline members for offences including actions 'detrimental to the interests of the union'. This was directly aimed at miners who continued to work, as in Nottinghamshire. And it was Nottinghamshire that took the first of many actions in the High Court, to obtain an injunction on 10 July to stop the union doing this. The next day a special conference of the NUM ignored the injunction and went ahead with creating a disciplinary 'star chamber'.

This decision enabled MacGregor to issue a statement on 12 July saying that rebel miners would not lose their jobs if they were thrown out of the NUM. At a stroke he rescinded the miners' closed shop, which for generations had ensured that their union was strong. This, like the breaking of the Dock Labour Scheme, would at normal times have been an earthquake in the industry. In the fever of the times it too went almost unnoticed; but without this decision, the breakaway union that eventually hammered the last nail into the coffin of NUM power would have been impossible.

As he battled through the long, hot summer of 1984, Scargill, like many other generals in history, waited patiently for General Winter to thrust victory into his hands. The passing of the longest day in the year, 21 June, was greeted as though it was the turning point, and on 30 June Scargill wrote a signed front-page lead in *The Miner* headlined TIME IS ON OUR SIDE NOW.

'The strike pendulum has now securely swung to our territory,' he wrote. 'The most crucial date in the calendar – June 21, the longest day – is passed. From here on in, the days get shorter and the nights longer.

We shall be entering autumn in an immensely powerful position with coal stocks at approximately 15m tonnes – well below the 17m tonnes level at which the three day week was introduced 10 years ago.' But that was ten years ago. There was a lot less oil about then.

Such stuff did not impress the print union leader Bill Keys, who was acting as the unofficial emissary of the left wing of the TUC General Council to the NUM. Keys was desperately worried about where the strike was going. Scargill, he confided to his diary on 29 June, the day before Scargill's article appeared in *The Miner*, 'wants a total victory, industrially and politically, and refuses to see that he is dealing with a different situation [from the one] that existed in the two previous miners' disputes.' It worried Keys that 'in talks I have had with him, there has never been any suggestion at any time of him modifying his attitude'.

Keys had never been in a dispute where he achieved total victory. Scargill 'will fight to the last miner, and in doing so destroy the NUM . . . I just wish the man would discuss a resolution with the friends of the miners.' Keys predicted the emergence of a breakaway union in Nottinghamshire, though he did not have access to the private evidence possessed by Thatcher, Gregson and MacGregor.

Bill Keys was a larger-than-life figure. In the powerful print and newspaper trade unions he had an almost mythical status, and the first reaction among them to any proposal, however unimportant, was generally: 'Have you asked Bill?' He knew it and encouraged it. He was once heard shouting to the President of the NUJ at a TUC Congress in Blackpool, in his uncompromising South London accent: 'I wish you'd bloody arst me before you put down bloody motions on bloody agendas.' His legendary correspondence was typed exactly as he dictated it, so his letters carried the stamp of his personality. One, to the NUJ General Secretary Ken Morgan when the two unions disagreed about something, began: 'Now, look here, Ken.' The classically educated Morgan reported it to his executive with the comment: 'Bill Keys moves directly into the vocative case.'

He was one of the many union officials – you can find examples even today – who seem to model themselves on that greatest of union barons,

Ernest Bevin, the creator of the TGWU in the 1920s: at once blunt and devious, lovable and a bit of a bully. Keys was a left-winger, but he used his union's considerable power carefully: a realist and a pragmatist, he knew just how tenuous that power was. He understood that print union power could one day evaporate like the morning dew – as it did, not so long after the miners' strike, though he had retired by then.

An erect, stiff figure with a face that looked ever so slightly like a seal's, Keys was a chain-smoker and a deal-maker, sometimes accused of being too elaborate in spinning out negotiations, but always trusted to deliver what he said he would deliver – which was the real key to his power. He was an old-style union leader in the Bevin mould, tough and noisy, full of bravado and a kind of simple cunning, conspiratorial, ego-tistical, but consumed with a passion for justice. He remained true to his working-class roots while unashamedly enjoying the fine wines of the ruling class.

In his own print union, Keys launched a campaign to get branches to adopt local pits and open up their homes to miners' families. He decided on the slogan: 'They shall not starve.' In August he took enor-mous satisfaction in despatching the result to Yorkshire – £100,000-worth of food.

As July opened, Scargill had, for a very short period, a ray of hope that the strike might spread to the docks. On 9 July a row over the use of 'scab' labour to unload coal at Immingham Docks threatened a national dock strike. The National Dock Labour Board moved swiftly to resolve the dispute in favour of the TGWU, and ministers insisted that the National Dock Labour Scheme was safe. But just for a day or two, the second front – one of Scargill's most desired outcomes – looked as though it might happen.

In government circles there was immediate concern. A memo[4] written by David Normington, then principal private secretary at the Department for Employment, to Andrew Turnbull, Margaret Thatcher's private secretary, included a special briefing for ministers of 'points to make' to the media that weekend. The top line was: 'Cannot see why the unions and employers should not settle this quickly through their normal negotiating machinery.' It emphasized that ministers should say the unions had already won their point.

Nothing was left to chance. A memo from Robin Butler, Thatcher's principal private secretary, on 17 July showed she had already ordered the immediate setting up of a special group chaired by Employment Secretary Tom King to co-ordinate action against any strike, alongside two other special groups that met daily under Peter Walker and the Transport Secretary. In the event the strike fizzled out by 21 July, but Thatcher's reaction showed how jumpy ministers were.

In the meantime there had been a secret review of the five collieries identified by the NUM as intended for closure by the NCB. The report on Polmaise, Herrington, Bullcliffe Wood, Cortonwood and Snowdon prepared by engineers and sent to Ned Smith and Kevan Hunt is the one that contained the extraordinary fact that Cortonwood, whose closure started the strike, should never have been included in the closure list in the first place.[5]

The talks brokered by Stan Orme resumed on 18 July at the Rubens Hotel in London, and centred on the terms of future pit closures. The two sides had prepared draft agreements. Both sides accepted that pit closures should be negotiated if a pit was exhausted, unsafe or for 'other reasons'. It was the definition of 'other reasons' that became the sticking point: the NUM had previously accepted poor geological conditions and poor quality coal as reasons for some closures but was not prepared to go further, and certainly would not give a blanket agreement to closures of 'uneconomic' pits. As a compromise, it was suggested that pits could close if they could not be 'beneficially developed'. That phrase formed part of the thirteen hours of talks before they collapsed. According to Stan Orme's diary it was not Scargill who stopped talking; it was MacGregor, 'convincing Scargill and Heathfield that he had been stopped in his tracks by the government'. Geoffrey Goodman observes: 'There was strong evidence then . . . that the Cabinet feared MacGregor was making too many concessions to the NUM and stood in danger of handing Scargill a political victory.'[6]

But in TUC circles it was being claimed that the fault for the breakdown lay with Scargill. There was briefly, they said, a form of words available which he could have proclaimed as a victory. The idea that a pit might not be closed while it could be 'beneficially' worked was a long way from the idea that it could be closed if it was not economically viable. Had Scargill been a proper negotiator, they said, he could have grabbed the chance before Thatcher had time to whip it away from him. This view was expressed most forcibly by the EMA leader John Lyons, who always maintained that Scargill had been offered the nearest thing to a victory that any trade union leader can ever expect. 'It was 95 per cent of what they were after.'

In public MacGregor and Peter Walker were adamant that talks could not continue. MacGregor said to journalists a little after midnight: 'The trouble with Arthur is that his rhetoric has put him out on a limb, and the problem for me is that all I have got to help him is a saw.' Walker was more prosaic and predictable. 'It can only be the desire to impose on Britain the type of socialist state that the British electorate constantly rejects, that motivates Mr Scargill to continue to do so much damage to his industry.'[7]

Walker launched a very personal attack on Scargill in *The Times* that same day, making it clear that the immediate cause of the strike was no longer the government's main concern. Ministers had launched a crusade to destroy Scargill and all that he stood for. 'Readers of the magazine *Marxism Today* in 1981 were left in no doubt of Mr Arthur Scargill's contempt for democracy,' Walker began. There was much more: 'This contempt for parliamentary democracy and desire to seize power through the militancy of the mob . . . The British people need be in no doubt that we are facing a challenge to our whole way of life . . . If the NUM was led by a union leader who was not concerned with playing the political fanatic . . . It is time for the Labour Party, if it is going to survive as a party believing in parliamentary democracy, to denounce both the political objectives and the violence . . . This is not a mining dispute. It is a challenge to British democracy and hence to the British people.'[8]

London during the 1926 general strike.

On our way, brothers – miners greet the announcement of the strike with optimism, March 1984.

(*top*) Attacking the police vans carrying strike breakers.

(*above*) Arrests of pickets were not done gently.

(*right*) A wounded miner, Yorkshire.

The Battle of Orgreave, 1984: 'when you've got two tons of police horse ridden at you, you don't hang around.'

(*top*) Scargill and Mick McGahey acknowledge the applause during the 1984 Trades Union Congress. Behind Scargill, with beard and glasses, is Roger Windsor.

(*middle*) 14 October 1984. Scargill with TUC General Secretary Norman Willis in London, fending off the media after one of their increasingly difficult meetings.

(*bottom*) At a 1984 Labour Party rally with Kinnock (far left) trying to look cheerful as Scargill takes the applause. Besides Kinnock is Ron Todd, leader of Britain's biggest trade union, the Transport and General Workers'.

Margaret Thatcher at the 1984 Conservative Party Conference, determined to defeat 'the enemy within'.

Coal Board chief Ian Macgregor.

Striking miners manage to give their families a Christmas at a Yorkshire soup kitchen, 1984.

Yorkshire: Women on the picket line.

Whittle miners' wives support group take their turn at picket line duty.

(*above*) NUM chief executive, and Scargill's emissary to Colonel Gaddafi, Roger Windsor

(*right*) Print union leader, Bill Keys, who nearly succeeded in brokering a deal.

(*below*) Betteshanger Colliery in Kent, after a year on strike. The Kent miners are among the last to return to work following the calling off of the pit strike by the NUM on 11 March 1985.

(*right*) A closed down mine, Durham 1987.

(*below*) Winding gear broken up and recycled, 1989.

But this was nothing compared to what the Prime Minister said soon afterwards. Choosing her words carefully when she was addressing the 1922 Committee, the powerful Tory backbench committee, at its last meeting of the Parliamentary session, Mrs Thatcher said the miners' leader posed as great a threat to democracy as General Galtieri, the deposed Argentinian leader, whom Britain had defeated in the Falklands War. In words which would be remembered as one of the key phrases of the strike, she said her government had fought the enemy without in the Falklands and 'now had to face the enemy within'. She described the pit strikers as a scar on the community.

Nor was this an isolated comment. The *Guardian* reported the next day: 'Her speech was echoed in a remarkable chorus of ministerial harangues in the country outside with the Home Secretary, Mr Leon Brittan, the Chancellor, Mr Nigel Lawson, the Energy Secretary, Mr Peter Walker, and the Party Chairman, Mr John Gummer, opening a drum fire of abuse against Mr Arthur Scargill, the NUM President, and Mr Neil Kinnock, the Labour leader.'[9]

The attacks left nothing to doubt. Thatcher was fighting for a long-term victory and was not interested in any face-saving settlement. Scargill was also in it for the long term, hoping that a cold winter in the months ahead would give him the upper hand.

There's an old joke about the 1967 Six Day War in the Middle East. An Egyptian general is being asked how the Israelis could overrun his country so fast. Did their Russian military hardware fail? No, says the general, the weapons were fine, it was the Russian military textbooks that let them down. 'The textbooks said: draw the enemy into your own territory then wait for the winter snows.'

Scargill seemed to have been reading the same textbooks – or that was how a worried group of left-wing TUC General Council members saw it. They met secretly on 24 July at the NUR headquarters in Euston, in Central London, joined by Scargill, Heathfield and McGahey. The meeting was called because they were frantically worried at the break-down of talks six days earlier. Bill Keys asked: 'Do you honestly believe you can win an unconditional victory?' He got no answer that made sense to him. He wrote despondently in his diary afterwards: 'We considered all the aspects, but it was obvious almost from the start that Arthur was not for moving . . . Arthur has no doubt he can win on his own. We listen about General Winter, which all runs contrary to what the coal board are saying about coal stocks being available for the whole of the winter. There was little reason in getting into an argument with him, for so far as he was concerned, we were there to listen. Meanwhile the union is in deep trouble financially as he had to admit, and the miners' families in dire need of clothing and food.'

After the meeting Keys went for a quiet drink with a couple of other general secretaries, and they agreed that if they had had the NCB offer, they would have used it as a foundation stone to build upon. 'How can we help such a man, he does not want TUC involvement and yet it is obvious that if complete disaster is to be avoided a third party has to come into the arena.'

They went despondently to the TUC General Council meeting the next day. McGahey, the only NUM member on the General Council, seemed very different without Scargill and Heathfield. 'Strangely Mick said that the miners were prepared to talk, but did not define on what basis they would talk,' recorded Keys. He wondered whether McGahey was hoping to get the NUM executive to take a less hard line than Scargill's. The day after that, Keys went to see Neil Kinnock, and established that the Labour leader was thinking all the things he himself was thinking.

The government also remained pro-active during August, as Cabinet Office papers released under the Freedom of Information Act reveal. Peter Gregson, in a long memo to Sir Robert Armstrong, then Cabinet Secretary, and Sir Robert, in a memo to Thatcher, show that, while the rest of Britain might have been on holiday, the PM was determined that the government should remain vigilant and not lose the initiative. The memos reveal that Bernard Ingham, the PM's volatile and blunt press secretary, had drawn up detailed plans, and put his deputy Romola Christopherson in charge of media co-ordination while he was away.

Sir Robert's memo records that Peter Walker chaired a daily meeting to co-ordinate action during the strike with senior officials from the Home Office, Employment, Transport and the NCB and CEGB. Twice weekly, on Mondays and Wednesdays, Thatcher herself chaired MISC101, the ministerial group on coal. Its purpose was to exchange information, give a ministerial steer to the line with the media, and work out policy.

Armstrong suggested standing down MISC101 during August after an early meeting chaired by Thatcher, though if any issue was to arise Lord Whitelaw could chair a meeting while she was away. Meanwhile, even in the quiet days of August, Armstrong proposed to Thatcher that Peter Walker's meeting should be twice a week, on Tuesdays and Fridays, to co-ordinate action. Regular telephone contact was to be maintained with all key ministers and officials, with Christopherson having direct access to Thatcher if it was necessary to co-ordinate a media response. In the meantime a tough line was circulated to all ministers from the Department of Energy, urging them to continue the attack in the media.

The agreed line on Scargill read: 'What more does he want? A blank cheque from the taxpayer so that no pit should close, no matter how uneconomic it is? This is ludicrous. It would cripple the industry's prospects for ever.'

A more private line was added by Hector Laing, the chair of United Biscuits, and a Tory donor and supporter, in a letter to Robin Butler on 23 July. Starting from the point of view that Scargill's action had a political end, he recommended more drastic action. He urged Thatcher to give redundancy to the 20,000 miners who wanted to leave, even though this could lead to an exodus of moderates. 'I think that is a risk worth taking.'

He also called on the NCB to publish a list of pits likely to be closed over the next five years, on the principle that 'uncertainty is always more damaging to morale than even unpleasant fact.' This should be coupled with a new expansion programme for coal, emphasizing high pay. 'When we announced the closure of our Liverpool factory we made the benefits to the remaining biscuit factories very clear to them [the employees] and while that was of course no comfort to Liverpool, the others saw the advantages to them.' He also included an unpublished graph showing a 'super future' for coal, predicting that by 2000 it would still have 24 per cent of the market, while oil would fall from 58 per cent to 36 per cent of European energy demand.

But Laing's advice was not wanted. According to Turnbull and Lord Wakeham, Thatcher's Chief Whip, it was pigeonholed and never seriously considered.

The situation during August was not as calm as might appear. The supply of coal was not plentiful everywhere in the UK, and particularly not in Northern Ireland. On 7 August, Jim Prior, the Northern Ireland Secretary, got his minister of state, Adam Butler, to write a secret letter to Peter Walker. In it he warned of an 'awkward' problem in the province that could rapidly alienate public opinion and give potential support to the NUM: the price of electricity.[10] 'Supplies of coal to the Northern Ireland Electricity Service have dried up completely and the Service, which had previously been maximising its coal burn, has had to switch to oil-fired generation, with a consequent increase in costs currently running at about £800,000 per month . . . the natural course of action would be to increase electricity tariffs by 3% if it assumed that coal supplies will be resumed on October 1 or by 4% if the date of resumed supply is assumed to be 1 November.'

If this went ahead in Northern Ireland alone it would cause a political furore, so Butler wanted Walker to consider a general rise in electricity tariffs across the whole of the UK. He warned that, if this was delayed, the difficulties in Northern Ireland would multiply. He hinted that delaying a decision to 1 January would mean tariffs going up by 9.5 per cent. The other alternative was to find money from a cash-limited budget to subsidize the industry further. 'It is that impossibility which is at the heart of the problem.'

A week later he received a firm rebuff from Walker. 'There is no plan to raise electricity tariffs in Great Britain during the strike. This conclusion was reached after careful consideration of the impact of any such move on the handling of the strike itself and of the scale and nature of the extra costs arising from it. The position will be reviewed at the end of the strike.'

The statement is revealing. It shows that the strike, contrary to public statements, was biting already, even in high summer, and that the government was quite prepared to fund extra costs until the miners were brought to heel, even if it was going to be a long haul. Expense was not to be spared.

Two weeks later a more cynical approach to mundane matters was revealed. For years the government had run an energy-saving advertising campaign, encouraging the public to switch off power and save money. A letter from Peter Rees, Chief Secretary to the Treasury, reveals that Walker wanted to step up that campaign, in order to 'extend endurance . . . if the miners' strike were to last through the autumn.'[11]

Rees told Walker that he would agree additional expenditure, but on conditions. Walker had to secure all the necessary savings from within the cash limits of this expenditure. The government itself was short of cash: 'The state of the contingency reserve is such that we cannot use it to meet any part of this expenditure. If the strike ends earlier I suggest we reconsider the case for additional spending.'

This little vignette shows how fighting the miners' strike was dominating everything, even routine energy-saving campaigns. It also shows that ministers would use everything at their disposal, even encouraging people to turn out the lights, but would not be unduly bothered once the strike was settled.

On the strike's front line, picket-line battles were commonplace, but there was now no doubt who was winning them. According to Kevin Barron, a former miner and NUM leader and by then an MP, 'The police were acting as judge and jury.' But Barron adds that pickets were not blameless; Scargill's denials that any violence had come from his side were foolish and self-defeating, he says, for everyone could see on their television that he was not telling the truth. Even the loyal Peter Heathfield could see it, says Barron, who recalls being at a public meeting with him in Blackburn, after which they watched Scargill on television saying: 'I've not seen anyone throwing stones.' Heathfield, says Barron, put his head in his hands.

The truth was that miners still on strike were desperately frustrated by their powerlessness to stop the drift back to work, which newspapers were gloating about, using often grossly inflated figures, but which Ned Smith was still privately charting twice a day with lethal accuracy. Whatever rubbish the public were fed or Scargill chose to believe, Smith's colleagues knew the real position.

Yet the extraordinary thing is not how many men were going back, but how many were still out. In August journalist Barbara Fox visited the Crigglestone and Hall Green miners' support group near Barnsley in Yorkshire, and provided some insight into why this was so:

> The village is not big, nearly all the 300 workers in the pit live here
> with their families. The wages were never very high . . . but they have
> cars and many own their little houses. The village with its well tended
> gardens, pretty curtains and tidy streets looks nice, almost
> prosperous. If this pit were to close – and it is on the list of pits to be
> closed – then the 300 men would be without jobs, and the chances of
> finding other work do not exist here. They say: 'We just want to be
> allowed to continue working. When this pit closes, there'll be nothing
> for us, and nothing for our sons . . .' It is the fear of a future without
> work, the vision of deserted villages and towns, which keep the
> workers on strike.

Another NUM special conference was held on 10 August, which confirmed the rejection of the NCB offer and appealed for £500,000 a week from other unions. There were, of course, no delegates from the rebel areas of Nottinghamshire, South Derbyshire and Leicestershire, which made the defeat of the offer more certain, but also less impressive. As for the £500,000, other unions were already fundraising furiously and sending as much as they could.

It was in the aftermath of this conference, and of the rejection of the NCB offer, that the idea began to emerge of Bill Keys, one of the most able and experienced wheelers and dealers the trade union movement possessed, taking a hand and trying to broker a deal. It was not conceived as an alternative to Stan Orme's efforts; the two would keep each other informed. Between them, they would know every possible avenue that might be tried. TUC General Secretary Len Murray and Labour leader Neil Kinnock were keen. Others consulted at this early stage were the train drivers' leader Ray Buckton, a leading General Council left-winger, and Ron Todd, who led the TGWU. Just four days after the miners' special conference, Keys and Todd were meeting Scargill and Heathfield at a London hotel, and Keys was briefing Stan Orme.[12]

Meanwhile, on 13 July, when talks were still going on between the NUM and the NCB, a new figure burst on the scene – Robert Maxwell. On that day Cap'n Bob, as he liked to be known, took over the *Daily Mirror*, the paper that had until then backed the miners but not the tactics of Arthur Scargill.

A larger-than-life figure, a bully, a spy who certainly worked for British Intelligence during the fall of Berlin, probably for the CIA and Mossad, and possibly for MI5 and MI6 during this dispute, Maxwell had a mission. He was going to solve the miners' strike single-handed and bring great glory to his new acquisition. He had even written the headline in his mind: 'The *Mirror* solves the Miners' Dispute.'

The *Mirror*'s industrial editor, Geoffrey Goodman, had excellent contacts on both sides of the dispute. So he was less than amused when his new proprietor, arriving back after a good dinner and somewhat the worse for drink, decided to rewrite Goodman's column himself overnight. His efforts destroyed a revelation in the copy that Margaret Thatcher and Sir Keith Joseph had both voted against Edward Heath when he decided to go to the country in 1974 on 'Who governs Britain?' The offending copy changes, since this was the pre-computer age and required much hammering of hot metal, did not appear until the late London edition, but the damage was done. The next day a somewhat abashed Maxwell invited his industrial editor for a drink in his office, hugged him and apologized. 'I promise it will never happen again. I behaved stupidly' are the words Goodman recalls.[13]

So as the annual TUC meeting opened at the start of September, there were three peace initiatives running at the same time, steered by three very different men: Stan Orme, Bill Keys and Robert Maxwell.

Scargill had wanted the TUC to stay out of the dispute, even though he lambasted the trade union movement for not giving enough support. By this time his relationship with the TUC General Secretary Len Murray was strained, to say the least. According to John Lyons, General Secretary of the EMA, Murray said to Lyons that the miners' strike was against 'the coal board, the government and the TUC'. Geoffrey Goodman recalls that Murray asked Scargill for his home telephone number, so he could contact him directly if he needed to in a crisis, and Scargill refused to give it to him.[14] But with a new General Secretary, Norman Willis, due to take over at the end of the week, there was a chance for change.

Scargill set the scene himself in an article in the *Guardian* on 3 September. This was no ordinary solidarity call to fellow workers fighting an industrial dispute. He called the dispute a fight against the government to save communities. He recalled Nicholas Ridley's blueprint of 1975, when the Tories were in opposition, to privatize nationalized industries, and insisted that the government wanted to close seventy pits and destroy 70,000 jobs.

'Our members will not submit to the butchery of their livelihoods and their communities. There was only one course of action: to fight,' he wrote. 'That fight has been an inspiration to working people around the world. Here in Britain, it has awakened the very soul of the trade union and Labour movement from a state of helplessness. Ours is a campaign unique in many respects, two of which deserve special mention. One is the mobilisation of young miners, fighting to save jobs which they regard as a trust, to be held and passed on to the youngsters of tomorrow. They utterly reject the horrors of the dole. The other inspiring feature of the dispute is, of course, the regeneration of community spirit – a phenomenon in which women have played a crucial role.' He made it clear that he intended to break anti-union laws – a decision that brought fears of the sequestration of union funds, and was certain to alarm other unions.

The article set the scene for further confrontation at the TUC between the NUM and other unions, and again at the Labour Party conference the following month.

Maxwell was still determined to appear as the saviour of the day. He badgered Goodman to set up secret meetings with the key figures and planned a big role for himself in mediation. It came to a head at the TUC conference in Brighton, on the Sunday before the conference opened on Monday. That day Maxwell had persuaded Goodman to organize a secret meeting in the basement of the Bedford Hotel, to be attended by Scargill, Mick McGahey and Peter Heathfield. On the *Mirror*'s side were Maxwell, Goodman and editor Mike Molloy.

Goodman had warned Maxwell to be 'very careful' about trying to organize such a meeting and was 'very uneasy' about success. But Maxwell was determined. Midway through the talks he insisted that Goodman ring Ned Smith, the NCB's labour relations director, at home. Dragged off a golf course to take the call (there were no mobile telephones then), Smith agreed to contact MacGregor, and to Goodman's astonishment MacGregor agreed to come to a meeting the next day at a hotel near Gatwick Airport to meet the miners' leaders.

The Sunday meeting went on for two hours, and Maxwell spent the rest of the evening in his hotel room, trying to get Thatcher on the telephone, and ending up calling Robin Butler, her principal private secretary.

But the meeting the next day came to nothing. It was quickly clear that the sides were still as far apart as ever, and, despite a further call to Number Ten, they reached an impasse. As Goodman writes: 'The sight of Cap'n Bob ambulating up and down the Brighton sea front looking for peace formulae was as irrelevant to both Thatcher and Scargill as counting pebbles on Brighton beach.'[15]

Future meetings were also to be futile. David Seymour, then a leader writer on the *Mirror*, said: 'They always broke down once both parties got together and realized instantly that what Maxwell had said each side was committed to change was completely wrong.' The truth was that, at the TUC in Brighton, Maxwell was a sideshow – a noisy sideshow, and one that attracted a lot of publicity, but a sideshow nonetheless. The real business of the Congress was to see what, if anything, the rest of the trade union movement could do to help the miners.

The 1984 Congress saw the retirement of General Secretary Len Murray. There comes a time, he told Congress, to move on 'and make way for a more substantial man', looking at the portly figure of his successor Norman Willis.

Willis, kindly, jovial, popular, with an impressive portfolio of jokes with which he had delighted fellow trade unionists and journalists for years, was widely considered a lightweight, appearances notwith-standing. He got the job on the 'Buggins's turn' principle, as Murray's deputy and as a man who had come out of the most powerful of the unions, the TGWU. But Jack Jones, formerly the TGWU General Secretary (he had retired in 1979) and one of the two most powerful union leaders Britain has ever known, was among those who urged that, in this crisis, Buggins's turn should be abandoned. He wanted a stronger figure: his candidate was the formidable white-collar union leader Rodney Bickerstaffe.

But Jones' successors, who lacked his stature and strategic intelligence, insisted on Willis, partly because they did not want the TUC General Secretary to be too powerful a figure: it might reduce the power of big unions like the TGWU. As for Bickerstaffe, though he almost certainly thought he would be better than Willis, he was unwilling to leave the union he led, the National Union of Public Employees, and did not think his supporters had enough votes in the bag to defeat Willis.

Norman Willis may have been thought to lack gravitas, but he did not lack courage. He knew that if the miners went down to total defeat, the power and influence of the trade union movement would go down with them. He had already been advocating a more interventionist approach to the dispute. Murray, having been firmly told to keep out by the NUM leadership, had agreed to do so, but Willis had already

```
*** TRANSIT SLIP ***
*** DISCHARGE ON ARRIVAL ***

Author: Beckett, Francis, 1945-
Title: Marching to the fault line : The 1984 min
ers' sti
Item ID: 1900188124
Transit to: BNRAD
```

quietly made informal contact with Scargill and Heathfield to find out what their situation was and what they were thinking. What he heard alarmed him.

In the run-up to the Congress, he was even more alarmed to see the proposals the NUM wanted to bring to it: a pledge that every union member – not just the transport unions – would refuse to cross any NUM picket lines; a ban on the use of any material that had been handled by non-union labour or soldiers. At first the miners also wanted a tenpence-a-week levy on every member of every trade union, but they abandoned this.

The problem, quite apart from the fact that these demands would split the Congress down the middle, was that they were completely undeliverable. Delegates sitting in the Brighton conference centre might put up their hands to vote for them, but nothing would happen. They would make not a jot of difference in the real world. They were gesture politics. The aim of the NUM's demands, it seemed to Willis, was not to help the strike but to show the workers that the TUC leaders were not really on their side; to brand Willis and his colleagues as class traitors.

At the beginning of TUC week, Murray and the man who was to take over from him less than a week later tried to broker a compromise. At first Scargill and Heathfield refused to meet them, or even to come to Brighton, but McGahey, the miners' representative on the TUC General Council, telephoned them from Brighton the day before the start of the Congress and said: 'Comrades, you've got to come tonight.' They agreed, reluctantly. They might not have done so had they realized that Norman Willis was in the room with McGahey when he made the call. If they had not agreed to come at McGahey's instigation that night, they would not have been available for the meeting with Maxwell described earlier.

They drove to Brighton. After their meeting with Maxwell, they saw Bill Keys before going into a meeting with the TUC top brass. Keys told them that he, too, thought their motion unworkable. Then, on Sunday, 2 September, at 8 p.m., in the splendid Louis XV suite in Brighton's

Metropole Hotel, the TUC team – Murray, Willis and their top officials, TUC Chairman Ray Buckton and David Basnett, leader of the GMB (General, Municipal, Boilermakers and Allied Trade Union) – met the three NUM leaders. Murray opened. He said the TUC wanted to help, but complained that the NUM seemed determined to appeal over its head to trade union members: a strategy, as he knew but did not say, which was doomed to failure. He added that the miners were not helping their case with other trade union members by picket-line violence.

McGahey said there was no intention to snub the TUC (though everyone thought that his President had precisely that intention). Scargill told them how solid the strike was, how the NUM was acting in accordance with the 1974 Plan for Coal, how the NCB had sabotaged peace talks, how he could not condemn violence while members were suffering 'great hardship, frustration, and in some cases provocation', how there was great hardship in mining areas and a desperate need for financial help, and how what they wanted from the TUC was for power supply unions to give wholehearted support. None of this can have come as a surprise to the TUC team.

Basnett opened for the TUC. A tall, stooping man with a slow, deliberate style of speaking, he must have sounded to Arthur Scargill like the worst sort of middle-class compromiser. His union included many workers in the power supply industry, and he said he could not accept the demand to respect picket lines. It would divide the unions without achieving its objective.

Four hours on, the sometimes bad-tempered argument produced an uneasy proposal for a 'concerted campaign' to raise money, and a compromise on picket lines. The compromise said that union members would not move coal, coke or oil substitute for coal and coke across NUM picket lines, and would not use them; but the decisions would only be implemented after detailed discussions with the TUC General Council and affected unions.

Even in this form it divided the Congress. On Monday afternoon in the conference hall, Scargill produced his usual oratorical *tour de force*, saying all the easy things that everyone wanted to hear, and was cheered to the rafters. The engineers' leader Gavin Laird was jeered when he said: 'The NUM saw fit for many months to ignore the general council and the government of the trade union movement' and there was 'no excuse for violence on the picket line'. Engineering union leader John Lyons also spoke against the agreed proposal, to cries of 'scab' and 'Tory swine'. Lyons, Bill Sirs of the steelworkers and Eric Hammond of the electricians all led their delegations in voting against it. But the big battalions – the unions with the votes, Basnett's GMB and Moss Evans's TGWU – ensured that it went through. It was, of course, meaningless, because it was undeliverable, and Norman Willis quickly regretted that they had not taken the chance to tell the miners' leaders firmly that their position was hopeless, and they must be guided by the TUC if they expected any support.

Lyons was privately furious with Basnett, whom he considered weak and vain, for agreeing to something that the unions with members in power supply could not deliver. 'It was criminal for the TUC General Council to go in for kidology with the miners on strike and suffering. The General Council knew it was a sham. Lionel Murray framed a resolution with weasel words in it,' he told one of the writers shortly afterwards. His speech, he said, brought him more letters of support from his members than anything else he ever did as General Secretary.

'The TUC wrote out a cheque and forgot to sign it' is John Monks' assessment today. But the miners' leaders left Brighton with the cheers of delegates ringing in their ears. Much good would it do their members. Yet Scargill seems to have had some hope that something helpful would come out of Brighton. After Orgreave he had been focusing more of his attention on leaders of other trade unions. The power unions could, in theory, deliver a decisive blow to the Government's hope of getting through the winter without electricity cuts. And, on one well-informed left-wing analysis, 'involving the TUC in the strike would mean that, if the miners were defeated, responsibility would be seen to fall on the shoulders of the trade union leaders.'[16]

Outside the conference hall, hundreds of demonstrators chanted, 'General strike now.' Under the WRP banner were Mark and Doreen Jones, parents of the first picket to die, David Jones. They had hitched to Brighton to lobby the TUC. On their return to Yorkshire they found a letter from the National Working Miners Committee, offering sympathy and a cheque for £250. They were hard up and £250 would have meant a lot, but they tore it up and sent it back with a letter saying it was an insult to their dead son.

Just after the Congress Neil Kinnock met the industrial correspondents and told them that the possibility of talks was getting stronger. 'I would say weeks not months. The NUM has been committed throughout to attending negotiations, but if possible they're even more committed since the TUC. The less attention to Thatcher the better . . . By investing her credit in "no surrender" she has introduced an inflexibility which even the Board doesn't welcome. The NUM cannot compromise on twenty pits and 20,000 jobs. That would tear up previous agreements; would say, uniquely in British industry, that management can close units of production like picking apples off a tree. It is clear that you close pits which are exhausting or exhausted, and pits which are unsafe.'

A journalist asked if he had his own formula for ending the strike. Yes, said Kinnock, he did, but he was not going to say what it was. But of course, he had none.

Downing Street was not sitting back after the TUC conference either. On 4 September Peter Gregson wrote another secret memo to Mrs Thatcher on the next round of NCB and NUM negotiations.[17] He said she had three choices: wait for an NUM counter proposal; table again the NCB's July text; or try a new approach. The last option could involve giving up an agreed definition of pit exhaustion, seeking agreement to get rid of X million tonnes of coal or going ahead with the closures anyway.

Waiting for the NUM to put forward a counter proposal had the advantage of putting the onus on the NUM to negotiate constructively. But the NUM might simply propose the July text without the words 'beneficially developed', and in this way 'it may be able to appear [under-lined] constructive', while simply ignoring the problem of loss-making pits. The NCB would then be faced with trying to negotiate extra words back into the text.'

Retabling the NCB text had the advantage of putting the NUM in the position of having to justify exclusion of the words 'beneficially devel-oped' or to substitute others that acknowledged the need to close loss-making pits. But it might imply that the NCB was prepared to make further concessions of substance.

Gregson also toyed with a new approach altogether, on the grounds that it could 'rescue both sides from an argument about words and formulae which is becoming sterile and unproductive'. But he was put off by major disadvantages. It could have given the NCB a new line but 'badly handled it could lead to a rout'. A new approach would probably be even harder for the NUM to swallow if it included new concrete arrangements such as timetables and quantities of coal to be produced, while 'a change of approach by the NCB would be much harder to explain publicly and could be presented by the NUM as a wrecking move'.

All in all, he thought the best thing was for the NCB to table the July text again, 'making it clear that any agreement has to deal with the prob-lem of loss-making pits, but indicating a willingness to consider alternative forms of words which deal adequately with the problem'.

He also raised other issues from Scargill's speeches, asking whether the settlement of the pit closures dispute would not just lead to other disputes, for example about pay. This was one more reason why 'it will be vital to pin the blame for a breakdown on NUM intransigence'. This might be crucial in the government's efforts to last out the strike, because it would affect power union members' willingness to give effect to the TUC resolution. So he wanted to be sure that the NCB had plans 'to ensure that the right message gets across to the media immediately and effectively'.

Thatcher followed Gregson's advice. She was adamant that there should be no change. Neil Kinnock wrote to her demanding a recall of

Parliament. He noted that the PM had said she could not leave the country for a tour of the Far East because 'it would not be right for her to be so far away from Britain', and he urged the government to become actively involved in seeking a resolution to the dispute. He received an icy reply saying a recall of Parliament would not serve any useful purpose. She said that the same pit closure procedures had been agreed by Labour in its Report for Coal and the dispute could be quickly settled if the NUM negotiated with the NCB along the same lines. To rub it in, she sent him the NCB press release at the end of July explaining why talks had collapsed. She stuck firmly to the NCB line.

Nevertheless talks between the NCB and the NUM continued, despite the collapse of negotiations in mid-July. They seemed to be getting somewhere, but collapsed again on 14 September. The fault this time appeared to be Scargill's intransigence. The Board tabled two amendments to the proposed closure procedure. The NUM insisted that the closures could only take place on grounds of exhaustion or for safety reasons. The NCB were determined to allow closures on economic grounds. But the Board did agree to modify the wording of the closure procedures, removing the use of the word 'beneficially' and including a proposal for a joint examination of potentially doomed pits by mining engineers. This was rejected by the NUM but, after a second attempt at a redraft, the NUM appeared to be about to agree.

When talks were adjourned on 13 September, the only difference was between 'satisfactory' or 'acceptable'. But the next day the NUM stepped back from what they agreed, and talks collapsed. The NCB put out a press release saying the dispute was 'quite unnecessary' and repeated pledges for a future stable industry, no compulsory redundancies, an offer of new jobs for everyone at closed collieries plus generous transfer payments, improved redundancy, a 5.2 per cent pay rise and continued high investments, specified as between £700m and £800m in 1984/85.

Meanwhile ministers continued to fret about coal supplies. Peter Walker received a letter on 6 September from Patrick Jenkin, the Environment Secretary, about whether to use the crisis to remove more than 1,000 tonnes by road from an open-cast site in Staffordshire. Staffordshire County Council objected on planning grounds to lorries removing so much coal in April, but now ministers were desperate to get as much coal stockpiled as possible. Jenkin even speculated on breaking the planning laws to get the coal moved, though it ran the risk of a local council taking enforcement action, which would place the government in the position of committing a criminal offence.

On 17 September there was a key personnel change in the government. Giles Shaw, Parliamentary Under-Secretary at the Department of Energy, stood down, weary of all the stress and problems. His replacement added a new dynamism to the scene. David Hunt, a close colleague of Peter Walker and then a Tory Party vice-chairman in charge of candidates, was Walker's chosen replacement, and Walker persuaded Thatcher. Hunt was to bring a new energy and relish for the conflict to the Department, and Walker trusted him absolutely.

His appointment was marked by both drama and comedy. On that day David Hunt was at Conservative Central Office dealing with one of the most difficult and delicate problems any vice-chairman in charge of the candidates list could expect in his career. He was interviewing Sarah Keays, the mistress of Cecil Parkinson, who had hit the headlines the previous year when the Cabinet minister had to resign after it was revealed that he had fathered her daughter Flora.

Sarah Keays – who was to become increasingly embittered – had political ambitions and wanted to remain on the Tory parliamentary candidates list. Thatcher, who had been forewarned, did not want her there. So Hunt was charged with telling Keays that she had no future with the Conservatives. Just as he had reached this delicate point the telephone rang. He was told it was the Prime Minister who wished to speak him. 'David, I am appointing you the new minister for coal,' she told him.

But Hunt did not believe he was really speaking to the Prime Minister. He told us: 'John Gummer [who was then Party Chairman] often used to play pranks on people, by getting people to ring you up pretending to be someone else. I wasn't certain whether this was another of his jokes, so I started cross-questioning the PM to make sure she really was the person on the other end of the line.'

'When will I take up this job?' he asked. 'Six p.m. tonight' came the immediate reply. Hunt began to realize it was true.

The government, in September, was willing to look at ways of ending the strike which, though they must not be capable of being interpreted as giving Scargill victory, might at least have the appearance of compromise, and leave the miners with their spirits and their union unbroken. Now, it seems, it was Scargill who was determined not to settle. Privately, Mick McGahey told mining MP Kevin Barron: 'Something has taken Arthur over.'

CHAPTER 6

PIT MANAGERS, MOSCOW GOLD AND A FATAL LIBYAN KISS

2 OCTOBER TO 13 NOVEMBER

Nineteen-eighty-four was one year when Neil Kinnock could have done without the relentless arrival of the Labour Party's annual conference. Most years, for the Leader of the Opposition, the annual party conference is a chance to make some headway in the opinion polls. But Kinnock went to Blackpool in the first week of October knowing that all he could hope to do was limit the damage the week was going to do to his party.

It was increasingly obvious that Scargill was going to clash with the courts, and that he would choose to defy them, opening up endless possibilities for embarrassment for a Labour leader who was straining every nerve to sound like a safe pair of hands whom the electorate could trust. Neither Stan Orme nor Bill Keys could yet offer him hope of a solution. Scargill's trust that General Winter would come to his aid, a faith shared by few other trade union leaders, seemed undimmed, and neither the government nor the NCB seemed to have any strategy except to grind the miners down.

It was a bleak prospect for a Labour leader whose party was closely identified with the unions, and who was himself closely identified with the miners. And Kinnock did not yet know the worst: that Arthur Scargill was sending an emissary to Libya – just months after a policewoman had been shot dead from the windows of the Libyan embassy – to beg for money from the most potent hate figure in the world, the Libyan dictator Colonel Gaddafi, a public relations blunder of extraordinary magnitude; and that Scargill's efforts to keep his union and the strike alive financially were to engulf the NUM in yet more damaging controversy.

Kinnock had to walk a delicate line between splitting his party irrevocably by failing to support the NUM, and committing electoral suicide by failing to support the police. 'I condemn the violence of stone-throwers and battering-ram carriers and I condemn the violence of cavalry charges, the truncheon groups and the shield-bangers,' he told the conference, mollifying no one.

The headlines from the conference were mostly Scargill's. It passed a motion calling for full support for the strike, which mattered not a jot in the real world because there was nothing of value that the conference could deliver, but was a symbolic victory for the strikers. Scargill had the drama of a writ being served on him in the conference hall, which ensured that he was the centre of attention, whatever worthy motion might be being discussed by the platform. The Friday before the conference, Mr Justice Nicholls delivered his judgement that the strike was unlawful in Derbyshire, and Scargill and other officials must stop calling it official. Scargill went on Channel 4 News to say that it *was* official, whatever the courts said, and on Monday morning David Hart obtained a writ demanding that Scargill appear before the court within forty-eight hours to explain himself. Once he had the writ, Hart immediately chartered a helicopter to fly a writ server to Blackpool and present it to Scargill as he sat in the conference hall.

'I want to make it clear', Scargill told a fringe meeting, 'that if the offence I have committed is contempt, I plead guilty. Because the only crime I have committed is to fight for my class and my members.' Cue wild cheering, then more when he declared that he was prepared to go to prison, but the truth was that no one expected Scargill to go to prison. It was the union, not its President, that was going to suffer for Scargill's moment of glory.

Scargill again told the meeting that he had not seen anyone throwing stones. Kevin Barron MP knew perfectly well that striking miners had thrown stones, and told Scargill, when they met in a Blackpool corridor outside the conference hall: 'I'm not going to go round denying it.' Scargill was flanked by his faithful acolytes Nell Myers, Jim Parker and Roger Windsor, and, says Barron, there was a deathly silence from all of them. The next day the equally faithful editor of *The Miner*, Maurice Jones, told Barron: 'Arthur's not very pleased with what you said.' Arthur being not pleased was serious for an NUM-sponsored MP who wished to keep his union sponsorship.

But Barron knew what he was talking about. When he met Scargill, he still had his badly bruised arm in a sling after his own experience on the picket line. At the end of September he had been to a mass picket in Maltby, stood behind the police lines and saw stones being thrown. Then he and a local vicar went to speak to the pickets, wearing a helmet as the police advised him to do.

He described for us what happened next. 'Suddenly the police charged and they just started lashing about. The vicar ran, I tried to get my ID card out and saw a truncheon coming down on my head, so I lifted my arm to protect it, and I got two cracks on my arm from the truncheon. Then I ran, watching hand-to-hand fighting all the way and a man lying on the ground who I thought was dead.'[1]

So he knew Scargill was talking rubbish. But it did not matter a lot what Scargill said any more. His loyal members were listening, but the television reporters, who, for the first six months of the strike, had made what looks like an honest effort to be impartial, had become 'in effect the cheerleaders for the return to work', as the BBC's industrial correspondent Nicholas Jones puts it. 'Lining up in support', Jones adds, 'were the newspaper proprietors who realized that defeat for the NUM would pave the way for their own subsequent confrontation with the print unions.'

'Each weekend as the strike wore on', writes Jones, 'the newspapers were full of stories warning the miners they were fighting a lost cause; this was backed up by new offers of increased redundancy money for those willing to return. The aim was to put pressure on the men's wives to persuade their husbands to give up the struggle.'[2]

Not that the government got everything its own way. The police action against the miners and the intransigence on the government side had angered the church hierarchy, and even, if reports were to be believed, the Queen. The most dramatic intervention came from David Jenkins, newly appointed Bishop of Durham. A controversial figure, he had already caused a row in the Church of England by questioning the resurrection, the virgin birth and Christ's ability to perform miracles.

In a sermon at his enthronement he denounced MacGregor as an 'elderly imported American' and called for his dismissal. Later, in his autobiography,[3] he retracted the phrase as 'a hostage to fortune' and because he had learned that MacGregor was born in Scotland. But he never retracted his view that neither side should have total victory. He describes the strike in his book as a battle between MacGregor's belief in Darwinism and Scargill's Marxist analysis. His comments caused a furore among traditional churchgoers and the Tories.

Publicly the Prime Minister and Energy Secretary Peter Walker refused to be drawn into the controversy surrounding the speech, Thatcher merely saying: 'I don't think I should be too fussed about getting involved in that.'[4] Privately it was a different matter. The government was livid. Walker opened a correspondence with David Jenkins and took great pains in a seven-page letter on 5 October to try to persuade the controversial bishop to change his mind.[5] The letter was copied to Gregson at the Cabinet Office and to Brigadier Budd, head of the Civil Contingencies Unit.

Walker chastised Jenkins for arguing that the government 'did not seem to care for the unemployed'. The Tory Cabinet minister wrote: 'I know of no problem which so dominates the thinking and the anxieties of myself and the government. As somebody whose father was an unemployed factory worker in the 1930s, there is nothing that I hate more passionately than the despair of unemployment.' He listed government measures to tackle training, housing, enterprise and community programmes.

He responded to the bishop's criticism of the government's record in failing to care for the elderly, embarking on the Falklands war and spending more on the police by saying: 'I hope I don't have to presume that, as an Anglican bishop, you would have allowed the military adventures of the Fascist junta in the Argentine to succeed, and the freedom of citizens for whom we have responsibility to be destroyed.' As for the police, 'There are 70,000 people working in the coal industry who are very relieved we have done that.'

But it was the bishop's attack on MacGregor and his support for striking miners that really angered Walker. He devoted nearly three pages to condemning the bishop for suggesting that MacGregor should go, and for not taking Scargill to task. The bishop's description of Scargill as having a 'personal intransigence' seemed to drive Walker to paroxysms of fury. Did the bishop not see that Scargill was on a political crusade, that this was contrary to what most Britons wanted, that he was putting demands which the government and the NCB could not possibly agree to? 'I must ask you as a Christian and as a Bishop – why do you think Mr Scargill keeps up mass picketing?'

And what did His Grace mean by saying that Scargill had strong support? It was 'seemingly never strong enough to ballot his members, seemingly never strong enough to rely on the peaceful picket as opposed to the mass mob.' As for the bishop's argument that redundancy payments are all very well but redundancy means no further jobs for the redundant and no jobs for their children, Walker had no time at all for it: 'And even if they [uneconomic pits] could last, you would be condemning tomorrow's teenagers to a working life deep in the ground in the most dangerous and uncomfortable four pits. I cannot believe that it is Christian charity to preserve these sort of jobs when, economically, there is no need.'

He lectured Jenkins on his Christian duty: 'As a Christian bishop in a mining diocese your objectives must be identical to the policies that the government are willing to finance . . . What as a Christian bishop you must not do is encourage the belief that if miners are deprived of the right to ballot and mob rule and violence are imposed, then demands devoid of logic and sanity will have to be fulfilled.' Why did he not tell miners' leaders that their cause could not be just if force and intimidation had to be used in its support? And why not tell Mr Scargill – 'if he listens to preachers of your faith'. This last phrase gives a sense of the harrumphing establishment anger many Tories felt at this apparently over-mighty union leader.

Walker helpfully provided a shopping list of issues which he thought it was the bishop's Christian duty to talk about: the absence of a ballot, the NCB's investment programme, the fine work of Ian MacGregor. And he told Jenkins 'as a Christian in your moments of meditation and prayer to ask why the 70,000 miners who were given a democratic vote, decided overwhelmingly not to strike . . .'

The government still had problems over coal supplies. A secret letter written on 11 October to Peter Walker by John Stradling Thomas, the minister of state at the Welsh Office, showed that school closures were a real possibility in Glamorgan because the coal they were getting was not a suitable grade. The NCB did not have sufficient alternatives to use in some 150 schools because of low stock levels, and Thomas warned of widespread disruption to education in the county.

Walker was resolute. In a tough reply on 17 October he said: 'There is plenty of coal in Wales which the miners could produce if they are anxious to avoid this particular form of suffering. I am sure we must convey very carefully to the public that it is the NUM's refusal to supply that coal which will create any problems.' The government and the NCB were largely managing to convey this message, with the help of a broadly compliant press and a sophisticated media operation.

But there was a ray of hope for the striking miners. If NACODS, the small but crucial trade union for pit overseers, could pull all its 16,000 members out in support, the industry might still be closed down, for without overseers to ensure proper safety procedures it was illegal to operate mines, and the NCB would have to close them. Both Scargill and Thatcher believed that NACODS held the key to victory in the strike, and the NCB was scurrying round making sure it did not unnecessarily antagonize the overmen and deputies: for example, by seeing to it that where possible they would be paid when they were unable to work because of picketing, so long as they could show they had tried to get in to work.[6]

So while the NUM and the Board were dancing minuets around each other at ACAS (where more talks started on 6 October), the talks that really mattered were happening in the Board's own headquarters. For NACODS members, surprisingly, had already voted by a substantial majority (82.51 per cent) to come out in support of the miners. Peter Walker privately blamed MacGregor for this debacle because of his bungling of the negotiations.[7]

This was a worry for Walker. He and Thatcher were sure that it was vital to buy NACODS off, and he knew that MacGregor was reluctant to offer NACODS anything. According to MacGregor's adviser Tim Bell, MacGregor 'didn't really see why such a union existed. He was quite prepared to bring in private staff, say health and safety staff and doctors, to take over their work. And he was not impressed with Peter McNestry and Ken Sampey, the two negotiators, referring to them as "Scampi and chips". He thought that with private staff he could keep the Nottinghamshire pits working.' MacGregor's autobiography dwells on a plan he had to let the NACODS strike go ahead, confident that Nottinghamshire could not come out – something neither Walker nor Thatcher believed for a moment.

This attitude was typical of MacGregor. He never seemed really to want a settlement. Tim Bell, who was called in to advise MacGregor about the same time as Hunt was appointed by Thatcher, recalls the extraordinary way he handled his board meetings. Not only was MacGregor occasionally out of step with the government, he had almost no rapport with his own board, whom he saw as part of a big consensual, subsidized state apparatus that ought to be swept away. Bell recalled: 'I used to come with him to board meetings, which always shocked the other board members. He would never have an agenda. He would start the meeting with "What shall we discuss today?"

'He often clashed with people, notably Ned Smith [the labour relations director]. Ned would say, "We ought to settle this dispute," and MacGregor would reply, "Why?" and he would say, "Strikes are a bad thing for the industry," and MacGregor would come back and say, "I disagree, sometimes strikes can be a good thing." So often any initiative from Ned would get nowhere.'

So MacGregor was a permanent worry to Walker. But Scargill was worrying him, too. Like many people, he probably overestimated Scargill's cleverness and subtlety, and he was preoccupied with the idea that the NUM President might be able to capitalize on the NACODS problem. These worries led to Walker's last-minute decision not to go to Brighton in the second week of October for the Conservative Party conference, but to stay in London to be on hand for the dispute. So he gave his room in Brighton's Grand Hotel, room 659, to Sir Anthony Berry MP, a junior minister. In the early hours of Friday, 12 October, the last day of the conference, an IRA bomb went off just underneath room 659, and Anthony Berry was killed instantly. Patrick Magee, the bomber, had planted the device a fortnight before, hoping to kill Thatcher.

Telling us this story, Walker said, perfectly seriously: 'Arthur Scargill saved my life.' If he had been in that room, much might have changed. Walker was a far more central figure in the dispute than most earlier accounts have given him credit for, and he was much more hardline than people have realized; he was not the Cabinet wet that his public image suggested, or as MacGregor liked to paint him. Also, his death would have linked the IRA to the miners' dispute in the public mind – wrongly, because the IRA did not particularly want to kill Walker, but inevitably all the same.

Just an hour or so before the bomb blast, in Margaret Thatcher's hotel suite in the same hotel, a key decision was being made. According to Tim Bell,[8] he had been talking at a reception earlier that evening with Norman Tebbit, the Industry Secretary, about how to handle NACODS. MacGregor had told Bell that whatever other people wanted, he had no intention of settling with NACODS.

Thatcher, more politically aware than MacGregor, briefed by Walker and advised by Tebbit, realized that, if NACODS came out, the working pits would close and any momentum in getting miners back to work would collapse. The central strategy for fighting the strike – the Whitehall code word 'endurance' – would be derailed.

Thatcher decided that MacGregor must be told in no uncertain terms to do everything he could to settle the NACODS dispute. She rang him from her hotel room to tell him, so there could be no doubt that was her view. MacGregor was forced reluctantly to agree, and not to proceed with recruiting private staff to replace the pit safety men.

One hour later the IRA bomb went off. If it had gone off earlier, MacGregor might not have received such an unequivocal personal message from the PM. As it was, MacGregor offered the NACODS General Secretary, Peter McNestry, an independent review body to which all pit closure proposals would have to go.

While negotiations were going on, ministers faced another problem that made a settlement with NACODS even more urgent. It emerged that social security benefits would be docked from working miners if they were laid off as a result of the NACODS dispute. The chief adjudication officer had ruled that working miners, like striking miners, would face savage benefit reductions of £15 a week if they were laid off.

A secret letter from Norman Fowler, the Health and Social Security Secretary, to Peter Walker was sent on 23 October warning him of the consequences.[9] 'The 1975 Social Security Act and the 1980 Supplementary Benefits Act require that somebody who has lost employment as a result of a stoppage due to a trade dispute is disqualified from benefit . . . unless he can prove that he is not participating in or directly interested in [underlined by Mr Fowler] the trade dispute which caused the stoppage of work. The legislation does not distinguish between different categories of people (i.e. those on strike and those laid off) who are directly interested in the trade dispute.'

Ministers were perfectly happy – in fact, delighted – that striking miners should be reduced (as many of them were) to scratching around on slag heaps for coal to heat their homes and stealing potatoes from the fields so they could have egg and chips, but horrified at the idea that hardship might also be caused to the working miners on whom their expectation of victory rested. If NACODS went on strike, not only would working miners in Nottinghamshire have to stop work, a disaster that the government had striven to avoid at all costs, but they would also lose benefits. This could turn them against the government.

Of course in theory the ruling would also apply to mines closed by NUM action, but heavy policing and bussing working miners into the pits had prevented this from becoming an issue. A NACODS dispute would make it into a very big issue indeed. This Thatcherite legislation was just about to skewer the very people who had been the bedrock of fighting the strike.

It was another reason why Walker was being very careful to keep NACODS at work. In a statement to Parliament on 18 October he was able to tell MPs that he had reached agreement with NACODS on two of their three requests. This included the guaranteed independent review of pit closures that they had asked for, and a reassessment of the twenty-pit hit list that had helped to trigger the strike. He made great play of agreeing further talks at ACAS with the NUM as part of the NACODS package. ACAS chief Pat Lowry had devised an amended proposal for closures, and the NCB had accepted it, but the NUM had turned it down. Scargill rammed the point home by saying he had not moved since day one of the strike on 6 March.

This was dreadfully frustrating for Neil Kinnock, who on 16 October had told Robin Day on BBC Radio's *World at One*: 'If the ACAS formula is acceptably near to the procedure which existed before March, and if the Coal Board understands the need for the withdrawal of the twenty-pit hit list, then the probability of a settlement is very strong.' Three days after he said this, and the day after Walker's statement to Parliament, Kinnock wrote to Thatcher. He was pleased that there would be a colliery review procedure, and had interpreted Walker's statement to mean that plans to force through a hit list of twenty closures had been dropped. 'If that is what Mr Walker is saying, then there is indeed a possibility of resuming negotiations.'[10]

Of course the government had never been keen on a colliery review procedure, but felt it necessary to keep NACODS members at work. Thatcher made the best of a bad job, insisting that the government had always wanted to keep a colliery review procedure and would always have looked at future coal production afresh because of the losses caused by the dispute. She concluded with a rhetorical question to Kinnock: 'Please will you now confirm that in your view there is nothing to stand in the way of a settlement of this dispute in line with the ACAS formula?'

It was a shrewd tactical blow in the battle for public opinion, a battle that was not going entirely the government's way, despite the barrage of media attacks on the NUM and especially its President. The day before Thatcher wrote to Kinnock, NACODS General Secretary Peter McNestry had written in Thatcher's most loyal paper, the *Daily Mail*, a scathing attack on her coal chairman Ian MacGregor. 'He has treated us with total contempt,' he wrote. At the ACAS talks, 'Mr MacGregor just sat there and said, "Nope." We tried and tried but he just kept saying, "Nope." Then, when ACAS decided to end the talks he said: "Good, now we can all go home."'

McNestry went on: 'It is his whole attitude – the way he treats people, proud people with a responsible attitude to their jobs. Every time he opens his mouth he puts his foot in it. He is not the man for the job . . . I am now certain Mr MacGregor wants to break trade unions, even unions like mine which in the past has only been involved in negotiations about such things as safety underground.'

Criticism in the *Guardian* might be ignored but the fact that the *Daily Mail* published such a furiously critical article forced a radical rethink of the NCB's public relations. Walker made it clear to MacGregor that his public performance would not do, and his evident failure to understand the unions was a growing problem. Too many people shared McNestry's perception. He was becoming a public relations liability.

So two days after the *Daily Mail* article, on 20 October, Michael Eaton was appointed as the NCB's chief spokesman, to deal not just with public relations but also negotiations. Eaton was in charge of the important

North Yorkshire division of the NCB and had therefore had considerable dealings with Scargill. His appointment was MacGregor's response to Walker's criticism, but MacGregor did not feel it necessary to consult Walker. Walker apparently felt he ought to have been consulted, an indication of how much this had become the government's battle, not the NCB's.

MacGregor's Deputy Chairman, Jim Cowan, was even more furious than Walker, and threatened to resign if Eaton was at the talks at ACAS. So Eaton was removed from them, even though his knowledge of the NUM and Scargill personally was one of the main reasons for his appointment.[11]

By 25 October the NACODS deal was done. It was a good deal for the small managers' union, eloquent testimony to the government's and the NCB's conviction that NACODS had the power to deliver something like victory to the miners unless it was appeased. This was one of many moments during the strike when Scargill, if he had acknowledged the reality of his situation, might have grabbed a settlement. Of course, it would not have been a victory – the review body was established, but it never saved a single pit that the Board wanted to close – but it could have been dressed up as a partial victory, and a negotiator like Bill Keys in Scargill's position would have done just that, in order to save his union.

There was never the smallest chance of Scargill doing that. Nor was there any chance of McNestry – accurately described by Paul Routledge as 'a talkative and sympathetic Geordie well to the left of the average pit overseer'[12] – being able to persuade his members to turn down such a deal. McNestry knew his members would want him to accept, and he did. McNestry, says John Monks, 'wanted to help Arthur out of a hole' but could not do so.

Scargill, predictably perhaps, did not see it like that. According to Monks, he 'saw NACODS as a lot of Quislings. He underestimated and undervalued it.' After the strike Scargill confided to a journalist from the WRP paper *Newsline* that he could never understand why the big vote in favour of a NACODS strike had not been implemented. He thought there had been dirty work somewhere. His close friend Ken Capstick believes that NACODS could have delivered victory to the NUM, and its rank-and-file members would have been prepared to do so; they were let down by their leaders.

But Scargill and Capstick on one hand, and Monks on the other, agree that this was a crucial moment. 'Margaret Thatcher did not give up on negotiations until the NACODS strike was called off,' says Monks. He adds that the TUC did its best to stop NACODS from settling. 'We could see that with the help of NACODS we could get a review procedure. NACODS could close down Nottinghamshire, where it had great loyalty.' But 'Pat Lowry [of ACAS] and Ken Sampey [the NACODS President, who was not as left-wing as McNestry] told us to get lost.'

The NCB knew what was going on. An internal message to Ian MacGregor reads:

> Tim Bell called.
> His informant at the TUC has confirmed what you said, i.e.
> 1. They are trying to stop NACODS from settling.
> 2. They are trying to rewrite the peace formula to accommodate Scargill.

The ACAS talks ground to a halt after four days. Scargill's account of them to Kinnock, as summarized by Kinnock's office, was: 'Following four days of discussion at ACAS HQ during which the NUM actually met the NCB for less than 1 hour, the Coal Board has broken off talks, destroying hopes of an early end to the dispute . . . One document accepted by NUM, other by NCB, 3rd accepted by NUM and NCB went away to think about it for the weekend. It is now obvious that their consideration involved consultation, and that, once again, the govt has intervened to prevent an early settlement.'[13]

Stan Orme tried again to get something moving on 1 November with a further exchange of correspondence with Peter Walker. He raised the issue of a report that a new hit list existed for pit closures in the North East. In asking specific questions, the man who rightly said he had 'done everything possible to enable a negotiated settlement to be reached' tried to get talks going. But Walker, replying the next day with his confidence reinforced by the NACODS decision to call off their strike, was having none of it. He told Orme, rather smugly: 'I know you would like this dispute settled and know that the Labour Party is deeply embarrassed at being closely associated with the methods and objectives of Mr Scargill. But I must repeat I think he succeeds in taking you and your party for a ride on frequent occasions.'

His long letter was designed mostly to score points and embarrass Orme politically, and it ended like this: 'Please let us have three answers – publicly declared. Then the country can judge whether you and the Labour Party are in favour of the two unions – NACODS and BACM [British Association of Colliery Managers] – who have conducted their procedures in the best traditions of the trade union movement, and the third of the NUM's members who balloted and acted in accordance with the view of the majority, or whether you and the Labour Party are in favour of Arthur Scargill. If this is the latter I must say that you will be in pretty unpleasant company both at home and abroad.'

The tone suggests a minister who no longer thinks he needs Orme's help, nor is interested in any formula Orme may have to offer. Orme must have sensed that the government was now out for absolute victory, especially after MacGregor, too, rebuffed him, just two weeks after Walker had done so. Orme had been to see MacGregor and had left some proposals with him. MacGregor wrote on 16 November to say that to consider the documents would be to negotiate, and he did not think it appropriate to negotiate with Orme. The Labour Party's peace initiative had failed.[14]

On the same day that McNestry did his deal with MacGregor, the NUM dug itself so deeply into a legal quagmire that there was no longer any real chance of it emerging without being crippled.

Two weeks earlier, when Scargill had been ordered to appear in court, he declined to turn up, and his union was fined £200,000, with a £10,000 fine personally for Scargill. Scargill's fine was paid anonymously, but he refused to allow the union's fine to be paid, so on 25 October Mr Justice Nicholls sequestrated – took away – the entire assets of the union, which had been listed at £10.7m in money and property before the strike began. How was the strike to be paid for now?

Scargill hoped that one source of money would be the Soviet Union. In 1926, the Soviet Union gave money to miners' hardship funds, and some mining communities were saved from starvation by Soviet money. In the mid-1980s, talk of 'Moscow gold' still had the power to chill the blood of readers of tabloid newspapers.

The NUM leadership was asking the Soviet Union for money almost from day one of the strike, and with growing urgency after the NUM funds were sequestrated. This was not Soviet government money but money raised by Soviet mineworkers who donated a day's pay (which they could ill afford, on their miserable wages) and gave it to the Soviet miners' union for passing on to the NUM. But the Soviet miners' union needed government permission to get hard currency out of the country.

Scargill and NUM chief executive Roger Windsor offered the Soviets several methods of giving money clandestinely, in an effort to prevent it from being seized by the Receiver or known about by the British government. But nerves in Moscow meant that by the time Scargill went to the Brighton TUC at the start of October, nothing had happened.

In Brighton during TUC week he met two well-placed Soviet Union diplomats, and they set up a meeting on 8 October at the headquarters of the Confédération Générale du Travail (CGT) headquarters in Montreuil, near Paris, with Soviet diplomats, together with the leaders of the CGT miners' section, including General Secretary Alain Simon, a former miner.

The French do not have one trade union centre, as the UK has the TUC: they have three main ones and two smaller ones, and what divides them is politics. The CGT was the biggest in several industries, including mining, and politically close to the Communist Party. Simon was also a key figure in the eastern bloc miners' international, MTUI, and an ally of Scargill in opposition to the western bloc international, which both men considered an agent of American imperialism. They had prepared the ground by lobbying key Soviet political figures on the NUM's behalf.

Four days later the Soviet Communist Party Central Committee secretly decided to allocate to the British NUM one million roubles – about $1.4m – in hard currency from the funds of the Soviet TUC. Authorization for the transfer was signed by Mikhail Gorbachev, then number two in the Soviet hierarchy.

They tried to put the money into an NUM account in Zurich, apparently unaware that all NUM accounts had been frozen. The bank returned it, while alerting the Receiver to the existence of the account. Then they hesitated, fearful both of the money falling into the hands of the British government and of the diplomatic consequences should the Thatcher government discover their intentions.[15]

They were right to be worried. Articles by the *Sunday Times* Insight team on 18 November and the *Morning Star* the following day alerted Sir Geoffrey Howe, the Foreign Secretary, to serious problems for relations between Mrs Thatcher and Mikhail Gorbachev, who was soon to pay an official visit to Britain. Support from the Soviet Union rang alarm bells in Downing Street, the Foreign Office and the Treasury.

On 20 November Colin Budd, private secretary to Sir Geoffrey, wrote to Charles (now Lord) Powell, Thatcher's foreign affairs adviser at Number Ten, commenting that the Insight article which quoted Scargill 'appears to confirm, for the first time since reports of Soviet miners' assistance were received in September, contributions in cash as opposed to food and clothing have been received.' The confidential letter[16] said Sir Geoffrey viewed such a move as (in Whitehall language) 'a matter of some concern'. So it was proposed that Norman Lamont, then minister of state for industry, should take the Soviet ambassador to task at a private lunch on the same day.

At the same time the Foreign Office was expressing alarm that a Donetsk coal-pit foreman, a Mr Strelchenko, who would be accompanying Gorbachev, was planning to go and address striking miners. The letter warned that if he did 'there would be a serious political row'

and the Russians should be informally warned of the possible controversy. The letter added that if the Soviet miners were giving cash to
striking miners, 'it would be most unlikely that the Soviet miners'
unions could have been given access to convertible roubles without
express Soviet official permission . . . the Soviet Government has, to
some extent, been involved.'

But it went on: 'At this end, we doubt whether the Russians could
have committed any irregularities. Legally, they could have passed the
money through a Soviet bank (and the Moscow Narodny have a branch
in London) direct to a TUC or regional NUM account and without, so
far as our lawyers can see at first glance, there being any risk of sequestration.' So at the beginning the cash was deemed legal. All the more
reason to stop it.

After the lunch Edmund Hosker, Lamont's private secretary, wrote
to Charles Powell with the outcome. It was pretty bad.[17] Lamont raised
the issue of £1m in Soviet miners' aid only to be told by the ambassador: 'The Russians recognize that the UK is a democratic country; the
UK must recognize that the USSR is a democratic country.' Pressed by
Lamont on the fact that the Russian government must be involved in
allowing the transactions, 'the Ambassador maintained that citizens
could transfer money for some purposes, and emphasized the importance and independence of Soviet trade unions . . . Refusal to allow their
rights to be exercised would have constituted unwarranted interference
by the Soviet Government in the Soviet miners' union's own affairs.'

A handwritten note from Charles Powell to Sir Robert Armstrong,
the Cabinet Secretary, on the top of the letter said: 'Mr Lamont got an
entirely predictable response.' 'Entirely so' is Sir Robert's handwritten
comment.

On 23 November Colin Budd wrote again to Charles Powell. This
time the FO had made much stronger representations to the Soviet
Embassy, with the agreement of Thatcher. He was able to assure Powell
that the Soviets did not want to interfere in British domestic politics,
and that Gorbachev had been advised not to visit any mining communities. As for Mr Strelchenko, the FO had a line, should the press get

too interested. They intended to say that he had been invited on a parliamentary visit and, as far as events organized by the Government were concerned, would be received in his parliamentary capacity. He would be expected to watch his step, and not to do anything that could be interpreted as interfering in Britain's internal affairs.[18]

Meanwhile Oleg Gordievsky, who worked undercover for the KGB in the Soviet Embassy in London and was a double agent working for MI6, warned his Moscow superiors that it would be 'undesirable and counterproductive for the Soviet Union to help the striking miners'. His warnings were echoed by the labour attaché in London, Yuri Mazur, who looked after relations with both the trade unions and the British Communist Party. He thought any help would leak out, and would damage both relations with the Thatcher government and the electoral prospects of the Labour Party.

On the other side, senior figures in the Prague-based trade union international, the World Federation of Trade Unions (WFTU), wanted to help the miners. But by the end of November, nothing had been received, and Thatcher was due to meet Gorbachev the next month. (Theoretically Gorbachev was only heir apparent to Konstantin Chernenko, but Chernenko was already very ill.) The Thatcher–Gorbachev meeting was to have a crucial impact, as we shall see in the next chapter.

Miners' unions in Czechoslovakia and Bulgaria secretly handed over money, in used notes, to NUM emissaries to deliver to the NUM's Sheffield headquarters. In one instance they stuffed a plastic bag containing $96,000 in cash into the hands of a surprised Peter Heathfield. Heathfield did not know what it contained, and forgot about it for a few days, while it languished in the boot of his car.[19] But nothing like enough was coming in, the strike was in a desperate state, and by the end of November nothing had been received from the Soviet Union.

Where else was money to be had? Scargill had what seemed to him a very bright idea, and what seemed to Mick McGahey, when he heard about it after the event, an amazingly stupid one. On the day of the sequestration, Roger Windsor, whom Scargill had personally appointed to be NUM chief executive, was in Libya. Only Scargill knew of Windsor's mission. Yet Windsor appeared on Libyan television embracing Gaddafi in his tent, and Gaddafi, according to British newspaper reports of the event on 27 October, 'expressed sympathy with the striking miners who suffer from abuse and exploitation'.

Just six months earlier, on 17 April, WPC Yvonne Fletcher had been shot dead from inside the Libyan Embassy as police surrounded the building, and Gaddafi was seen in Britain as the worst sort of international pariah. It was as though in 2003, shortly before the Iraq war, a trade union leader had gone to Iraq to plead for money from Saddam Hussein.

'Cannot Arthur see', wrote Bill Keys in his diary, the day the *Sunday Times* revealed the story of Roger Windsor's trip to Libya, 'that this type of activity is going to drive an even greater wedge between the unions and the public . . . How can one get through to Arthur, that he cannot win this dispute on his own . . .'[20] It is the one thing for which Mick McGahey, who remained, right up to his death, publicly loyal to Scargill, was prepared openly to criticize his President. 'We made a mistake sending Windsor to Libya. I blew my top. I was never consulted,' he told Paul Routledge.[21]

Presumably Scargill did not consult McGahey because he knew his Vice-President would oppose the idea. McGahey found out from one of the industrial correspondents, Donald McIntyre of the *Sunday Times*. McIntyre had had the story that morning from his newsdesk, and was covering the Scottish miners' gala at the time, so he asked McGahey what he thought about the Libyan money. McGahey, genuinely perplexed, said: 'What Libyan money?' He maintained impassivity in front of the journalist, but afterwards said to Ken Cameron, General Secretary of the Fire Brigades Union: 'The man [Scargill] is mad.'[22]

Roger Windsor is one of the strangest and most unexpected figures in this story. He was a bookkeeper who had worked in the small office of a trade union international, Public Services International, for ten years. According to Cyril Cooper, who was then one of PSI's top people and responsible in those apartheid days for ferrying large amounts of trade union money secretly to the African National Congress in South Africa, Windsor was a very minor figure in PSI. He did the books, and was responsible for handing Cooper the sums of money he took to South Africa and for booking his flights, but he would not have been involved in any decision about what Cooper was going to do with the money.

'I was amazed when he suddenly turned up as one of the key people in the NUM in such a senior job,' says Cooper. 'It was a far more important role than he had had with PSI.' Cooper adds that Windsor was not well thought of in the office. 'Whatever you were talking about, he was an expert on it.'

Windsor was eventually to denounce Scargill in the *Daily Mirror*, and Seumas Milne, the one journalist to whom Scargill speaks freely, now calls him 'a cold, fussy man'. At the time, though, he was known to be the one man Scargill trusted.

The CGT's Alain Simon worked with Windsor over the Soviet money and he, too, says: 'I never liked him. And he didn't like me either. But he was Arthur's right-hand man and I was obliged to accept this man.' 'Someone whom Arthur trusted' had asked Scargill to give him a job.

This must be a reference to Rodney Bickerstaffe, the new left-wing General Secretary of the public service union NUPE, and Tony Benn, who were Windsor's referees. Bickerstaffe today plays down this involvement. He met Windsor because NUPE was affiliated to PSI, and agreed to be a referee, he says, in the casual way that you do with a junior member of staff whom you know nothing against. He was as surprised as anyone when Windsor suddenly became a pivotal figure in the NUM.

For Scargill, Windsor's main attraction was probably that he was not in any way equipped to challenge his master, politically or intellectually. He had no power base in the union apart from what he derived from being Scargill's man. Perhaps his international experience and fluent French were also factors.

His appointment was very much in the Scargill style of choosing those closest to him, like Nell Myers for press officer and Maurice Jones for editor. None of these three was ever more than a creature of the

President. He never seemed to want strong, independent people around him, who might contradict him.

Arriving at NUM headquarters in November 1983, Windsor quickly became the President's right-hand man, and during the strike he became more important almost daily, until by the end he was consulted more than such pivotal figures as Mick McGahey.

He it was who, before the strike, had been told to prepare, in the greatest secrecy, a scheme to protect the union's money from sequestration, which involved putting the money in foreign bank accounts and setting up an independent trust to take over the NUM's assets. At the start of the strike, he set it in motion, and by all accounts revelled in the cloak-and-dagger atmosphere he was able to create. He spirited £8.5m from bank to bank, via the Isle of Man, through the financial systems of seven countries, finally leaving it in Dublin, Zurich and Luxembourg. From Dublin, £5m went to New York to buy Jersey currency bonds. Windsor then hired a small private aircraft and sent the Finance Officer, Steve Hudson, and a colleague to Jersey to pick up £4.7m of dollar bearer bonds and fly them to a Luxembourg bank.[23]

Windsor says he first heard about the Gaddafi project when he was in Paris at the headquarters of the CGT. Their host in Paris was Alain Simon. 'Scargill and Heathfield told me I was to represent the union and meet Colonel Gaddafi,' Windsor told us. 'Over lunch with the Libyan representatives in Paris, we were told that money could only be given with the authority of Gaddafi. We were led to believe it would be about £1m. Someone had to go to Libya. Scargill said, "It can't be me or Peter, is it OK if Roger goes?"'[24]

Scargill gave a rather different account to Seumas Milne. In this version, Scargill himself refused to go to Libya, saying that if Libya wanted to help, it should suspend strikebreaking supplies of oil. Windsor, on the other hand, 'declared himself more than willing to go.'[25] But this feels like an attempt to distance himself from an adventure that blew up in his face, and pin the blame on a subordinate. It is clearly nonsense to suggest that Windsor would or could have gone if Scargill was not very keen on him going.

Windsor flew from Manchester to Tripoli. 'I was told I would see the leader fairly quickly but in fact was hanging around for several days.' He spent the time mostly in his hotel, he says, except when Altaf Abbasi took him to meet some Libyan trade unionists. Abbasi had provided the NUM with an introduction to Gaddafi. He ran a grocery store in Doncaster, South Yorkshire, and, according to Seumas Milne had close connections with the Pakistani opposition group around Benazir Bhutto, for which he had spent two weeks in a dreadful Pakistani prison.

'All this time Arthur Scargill was phoning my wife every day, sometimes several times a day, asking, "When will he be back, will he be bringing something with him?"' says Windsor. 'Eventually one day a car came for me and I was driven for about twenty minutes to what I took to be an army camp, and we drew up at a tent. Somebody told me: the protocol is, kiss him on both cheeks. We spoke through a translator.'

Then came the moment that was to cause the NUM so much misery. According to Windsor it happened like this: 'Someone said to me, we always take a picture for the record. I gave my speech, the one Arthur and I had drafted in advance, he asked some questions, we kissed again. I don't know the route by which the pictures got into the *Sunday Times.* Perhaps the security services picked it up from Libyan television. When I got back to Manchester Airport, I phoned my wife and she said, "You are all over the *Sunday Times.*"'

He went to NUM headquarters in Sheffield and sat down with Scargill, Heathfield and Myers to write a statement on the purpose of the visit. 'We decided to say the purpose was to see Libyan trade unionism,' Windsor told us. 'It's called lying for the cause.' It's also called stupidity. Can they really have thought anyone was going to believe that?

Windsor collected the money that he thought had come from Libya. Then came a moment which, in the long term, was to cause even more trouble than the original trip to Libya. Years after the strike the *Daily Mirror* ran a story claiming that, on Scargill's instructions, Windsor brought the Libyan money in cash – all £163,000 of it – to Scargill's office. There he found Scargill and Heathfield. Scargill explained that the money had to be hidden before the Receiver took over all the union's accounts. He then counted out money to each of the three of them: £25,000 to clear his mortgage, which the union had given him; £17,000 for improvements to Peter Heathfield's home, for which the union had loaned him the money; and £29,500 to clear the bridging loan the union had made to Windsor for his home. Finance Officer Steve Hudson was sent for to pick up the money and provide all three with receipts.

That was the accusation made six years later, in 1990, by the *Daily Mirror*. And twelve years later still, the *Mirror* editor who had published it, Roy Greenslade, said the paper had it wrong. The reporter who got the story, Terry Pattinson, still insists they had it right, and has been published in the *Guardian* repeating his accusation. Greenslade now calls Pattinson, the man he once trusted to report on this major story for his newspaper, 'testy and excitable'. He said he was now sure that Scargill had not taken Libyan money, and had not misused strike funds.

Greenslade does not explain his road-to-Damascus moment. The meeting the *Mirror* wrote about, where the money was divvied up between the three officials, did take place. The sum on the table was £163,000, and Scargill, Heathfield and Windsor did leave the meeting with the cash. Whether the money was all, or partly, from Libya, as the *Mirror* alleged, we cannot be certain because, as we shall see, a great deal of cash was getting to the NUM from other sources.

But did the three officials, as the *Mirror* alleged, take for their own use money that had been given for their desperately hard-up members? Here the case against them is very far from being proven, and it is unlikely that it can ever be proved either way, because so much cash was sloshing about, unaccounted for because any accounts might make it vulnerable to the Receiver.

It would have been a dreadful thing to do, a betrayal of everything they were supposed to stand for. To accept that they effectively stole from their members at a time of their members' greatest need would require a revolution in our view of Scargill, and an even greater one in our view of Heathfield. Anyway, Scargill had already paid off his mortgage, and Heathfield's home was owned by the Derbyshire area of the NUM.

Seumas Milne provides a detailed account of what happened to the money that was handed out round that table, an account echoed in a report by Gavin Lightman QC which the union commissioned.[26] It seems likely that the meeting, and the divvying up of the cash, was part of the extraordinary efforts that had to be made to keep the union afloat after its funds were sequestrated on 25 October. The union no longer belonged to the members and their elected leaders: control passed to a Receiver appointed by the court, and the Receiver remained in charge until 27 June 1986, when the strike was long over. Trade unions and others in Britain and throughout the world provided huge sums of money to keep the strike and the union going. They provided it in cash because that was the only way they could keep it out of the hands of the Receiver. No one is ever likely to be able to put a figure on the amount of cash that passed through the miners' leaders' hands and their various bank accounts, money that they struggled to keep from the prying eyes of the Receiver, but it was certainly many millions of pounds. It came from all sorts of places. Alan Meale, now MP for Mansfield, then a junior official working for the co-ordinating committee that was designed to act as a link between trade unions sympathetic to the strike, such as the Fire Brigades Union and NUPE, believes that altogether some £6m was redistributed to the NUM from other left-wing union leaders.

Left-wing union leaders, though they may have disappointed Scargill by not calling their members out at his bidding, were generous when he came to them for money. Ken Cameron of the FBU, which had already given the miners money, recalls an early morning telephone call from Scargill. The miners' President told him that he needed £200,000 in cash. Cameron said that to loan such a large sum of money he needed authorization from his executive, which was not due to meet for another month. Scargill told him that unless Cameron could give him the cash that morning, he could not pay his staff. Cameron took the decision to give Scargill the money and clear it with his executive later. He went to the bank and, as arranged, met Scargill's driver Jim Parker there. Cameron and Parker went into the bank and the money was ready for them. It would not fit into Cameron's briefcase, so they found some cardboard boxes that had once held packets of crisps, and stuffed the notes into those. The bank manager asked what Cameron wanted the money for, and Cameron said: 'Where's the nearest bookie?'

As they drove away, Parker said: 'He's odd, that bank manager.' Cameron replied: 'He's stupid. He didn't ask the name of the horse.' Scargill had a flat in the Barbican, provided by the NUM for his use when he was in London, and that was where they took the money. Scargill emptied it out on the floor and thanked Cameron, who left for his next meeting.

Many unions, including the TGWU, found ways of channelling suitcases full of banknotes to the NUM. Rodney Bickerstaffe was another left-wing trade union leader who helped Scargill with money: his NUPE, like the firefighters, gave substantial sums of money during the dispute. Bickerstaffe also hid NUM money from the Receiver. Sequestration did not come as a complete surprise, and miners' leaders had made some preparations. Bickerstaffe recalled for us a lonely drive to a railway station, some time before sequestration. He pulled his car into the station car park alongside that of the leader of one of the NUM's regions. This man handed him a suitcase, told him it contained £100,000, and drove off. Bickerstaffe took the suitcase back to his office and called his finance officer in to be with him while he put the case, unopened, into his office safe.

'Shouldn't we count it?' asked his finance officer. 'Don't be so stupid,' replied Bickerstaffe. He told us: 'It was all done on trust. We trusted each other. We had to or it couldn't have worked.'

Overseas trade unions were very generous too. Ken Cameron led a small delegation to the USA in search of money, coming back with a respectable sum from such unions as the Teamsters, though the American TUC, the AFL/CIO, was not helpful, since it was at loggerheads with Scargill over his support for eastern bloc internationals.

But by far the most generous was the CGT. Not only did the CGT give generously from its own funds, it also appealed to its members for money for the British miners, and they responded with great generosity.

Jeff Apter had worked for the CGT. He had recently left, but remained in Paris working as a freelance journalist, which he still does – he is now the Paris stringer for English-speaking newspapers and magazines all over the world, and still has excellent trade union and industrial contacts there. Apter became the crucial link between the collectors in France and the NUM. There was a limit to how much foreign currency a French person could bring to the UK. So a team of French printers used to book their passage on a ferry to Folkestone, each carrying the maximum permitted amount of currency, and Apter booked himself on the same ferry. After they disembarked, one of the printers collected all the parcels of money and met Apter in a pub. The printer walked into the pub with a case, they had a drink together, and Apter walked out with the case. In a small side street, a car waited, usually driven by Jim Parker with Nell Myers in the passenger seat. Apter put the case in the car, and Parker drove away. And, as with the £163,000 that was divvied up in Scargill's office that day, no one knows exactly what happened to this money, or to the other millions of pounds in cash that found their way to the NUM from various sources. As Rodney Bickerstaffe says, 'It was all done on trust.'

Chapter 7

The Collapse of General Winter

14 November to 31 December

One of Norman Willis's first acts as the new TUC General Secretary was to attend a big miners' rally in Aberavon on 14 November – a symbol of his intention that in future the TUC was to be an active player in the dispute. And there something dreadful happened, something that showed the trade union movement was irreparably split and the hatred that had built up: a hatred not of the government, not of the NCB, but of the union leaders who Scargill told his members were class traitors, ready to betray the miners as their predecessors had in 1926.

It happened because Willis did something difficult and courageous. He spoke at the end of a day that had seen dreadful violence in Yorkshire, where striking miners erected barricades to try to stop the trickle back to work from turning into a torrent.

It was one of those big, fairly conventional halls, with a stage at one end and a table set up on the stage behind which sat the platform party – five or six union leaders including Scargill and Willis. Scargill made one of his barnstorming speeches. The text hasn't survived, but we can be certain that he told his loyal members that right was on their side, that they were on the path to victory, and that it was time for the whole trade union movement to come to the aid of the miners. He sat down to the torrent of cheering that always followed these speeches, and the stout man seated beside him rose and took the microphone. If Norman Willis was nervous, he did not show it.

Standing beside Arthur Scargill, he began by saying that he wanted to give the miners all the support he could. 'But the TUC is not an army and I'm not a Field Marshal,' he said, raising his voice to be heard above the shouts and jeers. Scargill looked straight ahead, impassive, and left it to his members to guess what he was thinking, which they had little trouble in doing. Willis went on: 'When I see the hardship, when I see the sacrifice, I wish I could guarantee you all the support you need. But I don't kid trade unionists and I'll never mislead the miners about the true picture.'

He condemned the violence of the police and the attitude of the government. And then, to howls of outrage, he went on: 'I could leave it there, but I will not. For I have to say that any miner, too, who resorts to violence wounds the miners' case far more than they damage their opponents' resolve. Violence creates more violence, and out of that is built not solidarity but despair and defeat. I have marched proudly before many miners' banners and I know there will never be one that praises the brick, the bolt or the petrol bomb. Such acts, if they are done by miners, are alien to our common tradition, however, not just because they are counter-productive, but because they are wrong.'

And as he spoke, a noose was lowered from the ceiling, to hang over his head. What was worse to Willis, the lifelong professional union negotiator, was that his fellow union leader Arthur Scargill sat beside him, still looking grimly straight ahead, saying nothing. A word from Scargill, as Willis pointed out afterwards, would have been enough to have the noose removed. He did not say it.

Willis had had enough of Scargill. He was feeling not personal pique but the impatience that a professional union negotiator feels for a man he considers a shallow populist. The professional knows that in some circumstances he has two choices: to do the business for his members, or to obtain their applause with an easy speech. What

Willis thought in his heart was that the miners' President had chosen the latter.

Neil Kinnock issued a statement in support of Willis. 'Norman Willis gave strong, truthful advice last night. When he restated the TUC's support for the miners and the mining communities, and when he condemned picket-line violence, he spoke for millions of trade unionists.'

The night Willis went to Aberavon, print union leader Bill Keys spoke at a miners' meeting in Birmingham with Stan Orme. Later that night, Keys and Orme dined together in Birmingham and discussed Orme's revised plan for a settlement. Both of them thought it might just be good enough. Keys reported the discussion to Willis, and Orme to Kinnock.

Orme understood that Keys was now the key player on the TUC side. One of the consequences of Willis replacing Murray was that Keys, without anyone actually saying so, moved from being simply the unofficial liaison between the left wing of the General Council and the miners' leaders to having a vital secret role to play on behalf of the TUC itself. He was co-opted onto the special committee of General Council members dealing with the miners' strike. Keys was a very sensible choice, because as a left-winger he had a better chance than anyone else of keeping the miners' confidence, while as a negotiator he was knowledgeable, well-connected, pragmatic and adroit. 'It seems that the miners are dividing the General Council into Goodies and Baddies,' he wrote in his diary. But, supreme realist that he was, Keys was quite happy to use his status as one of the Goodies, as long as it lasted, to try to get a settlement.

By the start of December, Keys' last-ditch peace initiative was starting to take shape. Willis asked Keys to come to Congress House to see him. 'He [Willis] is very much down in the dumps,' wrote Keys in his diary that evening. 'Norman tells me that he has spoken with Arthur, Peter, Mick, who all have different attitudes, but that Arthur while appearing worried gives the appearance of wishing to fight to the last miner . . .'

John Monks has told us what Willis was thinking at the time. 'Norman just wanted it settled. Trade unionism was more likely to lose than gain. Extrication was the name of the game. And that suited Norman's personality.' As for Keys, 'he took the left line but he was always trying to find solutions, he was on the phone all the time.' If those two couldn't find a way out, no one could. But Keys was starting to despair. He thought the miners had been out for far too long, and the cracks were showing. And he thought that no one except Arthur Scargill any longer believed that the miners could win on their own.

Keys would remain actively and energetically involved right up to the end, desperately trying to get a settlement, despite his own failing health. The day after he saw Willis, he saw his doctor, who told him to retire, quickly. Willis, who did not know of Keys' health troubles, asked him to cancel a planned visit to Russia later in the month, so as to be available to help with the crisis, and Keys duly cancelled it.[1]

As winter approached, the strike was visibly collapsing, as the on–off peace talks drained the morale from the striking miners and their hardship became every day a little worse. The NCB moved fast to exploit this, decreeing that men who went back to work could earn a considerable amount in back pay and a special Christmas bonus – a matter of no small importance to men already deeply in debt and foreseeing a bleak Christmas for their children. Nottinghamshire was at work, and men were even returning to work in South Wales and Yorkshire. On 8 November the first man had gone back at Cortonwood, the mine where it all started, and over the next few weeks he was followed by more. Scargill routinely denied that it was happening, but it was.

The electricians voted by a large majority not to take action to support the miners. 'This must be worth a peerage to [union leader Eric] Hammond,' Bill Keys commented sourly in his diary. Another miners' delegate conference on 5 November had voted to continue with the strike and made a series of demands of the TUC, and two days later Scargill, McGahey and Heathfield were in Congress House at a meeting of the TUC's Finance and General Purposes Committee, where Scargill agreed there had been a 'slight' drift back to work.

On 20 November, the TUC's two most important left-wing union leaders, Bill Keys and the train drivers' leader Ray Buckton, with a few other left-wing general secretaries, met Scargill, McGahey and Heathfield in London. They told the miners' leaders that the dispute was running into the sands and the miners should ask for TUC help to sort it out. Scargill said the TUC should stay out.

After another formal TUC General Council meeting a week later, Keys and other General Council left-wingers went for a quiet drink with Mick McGahey. McGahey was careful, but Keys noted: 'My own opinion from the talk was that Mick is far from satisfied with the way the dispute is being handled, but does not feel himself in a strong enough position to challenge Arthur.'[2]

McGahey of course continued to make the correct public noises. Just a fortnight before, he had told a rally of Scottish miners in Usher Hall, Edinburgh: 'No one, but no one is going to settle this dispute except the National Union of Mineworkers. If the TUC want to do anything, then they can activate the decision of the Brighton Congress fully. No scab coal. No crossing picket lines. No use of oil. Stop industry.'[3] But that, as we shall see, is not what he was really thinking.

It was an acutely difficult position for Keys. He was reporting to the special committee of General Council members, on which more right-wing union leaders like David Basnett wanted to take control of the dispute away from the miners. At the same time he was trying to keep the confidence of the miners' National Executive and their President, who were constantly expecting a 1926-style sellout. The folk memory of 1926 was the main thing that enabled Scargill to keep hostility to the TUC at fever pitch. And while doing all that, Keys had to make the most discreet enquiries possible to find out who in government he might talk to secretly.

Meanwhile the official TUC machine ground on. On 5 December the miners' liaison group of general secretaries, the 'TUC seven', met Energy Secretary Peter Walker. MacGregor was furious about the meeting, to which he was not invited. He thought it would delay the setting up of a rival union in Nottinghamshire, which by then the NCB was actively working to create. His Nottinghamshire friends would ask 'what was the point of sticking their necks out if there was about to be a sell-out to Scargill.'[4] Walker, of course, always thought it was MacGregor who could not be trusted not to 'sell out' to Scargill.

Walker, according to Keys' diary, told the TUC seven that it was Scargill who had chosen to go to war, a war he could not win. Coal stocks were high even though the winter was well under way. Miners were drifting back to work. All the same, Walker said he was prepared to move, so long as nothing was agreed that could be presented as a victory for Scargill. 'He stated that he was prepared to move,' continued Keys. But 'they were not prepared for Scargill to claim victory.' It was the old, old problem. Two days later the TUC group spent no less than seven hours with Scargill, McGahey and Heathfield. 'I could not but get tired of Arthur continuing to lecture us, fighting 1926 all over again,' wrote Keys. 'Does he not wish to grasp what is at risk?' Nothing was achieved.

'Mick [McGahey] obviously wanted to talk privately,' Keys wrote, 'but was not afforded the opportunity. Shall have to pick up on this. Had dinner with Norman afterwards. He praised me, but I am not at all certain we are going to find an answer this way.' A few days later two key players in the South Wales miners – Keys never revealed who they were – approached him quietly and urged him to see if he could find a way out with dignity. They were appalled at their President's actions, they told him.

There had to be another way, and Keys, who had spent a lifetime doing deals, was the best person the unions possessed to find it. Stealthily, he started making enquiries of his extensive and unlikely contacts in the Thatcher circle. It was David Young who told him that his best bet was Willie Whitelaw, which was fortunate because Keys had known Whitelaw for years and they trusted each other. All three – Keys, Whitelaw and Young – were on the Manpower Services Commission, where they worked closely together.

Nervously – he would have been bitterly condemned throughout the trade union movement if his mission had been known, and would have lost any influence he might have – Keys made his way to the House of Lords for a meeting in a private room with Whitelaw. He told no one but Willis, and Whitelaw told only Thatcher.

The meeting got off to a good start: Whitelaw had ready a silver container filled with what he knew was Bill Keys' favourite wine, a Chablis. That first meeting was very general. Whitelaw said the strike had caused economic problems for the government, and that there was scope for a deal, but it could not be one which allowed Scargill to claim victory. 'You mean, victory for Scargill – not the miners?' asked Keys, and Whitelaw agreed.

Keys wanted to know whether the Prime Minister knew about the meeting. She did, said Whitelaw. 'Margaret said, find a way out of this.' Whitelaw added that they were happy to talk secretly to Keys because he had the confidence of those on the right and the left.

Keys left feeling encouraged. His main worry was how long this window of opportunity would remain open, given the speed with which miners were now going back to work. Very soon the government would have no motive to give him anything at all, not even enough to save the NUM's face.

Naturally, at the special committee's next meeting with Walker the following day, Walker took a much harder line. But Keys knew better than anyone that what is said in formal negotiations often matters less than what is said in private, unminuted, non-attributable meetings – especially when he was having secret talks with someone who he knew had the Prime Minister's ear. And when Mick McGahey took an opportunity, after a meeting of the 'friendly' union leaders – Keys, Buckton, the rest of the left whom the miners considered their friends – to whisper that he would like a quiet word with Keys some time, Keys thought he saw a ray of hope.

He promised to get in touch, and telephoned McGahey at home on 2 January.[5] As we shall see in the next chapter, McGahey did indeed share his fears, and the Keys initiative became the only chance of a settlement with dignity that might have avoided the destruction of the miners' union.

Meanwhile Neil Kinnock was having his own tribulations with the NUM President. He had been asked to go to the Aberavon meeting where a noose was lowered over Willis's head, and had declined. Or, rather, he had received, via the Labour Party General Secretary, what amounted to a summons from Scargill to attend five miners' rallies in the first half of November, culminating with the one in Aberavon. He had replied to Scargill that he was already fully committed on those dates. So instead, he said, the Labour Party itself would arrange a rally at which Kinnock would speak, and at which Scargill would also be invited to speak – but as the Labour Party's guest, rather than the other way round.

Kinnock told us: 'I could not afford to be seen at Scargill's beck and call. If he rationally wanted the official moral support of the Labour Party he would have said, "Let us plan a few meetings together" . . . I had nothing against putting the case for coal but I couldn't afford to appear on his platform and the only way to do it was for him to appear on our platform. The one thing I regret is not being in South Wales with Norman Willis. If I'd known what was to happen I'd have been there.'

The meeting was arranged for 30 November in Stoke on Trent, and Scargill wrote pointedly to Kinnock: 'I have rearranged my diary in order to attend.'[6]

The anger Kinnock felt at Scargill did not extend to striking miners, with whom he felt a close and painful affinity. Kinnock not only came from a South Wales mining family and represented a mining constituency, but from the start of the dispute he and his wife Glenys had sent regular cheques to support Welsh miners' families. At first they went to the Welsh NUM headquarters, but quickly the Kinnocks realized that money that went to the NUM was not safe from sequestrators, and they cut out the middleman: they sent much of their money to Dot Phillips of the Newbridge Women's Support Group in Kinnock's constituency, and they stayed in touch with her. They also sent money to another support group, and to a few people they knew personally who were in difficulties.

They made all the recipients promise to keep it secret, and it has never been made public until now. 'I don't want publicity by the way,' Kinnock wrote to Dot Phillips. 'In our family you always help out anyone on strike as a matter of course without the chest beating that some of the middle classes are given to!!! Keep smiling, Neil.'[7] Great affection grew up on both sides. Kinnock calls Dot Phillips 'a tiny woman with an angel's face and sparkling eyes, but put her on a platform anywhere in the country and ask her to tell the case on behalf of the mining community and she'll melt everybody. Without affectation, she'd just say it like it was.' She wrote to him:

> We thought it was great of Glenys, Maureen [Willis, wife of
> Norman] and yourself to come along to the children's party. We
> would also like to thank Glenys and Maureen for their donations,
> I know you said you don't want thanks but it was very much
> appreciated. The promise of further support from you was also a
> wonderful boost for us . . . Today we fed over 100 men. They had
> corn beef pie, peas and potatoes or sausage peas and chips. After so
> many weeks people are finding things very hard and so the numbers
> will grow. There is no talk of going back though: morale is still very
> high. Neil I hope it is not taking a liberty to say that I feel I have
> known both you and Glenys a very long time and that you are
> valued friends.[8]

This sort of help was desperately needed. The Social Security Act 1980, one of the Thatcher government's first acts, had removed the right to welfare benefits from strikers. Benefits were therefore only available for 'dependants': wives (not cohabitees) and children. Single people and people with no children had no entitlement to money. To make it worse, the regulations assumed that strikers were getting some strike pay from their union, and money was accordingly deducted from the amount given to wives and children, even though the NUM was in no position to pay strike pay. The combined effect was to cause actual destitution in miners' families. Many people believed that the legislation was part of the Thatcher government's preparations for the strike – a way of ensuring that when the strike came, the miners could be starved back to work.

Women's groups like the one run by Dot Phillips distributed some of the food given by well-wishers from the UK and overseas and organized for the men to be fed. Many families could not have lasted without them. People were losing their homes. As winter approached they were to be seen collecting coal from slag heaps and digging potatoes from farmers' fields.

These women's groups received no funds from the NUM. Instead, the NUM made money available to the branches to support picketing and ease hardship. The Yorkshire area provided each women's group with £120 as a start-up grant, but nothing else. Often, the first action of a local women's group coming together was to hold a jumble sale.

As well as distributing food, they helped to protect miners and their families from the police. In Doncaster women threatened to picket the home of any miner threatened with disconnection, and made the gas and electricity boards back down. Pontefract women persuaded the local council to increase the school uniform grant for miners' children.[9] Jean Stead reports women pickets seeing a man on the ground vomiting as he was beaten by police and dragged across the road. They ran across and managed to stop the beating. Then they covered the man up and sent for an ambulance.[10]

Sometimes soup kitchens also became centres for strike organization, because they were the first places that men came to when returning from picket duty. 'With less than half the active pickets attending union meetings, the kitchen became an important place for the pickets to meet and discuss. As one striker said: "Coming here you learn more about the strike than you do at most union meetings. This is the place we get most of our information about what's going on."'[11]

There were occasional boundary disputes between soup kitchens. A kitchen run to feed North Gawber families was being used by a majority of Woolley branch miners. When the women asked for funds from Woolley, they were told to turn the Woolley men away.[12]

Women were sometimes in evidence on the picket line – Anne Scargill's stories in an earlier chapter are not untypical – but less so than might have been expected, for a very basic reason. When men picketed they got paid – a tiny amount, but important to men near the bread-line. Women did not, and this was a real disincentive when money was so short.

Neil Kinnock's secret activities did not stop at providing money for miners' families. If Arthur Scargill could have seen the correspondence Kinnock had in October 1984 with his old friend Philip Weekes, the NCB's South Wales area director, all his suspicions of the Labour leader's treachery would have been confirmed. Weekes wrote about the need to continue to supply coal to the Llanwern steelworks, marking his letter 'Strictly personal'. He described the rather cosy relationship he had, and continued to have during the strike, with the South Wales NUM leaders: Emlyn Williams, President, known locally as Swannie, or Em Swan, because his father kept a pub called *The Swan*; George Rees, General Secretary, a former Communist whom Kinnock describes as 'sensible and respected'; and Terry Thomas, Vice-President. The rela-tionship was maintained over discreet lunches described by Weekes as 'rather boozy'.

'Until June', wrote Weekes, 'we were by agreement moving 9000 tons/week prepared (washed) coal by rail into Llanwern . . . However stocks of prepared coal were rapidly being depleted and so I started persuading Emlyn that we should begin to wash some of the Gwent run-of-mine stocks. Emlyn privately saw the sense of this but knew that he would face problems with some of the wilder members of his executive.'

But the agreement broke down when Williams and Rees went to Sheffield for a meeting of the NUM National Executive and Scargill 'put the frighteners on them'. The NUM executive voted to end all dispen-sations to the steel industry.

Weekes thought that Emlyn Williams's view was that the strike 'must not be allowed to destroy the good relations that have existed between the Welsh miners and the Llanwern steelworkers for many years'. But that objective was in serious danger. Llanwern was operating below safety standards, and might be forced to cease. And this was a problem for the coal industry as well as the steel industry, for 'the future of at least five pits and 5,000 jobs are fully tied to the future success of Llanwern'.[13]

Kinnock sympathized with his old friend, but there was not a lot he could do except try to grease the wheels in South Wales. 'I knew the South Wales leadership could do little publicly without destroying their own reputation. They were as determined as I not to let Scargill have anyone else to blame.'

He added: 'Phil Weekes was a colliery boy from Tredegar . . . He should have been director of the NCB because he had huge technical skill, immense personal strengths which included great firmness and great humanity. He . . . perpetually counselled a measured and rational approach to the strike, he tested Scargill and Thatcher . . . He was just trying to keep the show on the road so that the overmen went into pits to make sure the pumps were operating, trying to mitigate damage and gathering of gas so that the pit could be returned to . . . He also tried to sustain relations with major customers, the power industry and the steel industry.'

Kinnock was also busy trying to prevent picket-line conflict developing in South Wales on the same lines as in Yorkshire. After a two-hour meeting with leaders of the miners' lodges, he wrote to Chief Constable J.E. Over of the Gwent Constabulary:

> The Lodge representatives registered very strong concern about the clashes between their members and the police and great anxiety about the general policing practice in the area in recent days . . . All the people involved in the discussion are known to me and I would regard them as responsible and experienced individuals.
>
> There was widespread feeling that among the police in the area last week, there were additions to the Gwent police from Yorkshire, Leicestershire and Wiltshire forces and the squad formation apparently adopted by some detachments has also given rise to the suspicion that soldiers have been used.
>
> There were allegations that some police officers have appeared in uniforms not carrying insignia of rank, number or force of origin.

Many reports of extensive and unnecessary impediments to movement in the Newbridge and Abercarn areas, of 'rampaging' by police through the streets and of very aggressive behaviour against small groups who were not running away or seeking to avoid pursuit in any way . . .

There is great concern about the treatment of alleged offenders at the time of their arrest . . .

Over insisted that he had only had some assistance from South Wales police and 'We have never used and will never use soldiers.'[14]

In Yorkshire the police had by now established domination. After Orgreave, miners sullenly recognized a stronger, better organized, better equipped and better fed enemy – and enemy was the word.

'At Highmoor on 10/12/84 Chief Insp Moore told the pickets that it was against the law to shout at the strikebreakers,' reported Sheffield Policewatch.

. . . Throughout the dispute the police have subjugated the men on the picket lines, exerting their total control through mass arrests, arbitrary law and excessive (and often unlawful) violence and threatened violence. Over the last few weeks the picket lines have become generally very quiet. We feel that the pickets have been forcefully convinced that they have no control of their own picket lines – very rarely are they permitted to speak to the strikebreakers as they enter the pits and frequently they are not allowed a position from which they can effectively picket.

Miners and their wives had by December grown to hate and fear the police. 'You can tell there's trouble when they [the police] adjust their chin straps – you know they're going to come straight at you with their truncheons, arresting people just anyhow,' one miner's wife told a journalist.[15] And here is another, celebrating a tiny victory:

We'll never forgive them [police] for what they did to us . . . We got
one over them, though. They were chasing a young lad, a picket, and
he rushed into the community house. We locked the door while he
stripped and got some clothes from the jumble. You could always find
plenty of jumble clothes here. By the time the police forced their way
in he was standing at the sink peeling potatoes, calm as you like. They
didn't recognize him. But we recognized one of the coppers, he was
on the picket line later, dressed as a striker, provoking the lads to
violence, trying to get them going.[16]

Allegations that some police were being used in this way as *agents
provocateurs* were very common. Here is another: 'I was walking home
alone (in Abertillery – not a big city!). I have to pass a crossroads on
the way, and as I did, a van pulled up just in front of me. It was dark but
I could hear the voices of men shouting out, "Slut, prostitute!" I turned
my head, actually to see who they were talking to: I honestly didn't think
that it could have been me . . . I suddenly realized they must have seen
all the badges that I was wearing . . . When I got alongside the van it was
full of policemen.'[17]

Frustration at the fact that the police had the strikers under their
thumbs, and were able to prevent them from mounting any sort of
picket that might make a difference, gave birth to one of the most terrible deeds of the strike. On 30 November a taxi driver carrying a
working miner to a colliery in Mid-Glamorgan was killed by a rock
dropped from a bridge.

Kinnock issued a statement: 'I feel complete horror at this
awful tragedy and send my deepest sympathies to David Wilkie's
loved ones. I ask whoever did this terrible thing to come forward
now. Others have died and been terribly injured in the course of
this dispute. Miners and their families are appalled by what has
been happening and I know that they, like me, want the violence
to stop.'

Thatcher's statement was more political, seeking to extract capital
from the death: 'My reaction is one of anger at what this has done to a

family of a person only doing his duty and taking someone to work who wanted to go to work.'

It was true that much of the self-righteous outrage in the press about this incident appeared in newspapers which had ignored the deaths of striking miners on the picket lines; and equally true that the police operation to find those who killed David Wilkie was a far more determined and successful one than the operation to find those who killed the striking miner David Jones. Nonetheless, it was a terrible act, and the two men who did it were found guilty of manslaughter and jailed for eight years.

By then Roger Windsor's carefully constructed cloak-and-dagger methods of hiding NUM money had all unravelled, and the sequestrator was bearing down on the NUM's money through the Luxembourg courts. The method of hiding the money 'was what you would expect of a used-car salesman', a city accountant was quoted as saying at the time.[18]

The NUM had nothing. It could no longer give its striking members the barest subsistence. The car in which the President drove around the country, the airplane hired to take him and Windsor to Luxembourg and Paris, the food for his members to have Christmas dinner with their children, it all had to be paid for from charity, that of other trade unions and well-wishers at home and abroad.

On 2 December the NUM asked the TUC to bail it out by taking a lease on a building in Sheffield which the NUM could use for its headquarters, its own headquarters now being in the hands of the sequestrator; by ensuring that any member of staff dismissed by the Receiver would be paid by the TUC; and by giving it enough money to get by from day to day.

It also wanted – and this phrase has Arthur Scargill written all over it – a General Council meeting to be called 'with a view to mobilizing the movement to take industrial action in support of the miners' union and ensure the Receiver is not allowed to hijack the NUM or indeed any other unions'. The next day another special delegate conference resolved not to pay the £200,000 fine for contempt, not to purge its contempt and not to co-operate in any way with the sequestrators or Receiver.

The TUC's legal advice was that, if it did what the NUM asked, it would be in contempt, and would itself risk sequestration. Individual members, of unions giving unlawful assistance to the NUM, could take action against their union. So Norman Willis and his colleagues declined to do what the NUM asked, thus feeding Scargill's conviction that he had been betrayed by the leaders of organized labour.

Meanwhile the hope of aid from the Soviet Union was receding. At the end of December, Mikhail Gorbachev paid his first visit to London as the new Soviet leader. At their meeting at Chequers, Margaret Thatcher made it clear that any approval of financial help for the miners would damage relations between the two countries severely. Gorbachev assured her that, to his knowledge, no money had been given. He did not feel it necessary to mention the abortive transfer to Geneva, since no money had actually reached the miners. Gorbachev went home and gave instructions that no money should reach them.

This was a dreadful disappointment to Scargill, who had created a bewildering number of ways in which secret payments could be made: through the Finnish trade unions; through an account controlled by the British representative at the WFTU; through an account in Dublin controlled by Nell Myers in her married name of Nell Hyatt; through the Sheffield Women's Action Group.

Scargill did not give up. He was in constant contact with the CGT General Secretary Alain Simon, who had excellent Soviet contacts, and who by now was regularly travelling to London or Sheffield to meet Scargill because the telephone was not secure. Normally he would see Scargill alone, but sometimes also Heathfield, occasionally McGahey, and occasionally (no doubt when there was money to deliver) Scargill's driver Jim Parker. It is likely, though Simon does not mention it, that Roger Windsor was sometimes present as well, partly to interpret, though Simon was now learning English, mainly so that he could talk to Arthur Scargill without needing Windsor to interpret. The meetings were mostly in 'bad, expensive English hotels near Sheffield'.[19] (Alain

Simon has a very French contempt for English catering, though on his visits to Scargill he has apparently warmed to Barnsley chops.)

Scargill sent a written appeal to the Soviet trade unions on 28 December. The NUM, he said, had spent £30m; it needed £300,000 a week to maintain pickets and day-to-day organization, and more for legal bills. It needed £10–£20m. He also had a new route to suggest: the money could go to a trust fund controlled by Alain Simon, Nell Myers or the Labour MEP Norman West.[20]

And that, at last, as we shall see in the next chapter, did produce some money – and, like so much else, the money produced more grief than relief for Arthur Scargill.

But no Soviet money had arrived by Christmas 1984, which looked like being a grim time for striking miners' families. 'At Christmas we had a toy and turkey appeal so that every child of a striking miner would get at least one toy and every family would have a Christmas dinner,' reported a member of one of the women's support groups. 'It was said that we would never raise enough money, but with the help of sympathetic supporters we did it – despite the turkey lorry getting confiscated at customs. There was even a convoy of toys from the Ruhr Valley in Germany.'[21]

It was done with real sacrifice. Anne Scargill gave us the flavour of it. She may have been the President's wife, but she saw herself as just another miner's wife and she shared their privations. She worked for the Co-op, not as a shop worker but in its administration. She needed to keep the job because Scargill was not taking his salary during the strike (though the exact state of the President's finances, as we shall see, remains to this day a matter of controversy).

'I used to finish work at half past five, come home and go to bed at six o'clock and then be off on the picket bus by eleven o'clock. We got to the picket and come back and I'd be at work for half past eight. I think now, how the hell did I do it? And then I also worked in the soup kitchen three nights a week, peeling potatoes and that.'

One writer who was close to the women's support groups believes that the generosity shown to the miners at Christmas was the last straw – it was the feeling of receiving charity that sent men back to work.

Children, she adds, adapted to Christmas. They decided that Father Christmas was a scab, and if he brought you a present then you were no better than a scab too. But at the last moment, two days before Christmas, French miners sent hundreds of toys. There was no way to share them out equally or distribute them fairly.[22]

Even though the miners' plight was desperate, the government did not think the dispute was over. David Hunt recalled that a special operation was mounted while the miners took their Christmas break. Knowing that picketing would cease, a big effort was made to transfer more coal to the power stations over the Christmas period. Whatever ministers officially said, there were fears that if there should be a bitter January and February, coal stocks could run out, handing a last-gasp victory to Scargill. So while the strikers settled down to their meagre Christmas fare, tens of thousands of tonnes of coal were moved to the power stations to make sure supplies would last. According to Hunt the exercise was successful.

Peter Walker was determined to keep as many pits running over Christmas and New Year as possible, despite strong representations from a now exhausted police force. Charles McLachlan, Nottinghamshire's Chief Constable, privately asked the Home Secretary for a two-week pit shut-down 'to give the police two weeks off over Christmas and the New Year'. The NCB decided to leave it to area directors, and the police eventually left it to the discretion of Chief Constables. McLachlan reduced his cover to dog handlers and effectively abandoned it on New Year's Eve.

On 5 December an internal Home Office memo disclosed that the Forward Planning Unit at New Scotland Yard had raised problems about the winter weather disrupting the police operations to block picketing. It said:

> Mutual aid units are billeted a long way away from the coalfields in which they are used and in bad weather conditions the units might be delayed or prevented from travelling altogether. PSU's [police support

units] travelling from Chilwell and Ruddington to Derbyshire face a journey of an hour each way, part of which takes them on a section of the M1 which is renowned for being affected by bad weather.

PSU's rely upon police motorcycle escorts to show them the way to collieries, but motor cycles could very quickly become unusable when the weather deteriorates.

In the end the Home Office official thought little could be done, 'having exhausted all possibility of obtaining accommodation close to the pits'.

But whatever problems the government felt it was having, the TUC was sure that the miners' troubles were more serious. As 1984 closed, it was clear to Norman Willis and Bill Keys that the miners' position was hopeless. Their only hope was a face-saving deal, which would probably have to be done, if it could be done at all, against the bitter opposition of the miners' own President. Could they do it?

CHAPTER 8

ELEVENTH-HOUR TALKS

30 DECEMBER 1984 TO 20 FEBRUARY 1985

As 1984 turned into 1985, the outlook for the striking miners was bleak. Their morale drained a little more every time another set of peace talks began and collapsed. The NCB's incentive payments to break the strike were now enormous: enough for a man to pay off his debts. The weapon of mass picketing, in which Scargill had put his faith, had been blunted by ruthless and often brutal police tactics. But still they fought on, with courage and conviction that seemed inspiring to committed left-wingers, and incredible to outsiders.

They fought on partly because they were fighting to save their jobs and communities, and perhaps because some of them – though fewer every day – still thought that their President, who sounded utterly confident of victory every time he spoke, might have a plan to achieve it. But mostly they fought on because of their loyalty to their union.

Scargill, without admitting it, had modified some of his positions as it became clear even to him that they were no longer tenable, and in doing so suddenly found himself, for the first time in his life, outflanked on the left, which he did not like at all. He urged limited co-operation with the Receiver appointed by the High Court, and was condemned by those who had believed him when he said he would never co-operate, led by Kent miners' leader Jack Collins.

The left-wing union leaders who had tried to support Scargill, men like Bill Keys and Rodney Bickerstaffe, were convinced that the NUM President was leading the miners to disaster, that there was no hope of real change from Scargill, and that he would drag their members down with his. Their concern now was to minimize the damage; to find a way out for the miners if they could; and, if they could not do that, then to make sure Scargill could not pin the blame for his defeat on them.

Privately, Scargill's own Vice-President, Mick McGahey, thought the same as they did, and he took action. McGahey went to his grave without ever admitting that he tried to put together a peace deal behind Scargill's back, but that is exactly what he did.

Bill Keys' meeting with Lord Whitelaw in December left him feeling that a settlement with the government might be possible, though Scargill would be unlikely to accept it, since it would be designed to prevent him claiming victory. It was still better than the outright defeat that Keys now believed was the only alternative.

He followed up his brief word with Mick McGahey by telephoning as agreed on 2 January. They arranged a secret meeting for 11 January in the Graphic Club, SOGAT's club for printers, in Edinburgh, where Keys arranged a private room and was able to ensure that no one else would be in the club to see who the two visitors were. It was the earliest time they could arrange without risking questions about unexplained trips. Keys could go to Edinburgh that day without arousing suspicion because he was to see off a food convoy for the miners, provided by SOGAT's Scottish members.

The club was freezing, and they both shivered and kept their over-coats on, for they could not go outside to a café where they would be seen together. Almost certainly they both chain-smoked, Keys holding his cigarette cupped in his hand behind his back. Had anyone seen them, they would have looked like a couple of conspiring mafia chieftains. But no one saw them.

This meeting is almost the only recorded time when McGahey allowed anyone to hear him criticizing Scargill – a testament to the trust he placed in Keys. Keys told us that McGahey said to him: 'There is a way out but the bastard is on a path of no return.' McGahey also agreed that the dispute was going badly, and could easily collapse.

He outlined for Keys the three points he considered to be the bottom line for an honourable settlement for Keys to take to the government. Exactly what they were, neither man ever subsequently revealed to anyone, but they must have included some minor buttressing of the colliery review procedure and a pledge of no victimization: striking miners as well as local strike leaders must be taken back to work. Keys wrote them down on a piece of card. 'I think we're in business,' he said. 'Can you deliver?' McGahey said he could.

This meeting was the basis upon which Keys went back to Whitelaw, who said he thought the three points could be delivered. It paved the way for the last desperate round of shuttle diplomacy involving the TUC negotiators, the Energy Secretary and the Prime Minister. That was how Keys had always done business, getting the deal sewn up privately before elaborately negotiating it in public.[1]

McGahey was working on another front too. He made an informal approach to Ned Smith, a man he had known and negotiated with for years. These two agreed that a form of words on what sort of mines might be closed should not be beyond the wit of experienced negotiators to contrive. Ned Smith later told Paul Routledge: 'We were in negotiations, proper negotiations. McGahey wanted a settlement.' Whether word reached the Prime Minister, or it was a coincidence, we do not know, but while they were talking she told a television programme that a lot of loss-making pits must close 'and there is no need to argue about the definition'. Smith must have doubted what he could deliver in view of the Prime Minister's growing expectation of total victory.[2]

It was this exchange between Smith and McGahey that led to a formal meeting between the NUM and the NCB on 21 January. By then it had of course been necessary to brief Scargill, and he must have had the crucial say in who attended for the union. His choice was a strange one. McGahey, probably the only man who could have done a deal and made it stick, was not there, nor was Scargill, without whose agreement any deal was probably doomed, nor was industrial relations officer Mick Clapham. Instead, the NUM was represented by Peter Heathfield and Roger Windsor. It was hardly the strongest team the union could field at this crucial time.

Ned Smith and Kevan Hunt on behalf of the NCB were not able to offer much. There was no movement on amounts of coal to be mined or on pit closures. Pits could be closed on economic grounds, and there would be no movement on that. There would be no question of an amnesty: the strikers who had been fired would stay fired. If discussions were to be resumed, there would have to be a quick settlement, and it was going to feel like a surrender, with perhaps the odd sweetener to help the miners' leaders to save face. According to the minutes, Smith and Hunt 'pointed out that there was a strong body of opinion that the strike was largely broken and would be ended by a return to work'. Heathfield and Windsor said 'that the main body of the strikers were still firm.' They also said that if there were to be further discussions, the full NUM executive would attend.[3]

This was an extraordinary way of negotiating, with an executive committee of well over twenty people. Scargill had done it once before, much to MacGregor's disgust, but why, at this dreadful moment, was the NUM insisting on it? Roger Windsor thinks it was Heathfield guarding his own back. Windsor also told us that they 'secured a framework around which discussions could take place', though the documents suggest that this is an exaggeration.

Out they came, and went round to NUM solicitor Michael Seifert's nearby office where Scargill was waiting for their report. There they saw that day's *Evening Standard*, and read in it that Kevan Hunt had put out a mildly optimistic statement. Scargill, according to Windsor, was furious, and at once dictated a statement designed to deflate Hunt's cautious optimism. MacGregor did the same.

Nonetheless, Heathfield reported to the miners' executive three days later, and wrote to Smith confirming their willingness 'to enter into negotiations without preconditions'. He added that he thought there was a chance of reaching an agreement, and that he and Smith should meet beforehand. Smith did not reply. He delegated the job to Merrick Spanton, who sent a very brief reply arranging a meeting between himself and Heathfield.

Quite quickly it all fell apart. Spanton and Heathfield met, then squabbled about what they had discussed, and on 30 January Spanton wrote to Heathfield brutally: 'The main purpose of our meeting was to tell you that the Board required the NUM to put forward proposals to provide a basis for the Board to determine that it was worthwhile to enter negotiations . . . and that in particular you would address the question of dealing with uneconomic capacity.'

Heathfield replied that same day, a long, careful letter. He asked for an amnesty similar to the one the NUM had had after the 1972 and 1974 strikes, and for undertakings on the five pits to be honoured.[4] A few months earlier he could have got these very modest demands. Now there was little chance.

Meanwhile Scargill was telling the press that the NUM had asked for talks, and on 4 February the Board put out a statement designed as a calculated snub. There were to be no talks, it said, because there was no indication of a change in the union's policy over uneconomic pits. Spanton said the same in an unbending letter to Heathfield. And that was that. Could Bill Keys and Norman Willis now pull a rabbit from the hat?

The NUM asked Norman Willis to continue to explore the re-opening of negotiations without preconditions, but the NCB was insisting on a prior commitment from the NUM to the Board's right to close uneconomic pits.

Willis told Keys that a form of words might be found which, in Keys' words, 'did not refer explicitly to the economics of pit closures, but recognized the Board's right to manage and the union's right to protect its members' interests'. Keys thought: 'Given goodwill on both sides it can save face.'[5] But the NCB wanted their firm agreement in writing before they would start talking.

Meanwhile an old friend and mentor was drafted in to try to reason with Arthur Scargill: Bert Ramelson, who had recently retired as the Communist Party's industrial organizer. He was more responsible than anyone for the rise of Scargill, and it seemed possible that Scargill would still listen to him. The Communist Party – once a power in the unions, now in its death agonies as its internal warfare crippled its effectiveness – could see the writing on the wall that was invisible to Scargill, and it calculated that if anyone could talk sense into the miners' President, it was Ramelson.

Ramelson was asked to draw up an appreciation of the position and present it to Scargill. The idea came from the Party General Secretary Gordon McLennan, but it seems likely that some non-Communist left-wingers in the unions such as Rodney Bickerstaffe were consulted as well. 'Some of us thought the strike might crumble and they had to go back in a disciplined way,' says one of Ramelson's closest colleagues in the Communist Party. 'Bert was brought back to have a chat with Arthur. He thought, one has to know when to call a halt. He wanted a strategy. Just standing firm wasn't a strategy.'

Ramelson took his work to Scargill. Scargill stopped reading after the first few lines, threw it on the floor and accused Ramelson of betrayal.[6]

Ramelson must have known of the negotiations for financial help from the Soviet Union, which, as he wrote his paper, were at last looking like yielding some money. The hope of Soviet money with which to rescue the apparently doomed battle looks like a hopeless last throw of the dice, and that, presumably, is what Ramelson thought. No doubt this is part of the reason why Scargill fell out terminally with the CPGB, while still trusting, and being trusted by, top French communists like Alain Simon, whose role was crucial in getting Moscow to help the NUM.

In any case, after the Gorbachev–Thatcher meeting, Moscow was not prepared to risk the diplomatic consequences of giving money direct to the NUM. But it was prepared to give money to a general international solidarity fund to be controlled by the Miners Trade Union International, whose largest affiliate was the Soviet miners' union. What

MTUI did with the money was, of course, a matter for its leaders. No doubt everyone, and especially Alain Simon, was perfectly clear which miners' union was going to be the first beneficiary of help from the fund.

Scargill and Simon agreed to establish the fund in Dublin, and Nell Myers flew there to set up the Miners Defence and Aid Fund (MIDAF). The trustees were Alain Simon and Norman West MEP. Simon and Scargill still had to calm nerves in Moscow and reassure the Russians that Thatcher would never find out what they were doing. At last, on 12 February, $1,137,000 was transferred to the fund by the Soviet Union. The East German miners' union had by then already put $100,000 into it. In addition to that, the NUM used the fund to put some of the money it had spirited away with other trade unions. Rodney Bickerstaffe was not the only union leader to have taken delivery of caseloads of cash and put them in his safe.[7]

But it was far too late. Most of the money arrived after the strike had been called off, and was kept to help found a new international, the International Organization of Mineworkers, with Scargill as President and Simon as General Secretary. This in the end exposed Scargill to yet more suspicions of misusing money intended to relieve the hardship of his members.

On 1 February, Norman Willis, just about to meet the NUM Executive, telephoned Ian MacGregor during the NCB board meeting.[8] MacGregor returned the call at 11.55 a.m., interrupting his board meeting to talk to Willis. Willis told MacGregor that little progress could be made with the NUM on the board's position: 'I am pretty sure at this stage that it will be unacceptable, but, of course, if that situation changes in discussion, I will send someone to let you know.'

He went on: 'There may be other words that we talked about that, if coming through, might have had a better chance. I am sorry if I perhaps misled you. I'm punctilious in carrying out what I've said and I don't want to close any doors.'

MacGregor: 'Well, I do. I would like to thank you for the consideration you have given to me in dealing with this, and you and Mr Graham [TUC official Ken Graham], as you say, have been punctilious in this.'

Willis: 'I'm sorry perhaps to have brought you out in order to keep doors open and be properly courteous but I take these things as being very important. I don't think that the NUM are disposed for any of the various formulas to come out . . .'

MacGregor: 'Well, Mr Willis, I think I get the impression that the situation hasn't reached what I might call the point where our friends are ready to face up to some of the things we have to do.'

Willis: 'Organizations and people are very funny and very odd. I will attempt to transmit what I can to you confidentially as soon as possible but, in case that was a long process, I just wanted to keep a door open and that's the way that I do it, if by perhaps excessive and sometimes intrusive courtesy.'

MacGregor: 'Well, you are nice to call us, but our board is rapidly coming to an end and the Directors will be dispersing . . . In the meantime, I want to thank you and I look forward to working with you perhaps when they are a little better ready to go back to what we originally had. Our industry had a system of dealing with the problems that we are talking about. It has only been disrupted by Mr Scargill's insistence that we don't do that. We'd like to go back to the past procedures, set them up, and have everyone agree that's what we want.'

It is quite clear that the two men were exasperated at this stage, but it was Willis who was desperate to keep communications going despite the NUM being determined to offer little in the way of compromise. MacGregor sounded confident of total victory, but made it clear that he did not want to alienate the TUC either.

A listener might have thought that the TUC leader was being rather obsequious to the coal boss, or that it was a crafty ploy to lure him into a deal that would get everybody off the hook – which he almost succeeded in doing, just two weeks later.

While Willis was working on MacGregor, Bill Keys was still in touch with Whitelaw. An NUM Executive meeting at TUC headquarters in

Congress House at the end of January gave Keys the opportunity informally to sound out some of its members, who thought a compromise was necessary to save the union. Keys wondered why this point of view could only be expressed in the hotel bar, never in the meeting itself.

After the meeting the miners' three national officers, Scargill, Heathfield and McGahey, met the TUC seven, and something very significant was said, according to Keys. Scargill said for the first time that it would be better to go back without an agreement than to accept what the NCB were seeking. Keys was horrified. 'It would mean total capitulation. A defeated army with nowhere to go. Any agreement is better than none,' he wrote in his diary. He redoubled his determination to try to get some sort of face-saving agreement.[9]

What Keys did not know was that Dr Kim Howells, research officer for the South Wales NUM, had already begun quietly canvassing the idea of a return to work without an agreement – with the secret knowledge and approval of the South Wales President, Emlyn Williams. Howells says he first heard the idea in the North East around Christmas.

When, at the start of February, Howells cautiously went public with a radio interview in which he said it might be the only way to secure an orderly end to the strike, Scargill phoned Howells in a fury, and the South Wales area council said that Howells should no longer be their official spokesman, though he remained their research officer.

South Wales was on the moral high ground in canvassing the idea, for the strike had been more solid there than anywhere else in the country, and much more solid than in Scargill's Yorkshire base. And this had been achieved without as much mass picketing as other coalfields had seen, for the South Wales leadership had doubts about its effectiveness and were keen to build alliances with such organizations as the churches, which would have been alienated by mass picketing.

Howells told Paul Routledge: 'Things had become inconceivably desperate, and many of us in the coalfields had recognized that there seemed to be a serious credibility gap between what Arthur and Peter were saying on public platforms at these huge rallies and what was happening on the ground. There seemed to be no recognition of the appalling problems which miners' families were suffering . . . A compromise didn't seem to be on [Scargill's] agenda. He was going for total victory and the corollary of that is total defeat. Many of us began to think how it might be possible to save the union.'[10]

Willis and Keys talked every day, churning over ways to salvage something from the wreckage. MacGregor recalled the series of meetings that led to a further attempt to solve the dispute, involving himself, Norman Willis, Ken Graham and Jim Cowan. As he recorded in his ghosted autobiography, MacGregor took great delight in holding the first meeting at the Ritz Hotel, on 30 January, just to show the unions who were the bosses.[11] Perhaps he should have paid as much attention to the detail of the talks, because Willis and Graham were running rings around him.

The serious negotiation began at MacGregor's flat in Eaton Square. There was a revised document and news of these secret talks reached Whitehall, to the growing alarm of officials and of Energy Minister Peter Walker and Coal Minister David Hunt. The rumours were that Willis had bamboozled MacGregor into agreeing to a deal which effectively gave Scargill what he wanted – a 'get out of jail' card that he could sell to his members, thus seizing victory from certain defeat.

By 12 February these discussions had provoked panic among government ministers. Peter Walker told us that he had been waiting for days for the draft documents but none turned up at his ministry.[12] Then at 4 p.m. they arrived. Walker and Hunt were aghast, because Willis had managed, with MacGregor's connivance, to achieve a form of wording that meant no pit could be closed unless 'deemed exhausted', with no agreement on who should decide that this was the case, the management or the unions. This wording would amount to nothing less than a climbdown by the board, as it would make it very difficult to close any pit that had remaining resources.

There was no alternative but a dramatic intervention. David Hunt was despatched by Peter Walker to MacGregor's flat, armed with some alternative draft papers which had been drawn up by Department of Energy officials. At the same time Walker rang Thatcher to give her the bad news that not only was her trusted coal chief drawing up a deal which could lead to victory for Scargill, but he was actually on the point of signing it with the TUC that very afternoon.

Thatcher was equally aghast. After months fighting Scargill and perhaps only days away from victory, MacGregor was about to ruin the entire carefully worked out Tory strategy of 'endurance' to defeat Scargill. Her government had resolved to spend whatever it took to defeat the unions, and had poured the nation's treasure unsparingly into the war. She was not now going to allow MacGregor to snatch defeat from the very jaws of victory.

According to Walker there was a brusque phone call between Thatcher and MacGregor – a detail missing from MacGregor's auto-biographical account of events. By that time Hunt had arrived. According to his account he was ushered into MacGregor's flat and made a cup of tea by Lady MacGregor, though MacGregor's book says she was away in Florida at the time.

Hunt persuaded MacGregor to leave the table where the negotiators were. He then explained in detail what MacGregor had done, and why it had caused panic at Westminster. According to Hunt 'MacGregor went pale and said, "I didn't realize. What shall I do?" Hunt replied, "There is nothing for it but for you to gather up all those papers. Tell them you need to look at them again for a moment." MacGregor did what he was told. According to Hunt the papers were replaced with ones from the ministry which carefully did not use the words 'deemed exhausted'. The government had been saved at the fifty-ninth minute of the eleventh hour from a grossly embarrassing situation.

MacGregor's account brushes the whole episode aside as 'largely a matter of semantics'.[13] This was certainly not Hunt's or Walker's view. That very evening Walker put down his view for posterity in a 'secret and personal' letter to MacGregor, starting by saying how disturbed he was by what had happened that afternoon.[14]

The last time he had spoken to MacGregor, he wrote, they were just discussing procedural matters with the TUC General Secretary – talks about talks. 'I did not know that you had negotiated with Norman Willis an overall agreement for the settlement of the dispute.' Then, just after

4 p.m., MacGregor had telephoned Walker to tell him that papers were on the way to Walker's office. 'By the time they arrived', wrote Walker 'you were actually in discussion with Norman Willis, and presumably had presented him with these papers. I would have thought that we could have been consulted on the wording of any paper which was going to form the final agreement with the TUC and through them the NUM.'

When Walker saw the papers, he was horrified. First, he was opposed to the linking of the deal to the 1946 Coal Industry Act because of the 'public interests' clause put in by the Attlee government. 'This of course would enable Scargill to claim that the most important aspects of public interest at the moment are those of unemployment and the impact of pit closures upon mining communities during a period of high unemployment.' Second, there was the use of the phrase 'deemed exhausted' in the context of pit closures. This could be taken to mean that the NUM had a veto over pit closures. Third, he was furious that there was a reference to the impossibility of a no-strike deal. 'Although one could argue [this] expresses the reality of not being able to obtain a no-strike agreement, it is drafted in such a positive way for the unions that Scargill could immediately announce he had obtained a settlement on the basis that the NUM will continue its policy of opposing the closure of pits for economic reasons.'

Finally, Walker expressed alarm over a clause allowing the NUM to delay agreement on a new independent body to review pit closures. He thought this would allow the NUM to delay any decisions as long as there was no agreement.

'I hope you have succeeded in not tabling these offers,' he wrote. 'I am very concerned that at the most crucial stage of this dispute I was given no opportunity of expressing any criticisms of the document you were tabling.'

Next day MacGregor defended his position. He thought what he was offering was no worse than the deal the government had already given to NACODS and offered at the time to the NUM – which may have been true, but the whole battle since the NACODS deal was signed had been fought on the basis that the NUM had already lost its chance to sign up to those terms. He had only been trying to get a procedure that enabled him to close uneconomic pits.

He added: 'You will realize that, built into the legislation under which the NCB operates, is a degree of consultation on a scale which I doubt is matched in any other industry. This already pre-empts much of the management's rights, and moving away from that is a task which will take a considerable time and much patience. We are attempting to take the first steps in restoring a balance in which management will have the chance to exercise their proper role.'

This did not save MacGregor from being the main casualty of the exchange. Walker decided that MacGregor must go within a year of the settlement of the dispute, which is what happened. According to David Hunt it was discussed that very evening. The near-disaster was regarded as the last straw, as bad as some of the other gaffes that had made negotiations difficult.

Norman Willis, baulked of his prey, sought to exploit what he could see was some disarray in the enemy camp – a task made harder by the disarray in his own, where Scargill still seemed determined not to compromise. On 15 February Willis called in the executives of both the NUM and NACODS. He told them the NCB still required, before talks could start, agreement that pits could be closed for economic reasons, but this need not any longer be in writing. He circulated another NCB document, which the board intended to be part of any final agreement.

Scargill wanted it thrown out, but for the first time his executive rebelled, though in a minor way: they asked the TUC seven if three amendments could be tried out on the Board. Scargill was furious. He said he would be the last miner to go back. And Keys saw an extraordinary private exchange between Scargill and McGahey: 'Mick saying that he will chain Arthur's mouth up for five years when all this is over.'[15]

The NCB rejected the NUM amendments. That negotiation was over. But Bill Keys still had his private channel to Whitelaw, and he managed to persuade Scargill to ask him to try again to talk to both the government and the NCB. For the first time, Scargill agreed that if the three amendments went in, the document would form a part of the final agreement. The TUC negotiators thought this a significant concession, and agreed to ask for a meeting with the Prime Minister, which Keys had reason to believe they would get.

Here then was the culmination of the Keys initiative, the meeting Bill Keys had been working towards ever since that first secret meeting with Whitelaw over a bottle of Chablis, and his conversation with Mick McGahey. Thatcher herself, no doubt as a result of Whitelaw's private urging, was going to sit down and talk to the leaders of Britain's trade unions and see if a deal could be done.

And Whitelaw, unusually, was to be at the meeting, staring across the table at his old union chum Bill Keys. He was there partly at the urging of John Wakeham, the PM's trusted Chief Whip. Wakeham, who had been trapped for seven hours in the rubble of the Grand Hotel after the IRA Brighton bombing which killed his wife, suggested that Whitelaw, the Cabinet's chief wet and Lord President, attend the meeting to show that the government was united on what he called 'the "who governs Britain" issue'.

Thatcher readily agreed to Whitelaw's presence, though Wakeham thinks that it was for another reason. She was very keen to demonstrate to the revered Tory establishment figure how she could be could seen to be reasonable in handling such a divisive issue without losing her cool or being overtly confrontational.

The TUC leaders sitting on the other side of the table may not have realized that her knowledge and reasonableness were based more on the need to demonstrate her command of the situation to the chief wet and the representative of Tory landed gentry than to demonstrate it to them. The Iron Lady, a shopkeeper's daughter made good rather than a member of the Old Tory establishment, still had a deferential streak when it came to its chief spokesman. Wakeham may not have realized the crucial role Whitelaw had already played in setting up the meeting, or that it was done in secret with that most overtly proletarian of trade union leaders, Bill Keys.

On the other side, Arthur Scargill was forced to do something he had vowed never to do. He asked the TUC effectively to negotiate directly with the government, rather than to act as a messenger boy or postman delivering the latest letter to ministers.

So both sides were readier to talk than they had been for months. Bill Keys, never a man to underestimate his own cleverness, was, with considerable justice, rather proud of himself.

Of course Scargill's decision reflects a certain desperation. The gloomy parallel with the 1926 strike, when the miners' union refused to allow the TUC to negotiate regardless of the outcome, was not followed to the letter. The TUC did, in the end, go in to negotiate. But the TUC leaders were wary of a sell-out by Scargill. They wanted to be sure he was not setting them up to be the fall guys. So they asked the NUM President to confirm that if the government accepted the three amendments put by the NUM, the NUM would ensure that it was part of the final deal. Only when he agreed and it was minuted by the TUC did they agree to approach Thatcher.

The meeting on 19 February was a historic one: the only time Thatcher met the TUC directly to discuss the miners' dispute and one of only sixteen (three of them being routine meetings of the National Economic Development Council) that the PM had had with TUC leaders since she won the 1979 general election, according to a chronology of meetings prepared by Andrew Turnbull, her private secretary.[16] Her last meeting with the TUC was almost nine months previously when she met leaders at the International TUC London Economic summit on 31 May.

While the TUC seven were preparing the ground with Scargill, Thatcher was receiving equally pertinent advice on how to handle the TUC leadership from Gregson, Turnbull and Bernard Ingham. The memo from Ingham was characteristically brusque and dealt with how to handle the media in the aftermath of talks. 'You cannot trust any one of those coming to see you,' he said of the seven union leaders, who included Keys, Willis, David Basnett, Ray Buckton and Moss Evans. 'The TUC will seize on the slightest sign of softening and weakening to suggest you are moving (and will blame you afterwards if there is a breakdown).'

His plan to promote the government's case was forceful. He did not want Thatcher to wait for Prime Minister's Questions at 3.15 p.m. (the talks were in the morning). 'You will not be able to control presentation,' he warned. 'It is vital that the Secretary of State for Energy [Peter Walker] gets on to the midday news bulletins with an authorized version, and that Mr Walker and Mr Hunt play the media strongly and firmly subsequently.'

At the NCB he suggested that spokesman Michael Eaton be given 'a confident line to deploy'. He disclosed that Eaton had been blocked from going on radio and television to persuade more miners to return to work. 'I told him I agreed absolutely and that he could operate confidently inside the NCB on that basis.'

Finally he warned that the lobby journalists would be at Downing Street in force. 'We shall pen them behind barriers. But we cannot avoid them, and we should not do so. We must carry our message to them, confidently and firmly.'

The industrial correspondents were being carefully nurtured and fed stories by the NCB, working closely with Ingham. Every Friday evening MacGregor would call in George Jones, political editor of the *Sunday Times* (and brother of Nicholas Jones), and Paul Potts of the *News of the World*, and give them a story for Sunday morning, normally about how many miners had returned to work that week. Ingham's clear-sighted view of media handling makes a sad contrast with that of the NUM, which had now thrown away such influence with the media as it might have had.

On the NUM side, the industrial correspondents were 'demonized' by Scargill, as the BBC's Nicholas Jones puts it. Jones was following Scargill around and, despite Scargill's view that the industrial correspondents were the enemy's front-line troops, was continually getting calls from the miners' leader at home, but the trouble was this: 'He played up the intrigue, and he did get useful tipoffs from people, but he would tell me about a document and never show it to me. So it was always his version. I had no way of knowing whether it was genuine.' That is why his tipoffs to Jones seldom resulted in useful coverage for the miners.

All the same, Jones was becoming increasingly unhappy about the way he felt he was being manipulated by the government and the NCB, used to exaggerate the drift back to work and hail every returning miner as a hero. The NCB, he knew, had been massaging the figures, so that fewer men appeared on the books, and the day on which it could claim that more than half of them had returned to work grew closer. He decided to blow the whistle, and the *Today* programme agreed to run his exposé. 'A week later', writes Jones, 'I was told to report to the secretary of the BBC governors as there had been a number of letters criticizing my story; my revelations were not regarded as having been "helpful".'

Jones was able to prove that, helpful or not, his story was true. But the only way he could get any more publicity for it would be if the NUM took up the story, and Scargill would not do that because it came from one of the hated industrial correspondents.[17]

Gregson's advice to Thatcher in advance of the meeting came in the form of a 'suggested game plan'. The bulk of the meeting should be taken up with the TUC outlining the progress they had made and the remaining points of difficulty. His section on tactics was illuminating. 'The main tactic must be to draw out the TUC on what they think they can deliver, and to manoeuvre them, if possible, into a position where, if the Government and NCB respond positively, they are prepared to put effective pressure on the NUM executive.'

The tone of the meeting should be firm, constructive and realistic. Thatcher, he said, should be 'dispelling the impression that it is the government which, for political reasons, is putting obstacles in the way of a negotiated settlement' and she should be 'offering a faint glimmer of light – for which responsibility should be pinned firmly on the TUC, thus increasing pressure on them – but avoiding arousing excessive expectations.' He proposed there should be a clearly identified next step after the meeting.

Andrew Turnbull's advice was more measured. His secret speaking notes prepared before the meeting give the flavour. He anticipated what

Norman Willis would say. He told the PM to expect 'a lengthy account' from the TUC General Secretary. Willis, he said, 'will emphasize the need for a negotiated [underlined] settlement. He will say that the TUC efforts have helped bring the first shift of opinion in the NUM executive, pointing out the NUM's acceptance of the NCB's right to manage, the need for pits to go through a colliery review procedure, and that the board has the right of final decision.'

He predicted that Willis would end by asking the government to agree that 'the gap is small and bridgeable and that if only the NCB were prepared to negotiate reasonably, particularly on points of text which seemed designed to humiliate the NUM, a settlement can be achieved.'

The PM was advised to 'take the opportunity to praise TUC's role again and disavow any intention of negotiating'. She was told to set out the government's objectives, and advised (surely unnecessarily) to be firm.

The key sentence was: 'There must be a clear resolution of the central issues which have been raised by the dispute. It is in no one's interests for strike to be settled in a way which dodges these issues.' The issues were then set out. A proper procedure for settling the dispute – with 'a substantial advance' by the NUM in accepting the independent review element first agreed with NACODS; an acknowledgement of the Board's duty to manage; and an acknowledgement that in making its decisions on the future of the pits the Board must take the economic performance of those pits into account.

The last was to be a major stumbling block for the NUM. But Mrs Thatcher was advised to invite the TUC to enlarge on how it could bridge the gap. Then, on cue, Peter Walker would be expected to insist that if the TUC were to come to an understanding with the NCB, the NUM should not use the position for further negotiation.

The briefing concluded: 'Tell TUC that you have found their views interesting and helpful. Recognize that still formidable difficulties to be resolved but undertake to convey the points the TUC have made to the NCB, who will consider them carefully.'

The Cabinet Office minutes of the meeting at Number Ten[18] reflect these briefings. Thatcher expressed 'her appreciation of the TUC's efforts to promote a settlement of the coal dispute'. She then, as briefed, invited Willis to tell her the position 'as he saw it' and he did, as expected, go on at length.

He described in detail the to-ing and fro-ing between the TUC, NUM, NACODS and NCB over the previous weekend. This ended with a Sunday morning meeting, where the TUC asked the Deputy Chairman of the NCB to consider the three amendments to the deal agreed at a meeting of the NUM executive. But the NCB had said their proposals were a fixed position.

He told Mrs Thatcher that in 'his judgement the last meeting of the NUM had seen a significant shift and he doubted whether this had been fully appreciated by the NCB'. He told her that the full executive of the NUM had 'accepted that it was the Board's duty to manage the industry'. He reported 'acceptance of the modified colliery review procedure' and 'acceptance of the NCB's right to take final decision'.

The TUC team made a detailed presentation. They showed that the deal now being offered to the NUM was far worse than the deal offered to NACODS, which at the time was also on offer to the NUM, and the NUM had rejected it. They said that the miners had moved a long way. The NUM was willing to recognize the NCB's duty to manage the industry efficiently; to accept the colliery review procedure as NACODS had done; to accept that the Board made final decisions; to commit themselves to reconciliation and a restoration of relationships. Could not the Prime Minister move a little too?

What was unacceptable was the right of the NCB to close pits on the grounds that they were uneconomic. Willis was firm: 'The union could not sign away such a right,' the minutes record, and he cited NACODS' opposition as well. He also pledged TUC help to get an agreed return to work once an agreement had been reached.

Thatcher is recorded as appreciating the TUC's efforts and is minuted as saying that she 'wanted to see the strike settled as soon as possible on a basis which allowed the industry to operate successfully'.

But then came the rub. This 'required a clear resolution of the central issues of the dispute'. She stressed that there must be no 'unclear document' as 'this would only be the basis for the next dispute with arguments about interpretation and bad faith'. Thatcher also challenged the notion that the NUM executive had really changed its mind. She accused the NUM of changing its mind on pit closures, first accepting that loss-making pits must close and now opposing any closures outright.

She drew a distinction between NACODS and the NUM, saying the former would fight closures but eventually agree that the Board had the right to make them, while the NUM might block plans for a new independent review body so that the present procedures would still apply. She described this as the NUM in effect having 'a veto on closures'.

Peter Walker then pressed Norman Willis on what he thought the NCB document meant. Was it a basis for negotiation or part of the final agreement? The answer was that it was to be part of the final agreement.[19]

Margaret Thatcher asked what authority they had. 'An interesting question,' noted Keys afterwards. 'To which we could only honestly say that our authority came from the NUM executive.' As a negotiator he was distinctly uncomfortable: 'The role we are undertaking could leave us to be attacked if there is no movement. In effect we are going into Downing Street as messenger boys on behalf of the NUM with no real powers of negotiation . . . It is a no-win situation for the TUC.'[20] Although they were now negotiating with the authority of the NUM, they could only undertake to recommend a settlement to the NUM executive: they were not empowered to agree one.

The meeting broke up with both sides emphasizing their final views. Mrs Thatcher said she thought a settlement was long overdue but 'that any agreement must deal clearly and unambiguously with essential issues of the dispute'. The TUC remained ready to help.

Geoffrey Goodman notes that Thatcher 'greatly impressed the TUC seven by her sympathetic understanding, her grasp of detail and her insistence that there should be no fudged agreement which might later lead to "accusations of bad faith".[21] The main reason, we now know, is that she had followed the advice of her private secretary and Peter Gregson to the letter, which suggests that she placed great trust both in the young rising star who would, like his boss Robin Butler, go on to be Cabinet Secretary and in the experienced Cabinet Office official who went on to become Permanent Secretary at the DTI.

The TUC team felt some hope. Keys noted that the Prime Minister listened, a rare occurrence in itself, and they went away feeling that 'we had done all we could in expressing the miners' executive's point of view.'[22] Thatcher's promise that Peter Walker would convey the TUC's position to the NCB gave them some hope. Talks were held between Walker and the TUC later that night and went on into the early hours of the morning.

The next day, 20 February, the TUC met MacGregor and Jim Cowan. And it was MacGregor and Cowan who gave them a letter, the final result of all the shuttle diplomacy that had begun when Bill Keys secretly met Willie Whitelaw in the House of Lords and then went to Edinburgh to talk it over with Mick McGahey.

It had been approved, down to the last detail, by Peter Walker, despite repeated government claims that it was not interfering in the dispute in any way. This time Walker was leaving no space in which MacGregor could botch the negotiations. 'I presume you will have this delivered to Norman Willis between two and two thirty in order that he can present it to the National Executive of the NUM whose meeting is due to start at 2.30,' Walker wrote to MacGregor, rather as though he was giving very precise instructions to a rather dim subordinate.

His hand-delivered letter continued: 'I have communicated these drafts to the Prime Minister who agrees that this is the correct response to the TUC following the meeting that took place at Downing Street yesterday, and further confirms that it is correct that the Government and the Coal Board make it clear that this clarification of your original document constitutes the final wording that will be offered.'[23]

The deal offered a minor revision of the words in their original document. It assured the negotiators that pits were not to be closed without the unions having time and opportunity to refer the closure to the independent review body which NACODS had been promised. It said this agreement would be implemented as soon as possible. It said existing procedures would apply until the new procedure could be created.

It also made crystal clear that this was the last word and it hoped the TUC would keep its side of the bargain. 'We note also that the TUC confirms that the Executive of the NUM had accepted the Board's duty to manage the industry efficiently; had confirmed its acceptance of a modified Colliery Review Procedure; and had accepted that the board would take the final decision on closures after completion of all the review procedures.'

It ended on a tough note: 'I wish to make it clear that this must now constitute our final wording. We hope that the NUM Executive will accept this as a means of ending the present damaging dispute and allowing all sides of the industry to concentrate their attention on the future success of the industry.'

And with that the TUC team trudged back to Congress House, where the NUM executive was waiting for them, and asked to see the three national officers, Scargill, Heathfield and McGahey.

CHAPTER 9

THE BITTER END

20 FEBRUARY TO 5 MARCH 1985

'I shall remember to my last day what then happened,' wrote Bill Keys bitterly in his diary on 20 February 1985. He and the rest of the TUC team had returned to Congress House, after long and difficult talks with the NCB, to present to Scargill, McGahey and Heathfield the revised document, with its minor amendments, including a small face-saving clause saying that they did not intend closing pits without the NUM having the opportunity to refer the closure to the independent review body.

'Arthur picks up the papers for the first time,' continued Keys. 'He flicks two pages in what could only be called a cursory glance and then tells us that the revised proposals are worse than the original. How the damn hell he could come to such a conclusion without detailed study I do not know. It was difficult to contain oneself. We tell the three (the other two had said not a word) that we intend to go up to the boardroom and present the document to the executive and then leave them to make a decision.'[1]

With that, they all trooped into the executive meeting. Norman Willis introduced the document, pointed up the minor differences from previous documents and answered questions. He said: 'It is the clear judgement of the liaison group that no further changes are achievable. That is the judgement of us all.'[2] This was designed to make it clear that left-wingers like Keys took the same view as right-wingers like Basnett.

Keys found himself seated beside two area secretaries who leaned across to him and said: 'This will do us, Bill.' When the TUC team left the executive to take its decision and waited in Willis's office, they felt a sort of desperate optimism that the nightmare might soon be over.

After an hour, Scargill, McGahey and Heathfield came to tell them that the executive had agreed unanimously to reject the document. 'Not even a question of clarification,' wrote Keys miserably. Questions of clarification were bread and butter to this veteran negotiator.

Had his two area secretaries not spoken up, he wondered? And what, he must surely have wondered but did not even confide to his diary, had happened to Mick McGahey? Years later McGahey said to Kevin Barron MP: 'There was a chance to settle and it should have been taken.' But at that last dreadful moment, he could not allow anyone to split him from his President.

'What the hell is happening?' wrote Keys. 'Why had so many in the past criticized the strategy as applied by Arthur, forgetting conveniently that they were part of the decision-making? . . . Does he have hypnotic powers over the executive, convincing decent people that they can still win? But how, there is nowhere to go. We are not just staring defeat in the face for the miners, but for the working class as a whole . . . All the group are terribly disappointed. Scargill is leading the NUM to disaster, and he will try and blame us.'

He was right. Members of the miners' executive joined the big group of banner-waving protesters outside Congress House shouting, 'Sell-out.' Although they had agreed to allow the TUC to talk to the NCB, they now attacked Willis and his colleagues for doing so.

It seemed inexplicable. It was not even as though executive members were not going through the hardships their members were experiencing. They were: long before, it had been agreed that they would not take their union salaries for the duration of the strike. Trevor Bell, who represented COSA, the white-collar section of the union, on the executive, told us: 'My mother had just died down in Royston and we had a little house to sell there, otherwise we would have been in big trouble financially.'

NACODS accepted the document, but the next day yet another NUM delegate conference at Congress House rejected it. Speaker after speaker condemned the TUC 'sell-out'. One delegate mocked the efforts of the TUC team: 'It's no good sending a boy to do a man's job.' The conference called on members 'to stand firm' adding: 'We call upon the TUC, the wider labour and trade union movement to implement the TUC Congress decision of last September and not to leave the NUM isolated.' It was, writes Geoffrey Goodman, 'a despairing, anguished cry from a dark corner'.[3]

Scargill told a rally to support the miners in Trafalgar Square: 'It's time that the TUC and the rest of the labour movement came to our assistance to make sure we can win.' Fifteen thousand supporters heard him, and 100 of them were arrested as they marched down Whitehall.

Less than a week later, on 27 February, the NCB announced that more than half the miners were back at work: 93,000 men had returned. What could the NUM say? It was true. Here is what Scargill did say, on Radio Four: 'We have already succeeded in stopping the pit closure programme in 1984. We have stopped the closure of five pits and shown that we can oppose the government's policies. That is also a victory. This has been the most courageous and determined stand by trade unionists anywhere in the world, arguing for the right to work.'

Events now moved fast to their inevitable tragic denouement. The TUC General Council met on 27 February and agreed that they could take up with the NCB some detailed points in the document. Privately, despite his denunciation of the TUC's efforts last time, Scargill telephoned Willis asking him to go to the NCB with some further amendments.

But the TUC leader had had enough of being messenger and whipping boy for Arthur Scargill. The jibe about 'sending a boy to do a man's job' had stung. After talking to the rest of the TUC seven, he decided to make no further effort to talk to the NCB unless the NUM request came in writing, with a clear statement of what they would settle for. They never again contacted the NCB or the government.

It began to look as though Scargill, without admitting it, might be hoping the TUC would pull that rabbit out of the hat for him. Willis told Keys that he had had 'a strange conversation' with Scargill, in which Scargill appeared to accept that the document the TUC had negotiated, which he had previously considered utterly unacceptable, might now be acceptable. The next day, on television with the NCB's chief spokesman, Michael Eaton, Scargill suddenly produced a copy of the agreement the NCB had made with NACODS, which he had scornfully rejected at the time. 'If Mr Eaton wants to negotiate, is he prepared to settle on television tonight the NACODS agreement in its entirety with the NUM? If so I'll accept it.'

But it was too late. Eaton's employers demanded total victory. There would be no agreement with an enemy they believed they had already defeated. An agreement they were prepared to make when they were still uncertain of victory was of no interest to them now.

In the South Wales area, NUM leaders were still quietly canvassing the idea of a return to work without an agreement, and the idea was starting to take hold elsewhere. At Easington in Country Durham, one of the biggest and most militant pits in the country, it was put to a mass meeting of 1,500 strikers on 25 February and carried.

Three days later the NUM executive met for eight hours, a long, anguished meeting during which they tried several times, unsuccessfully, to contact Peter Walker and top NCB officials. Their enemies, sensing imminent victory, declined to take their calls. They called yet another delegate conference for Sunday, 3 March. Everyone knew this was likely to be the end.

On the morning of 3 March, crowds of angry miners, accompanied by the usual supporters from the multitude of warring far left groups of the time, gathered outside Congress House from the early morning. The executive met first, and divided equally on whether to continue the strike, 11 votes to 11.

Arthur Scargill, incredibly, abstained. His vote could have given a clear lead to end the strike; or, if he really believed the things he said, his vote could have kept it going. He chose not to cast it. We have asked his closest friends and supporters about this behaviour, and none of them can explain it: they say we must ask Arthur, who is not answering questions.

It is impossible to avoid the damning conclusion that he knew perfectly well the game was up, but wanted to avoid his fingermarks being anywhere near the inevitable decision. It left him able to say, four months later: 'The proposal for a return to work without an agreement was a fundamental mistake.'

So, thanks to its President, the NUM executive had no clear guidance for the delegates, and its members were not even able to address the conference, because, procedurally, they could only speak in support of an executive recommendation, and there wasn't one. Even when the conference told the executive to go away and try again, they came back with the same result: a dead heat, with Scargill refusing to use his casting vote.

Terry Thomas of South Wales was one of many who were furious with Scargill for what they saw as abdication of leadership. He asked the executive to 'search your hearts, comrades, and make your minds up. The men are calling for leadership . . . either give them leadership and repay the loyalty they have given us, or sit back with your blindfold on and let the strike collapse around you. That is not leadership. We have got to live in the world as it is, and not as we would like it to be.' South Wales President Emlyn Williams, Neil Kinnock's old chum Em Swan, was more abrupt: he told Scargill he was a coward.[4]

We will probably never know why Scargill acted as he did. Here is his friend Ken Capstick's stab at an explanation, given to our researcher Dan Johnson as Scargill waited in another room at NUM headquarters for a meeting with Capstick.

'Possibly he felt that if the National Executive was that divided he probably felt it would have been wrong to do it. I'm trying to think how I would have acted in those circumstances. Would I have used the casting vote? He probably thought, leave it to conference because we came to conference . . . In a sense he did use the casting vote because the National Executive committee didn't have a recommendation. It didn't come to the conference with a recommendation because it was 11–11 so I don't know. I don't know. You'll have to ask him that.'

'I'd love to,' said Johnson, reminding Capstick that Scargill had refused to talk to us. He suggested Capstick go straight into the next room and ask him. But Capstick didn't.

Kevin Barron's explanation, unsurprisingly, is harsh. 'By Christmas Arthur had seen how it was going, and he wanted to be able to blame the TUC and others.'

Kent's proposal to continue the strike was heavily defeated, 170 votes to 19. Yorkshire wanted to keep the strike going until the 728 sacked miners were reinstated, which, since everyone knew the NCB would not agree to this, was effectively a motion for continuing the strike. Their motion went down by 98 votes to 91.

That left the South Wales motion for a return to work on Tuesday without any agreement. Scargill spoke neither for nor against, but he defended his refusal to sign the NCB document negotiated by the TUC, and he blamed the TUC and the other trade unions for leaving the miners isolated. He added, and this perhaps is the key to his political philosophy: 'The greatest achievement is the struggle itself.'[5]

The return-to-work motion was carried by the same majority as the one by which Yorkshire had lost, 98 to 91. The great strike was over.

Bill Keys was heartbroken and relieved, all at the same time. 'I feel so sad, that a cause so right has been lost,' he wrote in his diary that night. 'History will not forget that [the miners] were let down by the wider movement, but I blame the miners' leadership for this. As I also blame the miners' leadership for the strategy they adopted throughout.' Keys, a seasoned professional negotiator, asked in despair:

> Why could not Arthur recognize many months ago one cannot achieve 100 per cent in a dispute, particularly one provoked by this hostile government. Now we will have the recriminations, which will do the miners and the wider movement no good.

These wonderful people, the miners and their families who have stood by them for 12 months deserved a better result. All the suffering has stood for naught. When is our class going to learn that it is only total unity that can promote their interests? Above all when is it going to be recognized by our people that the movement is greater than the self advancement of the individual leader?

Just one thing gave him pride and pleasure: that his union, SOGAT, had given about £1.5m to miners' families.[6]

The Kent miners' leader Jack Collins, who had opposed the return to work – the small Kent coalfield faced extinction – said as he left Congress House: 'The people who have decided to go back to work and leave men on the sidelines, to unload these men, are the traitors of the trade union movement.'

The recriminations started that very day. Outside, on the steps, young men and women from various ultra-left groups stood and screamed betrayal, as they had done before, whenever they sensed a deal in the air. NUM official Dave Feickert, for one, was disgusted. 'It is a day in my life I will never forget as there were Trot demonstrators outside the TUC accusing these wonderful guys of being scabs, when they made the decision.'

But they did not jeer Scargill. He had not voted for a return to work, and now he stood on the steps of Congress House and told the demonstrators, as well as the army of reporters and television crews gathered there to hear him: 'I feel terrific. The union has responded magnificently to save jobs and pits. The trade union movement in Britain, with a few notable exceptions, have left this union isolated. They have not carried out TUC conference decisions, to their eternal shame.'

Then he went quietly upstairs to Norman Willis's office. Willis wasn't there, but John Monks, head of industrial relations, was, and he made them both tea and said with his habitual quiet courtesy: 'How are you feeling, Arthur?' And Arthur Scargill replied: 'Pure. I feel pure.' He told Monks that he was satisfied he had done everything that he could possibly have done, and that if he had the chance to live the previous twelve months over again, he would do just what he had done.[7] And that, incredible as it sounds, is the view he has continued to take, with absolute consistency and apparent certainty, throughout the last twenty-five years.

Two days later, strikers marched back to work behind their branch banners, sometimes with bands playing. 'One could not but be proud of them,' wrote Bill Keys in his diary, 'as one watched them on television marching with dignity with banners flying back to work. They certainly did not deserve such leadership as AS gave them.'

Yes, there was dignity, but it was brittle and hard-won dignity, because there was also the bitter taste of absolute defeat, and defeat at the hands of a government and a Coal Board who were going to humiliate them and rub their noses in it at every opportunity. Lord Bell, the chief media adviser to Thatcher and MacGregor, said years afterwards: 'We wanted the strikers to drag themselves back to work, their tails between their legs. That was what it was about at the end.'[8]

In that spirit, a triumphalist MacGregor promised the miners would be punished for their 'insurrectionary insubordination'. There was no question of reinstating the miners the NCB had fired during the dispute. A few were taken back in South Wales, thanks to Neil Kinnock's old chum, the area director Philip Weekes, but none at all elsewhere.[9] No one was going to try to make their return to work easier. Here's what happened in one colliery, Lea Hall in Staffordshire, as told by a man who was there:

> We all met at the colliery gates on Tuesday morning as planned . . .
> The Women's Support Group was there with their banner, and many
> other supporters had got up before the crack of dawn to make the
> trip to Lea Hall. But the most important people of all standing beside
> the gate were the two sacked miners, Eric Lippitt and Peter Mayers.
>
> It was so important that Eric and Peter were there because we knew
> full well that they couldn't come through the gates with us.
> Nevertheless they were there to make sure that we carried out our
> union instructions . . .

With the cheers of our wives and supporters ringing in our ears we moved off as one down the pit drive. We'd timed the moment exactly so as to hold up the coaches that were transporting the scabs. For the first time in twelve months it was them who were forced to wait outside the gates.

Tiny victories like that were seized all over the country.

After we'd checked ourselves in we decided to wait in the canteen for management to come and discuss the situation. Whilst we were waiting the scabs began to arrive, but amongst them there was not one who could look any of us in the face.

We decided that the colliery manager should come and address us so that we could all get assurances about our position, rates of pay and job security. But in his typical fashion, he refused.

A delegation went in search of him, but all he did was waste ten minutes on saying he couldn't spend five minutes talking to the men.[10]

There was a reason why the management at Lea Hall would not meet the returning, defeated strikers. The idea that the union had a role in ensuring the men got fair treatment was to be a casualty of the strike. To the victor the spoils; and part of the spoils, for this employer, was that it was going to treat the men however it chose. Managers were encouraged to refuse to talk to the men.

The union found that its role at each pit, looking after its members and ensuring each individual was decently treated, had gone for ever. Branch officials no longer had what was called facility time: they had to get down the pit and work. Management changed shift times how and when they chose, instead of taking the men's view into account.

At other pits, men were sent home that first day back for being five minutes late because they had waited for the procession to assemble. At Ackton Hall in Yorkshire, the men were told to stop parading around with their banners or they would not be paid.

Kent miners, and a few others, refused to accept the return-to-work decision, and fanned out across the country to set up picket lines. They stopped the return-to-work march in Cortonwood, where the strike had started. And they stopped Arthur Scargill himself. Scargill, with a Scots piper, started to lead 1,000 men into Barrow colliery near his home town of Barnsley, but was stopped by a group of pickets from Doncaster and Kent. 'I never cross a picket line,' said Scargill piously, and turned round and led the men back again. They went in quietly the next day.[11]

But there was also a reminder of what dreadful work coal mining was. At Mardy colliery, the last remaining pit in the Rhondda, the 753-strong workforce, not one of whom had gone to work for even a single day, followed their colliery band and massed lodge banners back to work. At the end of the day, when her husband came home with his brother, one woman wept. 'The difference in those men in one day down that pit. You forget. You aren't used to seeing them that sickly grey. You have them off twelve months, and one shift, that's all it took.'[12] Others, particularly in Yorkshire, noticed that there were no longer any mice down the pits. They had all died because no one was bringing their 'snap' (packed lunch) down the mine, so there were no longer any crumbs to live on.

On the day of the return to work, Leon Brittan, the Home Secretary, wrote to Charles McLachlan, President of the ACPO and Chief Constable of Nottinghamshire, expressing his appreciation for all their work during the NUM dispute. On 27 March McLachlan and fellow Chief Constables were invited to a reception at the Home Office and addressed by Mrs Thatcher, who thanked them personally for all their efforts. But the police themselves seemed to be relieved it was all over. In his reply to Brittan, the ACPO President wrote: 'I know you, as we, are happy that the main effort of dealing with the dispute is over and we can once again return to a rather more normal form of policing.' He must have known that there were mining towns where the police's community relationships were dreadfully and perhaps irreparably fractured.

That was only a small part of the cost.

The price the miners paid in the strike was shown in an article in the *Police Review* on 7 June that year. It provided a chilling statistical list. Miners filed 551 complaints against the police, 257 alleging assault. Some 1,392 police officers had suffered injuries, eighty-five seriously. A total of 9,808 people were arrested and 7,917 were charged. Altogether 10,372 charges had been brought against striking pickets, including 4,107 for conduct conducive to breach of the peace, 1,682 for obstructing a police constable and 1,019 for criminal damage. At the other end of the scale there were three murder charges, four charges of criminal damage with intent to endanger life, three explosives offences and five threats to kill. One person was charged with possessing drugs. Some 682 miners were sacked for 'violence and sabotage'.

The cost of the police operation was estimated at £200m. Some 14m hours were worked by police officers controlling the picket, with thirty police forces providing aid to twelve areas of the country. Twenty thousand people were injured or hospitalized. Two hundred served time in prison or custody, and two were killed on the picket line, while three died digging for coal during the winter. Nine hundred and sixty-six people were sacked for striking.

At the end of the strike the government estimated that at 1980 prices it had cost £2.5 billion. Later this figure had to be revised to nearer £2.75 billion. But that was only for 1984–5. In the following four months the figures had to be revised drastically upwards as it became clear that the overhang from the strike had produced dramatic extra costs for the NCB and electricity industries.

Confidential estimates produced by the Treasury showed an escalating series of costs and the need to increase dramatically the borrowing requirements of nationalized industries to cope. By the end of August the net figure meant an extra £1.1–£1.3 billion.

If the losses were to include the effect on the country's GDP, including calculating the loss of production by miners, then, in the words of one treasury minute, they would 'push the cost well over £5 billion'.

This was an even higher figure than press speculation suggested. David Lipsey, then economics editor of the *Sunday Times*, using an analysis of publicly available figures by the London Business School, estimated it would be as high as £4.8 billion.[13]

The Treasury were embarrassed by the press speculation but also reluctant to release the extra costs – which by now included a further £26m for the police and £103m for the prison service coping with jailed miners. It also had to include extending the external financing limit by £800m to cover restocking the power stations.

The only way the public figure could be held down would be by including figures disclosing how investment by the NCB had been cut back during the strike, and how, if the strike had never happened, all that stockpiled coal would have to have been unloaded onto the world markets, depressing the coal price.

In the end the Treasury decided to keep quiet about all these extra costs until they could find a time to slip it out when public interest in the dispute had waned. A confidential Treasury minute of 23 August concluded: 'For the time being I am sure you are right to suggest that we should avoid being drawn on the 1985–6 figures. If ever we need to render an account of that element, I suggest it might be sensible to do so in the budget next year or at some other time when it might be drowned out by other news.'[14]

It is a perfect example of Whitehall finding 'a good day to bury bad news'. The phrase did not become public property until more than ten years later, when a New Labour spin doctor's confidential memorandum on 9/11 was leaked, but the idea was already well established in Whitehall in 1985.

CHAPTER 10

THE POST-STRIKE WORLD:
LOST MONEY, LOST INFLUENCE,
LOST REPUTATIONS

Almost the first thing Arthur Scargill did after the strike ended was call a secret meeting at the Holiday Inn Hotel, in London's Bloomsbury near the TUC, for the general secretaries of those trade unions from which he had borrowed money. He asked FBU chief Ken Cameron to arrive a little earlier and meet him at another nearby hotel, the Bedford. The two men sat at a small table in the bar, and Scargill told Cameron he could not pay back the £200,000 which Cameron had taken in cash from FBU funds for him. His lawyers had told him it would be illegal to do so. Cameron was furious, and swiftly Scargill backtracked. He said he could find a way of paying back the FBU's money, but he would not be able to pay the other general secretaries whom they were due to meet soon at the Holiday Inn. Would Cameron support him in explaining the situation to them, and getting them to see that he really had no choice?

No, said Cameron, he would not. He was very cynical about the legal advice Scargill claimed to have received. 'If you ask a lawyer to write something, they will write it,' he says.

The pair went on to the Holiday Inn, where, in a meeting room Scargill had booked, they joined other general secretaries who had done what Cameron had done: gone out on a limb to lend Scargill huge sums of their unions' money at an hour or two's notice, in cash, and with no paperwork.

There was Bill Keys, chain-smoking and glancing restlessly around the room, still wretchedly thinking of the chance to end the strike with dignity which he had created and Scargill had contemptuously thrown away. The railwaymen's leader Jimmy Knapp, tall, stooping, white-haired, who looked like a man in his sixties though he was only forty-five, and spoke gruffly in a Glaswegian accent so thick that it was often impenetrable to southerners. There was the biggest union baron of them all, Ron Todd of the TGWU, who sounded like a North London barrow boy and whose hobby was palaeontology. There were perhaps two more in the room.

Scargill repeated what he had told Cameron. There was a moment's shocked silence, then outrage. All these men had trusted Scargill with hundreds of thousands of pounds of their members' money. Now the miners' President was expecting them to go back to their executives and say that there would, after all, be no repayment.

They agreed to keep the matter secret, but none of them was going to let Scargill get away with it. Eventually, in some cases years later, they were all repaid, often by the NUM regions, which had frequently had the benefit of the money in the first place. Cameron got his money six years later, when Scargill asked him to visit him in Sheffield. There he took Cameron to the bank to see the full £200,000 laid out in banknotes. Cameron grumbled: why did he have to come to Sheffield, surely he wasn't expected to carry that lot back to London, couldn't the money be wired? 'I wanted you to see it,' said Scargill. Still grumbling, Cameron got back on his London train.[1]

Years later Scargill told the Lightman enquiry that he had kept the secret accounts he had opened during the strike active for five years after the strike because some of the unions had made five-year loans, which he wanted to repay from that account but could not until the five years were up. Peter Heathfield told Gavin Lightman QC, who conducted the enquiry, a rather different story. He said they were not five-year loans at all: it was just that after the strike Scargill asked for five years to pay and kept the accounts open. In fact, we now know that Cameron, Keys, Knapp, Todd and the rest would have been delighted with earlier repayment. Lightman wrote: 'I think that the deliberate decision was made to delay repayment as long as possible in order to retain hold of the funds in question and the interest thereon as long as possible.'[2]

About the same time as Scargill was meeting his angry creditors, Peter Heathfield was writing to the NCB to say the union would not attend the forthcoming Joint Consultative Council which, before the strike, was a regular industry forum in which the union had had a powerful voice. He said that the national officials saw no point, because the Board was going ahead with pit closures and redundancies, and MacGregor had told the press that the unions would not be consulted about it.

It is perhaps understandable that he did not want to sit down at a table with MacGregor, whose treatment of the defeated strikers was triumphant, triumphalist and brutal. Miners considered to have been key strike supporters were ruthlessly fired. The Board and the government seemed to be revelling in petty acts of meanness towards soldiers of the defeated army. One of these was to force miners who had been on strike for a year, and were near to penury and up to their necks in debt, to make good their contributions to the Mineworkers' Pension Scheme; and, just to rub their noses in it, they forced the union to obtain the payments from them. Heathfield huffed and puffed, but back came the reply from the Board's Kevan Hunt: 'The Board requires from the NUM an undertaking in principle to solve the problems with the Mineworkers' Pension Scheme.' Hunt also told Heathfield in November 1985 that there would be no pay rise in 1986, and that the NUM had only itself to blame for damaging the industry by going on strike.

For Margaret Thatcher, 1985 seemed like a year of unalloyed triumph. The defeat of the miners seemed to consolidate the victory of Thatcherism. She had defeated the enemy within. She signed an Anglo-Irish agreement at Hillsborough with Irish Prime Minister Garrett Fitzgerald which, for a short time, looked as though it might just pave the way for the peace in Ireland that had eluded her predecessors. Mikhail Gorbachev, with whom she had established such a satisfactory relationship that she called this Soviet leader 'a man I can do business with' – and who, as far as she then knew, had done as she urgently instructed him, and prevented any aid for the British miners arriving from the Soviet miners' union – was formally established as First Secretary of the Soviet Communist Party.

To complete the Prime Minister's satisfaction, her political opponents were in complete disarray. The strike had rendered the Opposition entirely ineffective, by reopening all the divisions in the Labour Party. The Tony Benn circle took the Scargill line that if only Labour Party and TUC chiefs had supported the miners, they would have been victorious. Neil Kinnock, having struggled since he became leader in 1983 to unify his party around a set of policies on which it stood a chance of being elected to government, found himself further from his objective than he had ever been.

Kinnock topped the Scargill demonology, the blacklist of traitors to the miners' cause. So he was surprised and very touched when, a few weeks after the strike, he had an invitation from Mick McGahey to speak at the Scottish miners' gala in Edinburgh. He knew McGahey would be furiously condemned by the NUM President for issuing it. For Kinnock, it was an invitation he could not refuse: 'If it had been my daughter's wedding I'd have had to go to that meeting.'

So he went, and over a quiet drink in his hotel bar afterwards McGahey confided that he had been effectively marginalized during the strike. Real control, he said, rested with Scargill and a few of Scargill's personal staff. (He meant, presumably, Nell Myers, Roger Windsor and Maurice Jones.) He was especially critical of Scargill's handling of money matters. He could not have said so publicly, he told Kinnock, because it would have made no difference to the result; it would simply have enabled his President to escape the blame, and to say his tactics would have been successful without McGahey's betrayal.

His President, meanwhile, was buying a fine new house. It might perhaps have eased the nagging pain of a defeat he has never acknowledged, but it probably did not, for that purchase, like so much else that looked hopeful for him, brought him grief. Seven months after the strike ended, he bought Treelands, a large detached house on the border of Worsborough. He paid for it with money loaned to him by the International Miners' Organization, of which he was President and his close friend Alain Simon was General Secretary. The purchase was in the name of his son-in-law, who transferred it to Scargill the following year, apparently to avoid publicity; Scargill felt, no doubt rightly, that miners who were close to the breadline might resent it.

Repayments were made to the IMO, apparently in cash. When Gavin Lightman QC was conducting his enquiry into NUM affairs, he was not able to find proof that they were made at all, though he thought they probably had been. 'That this doubt exists', wrote Lightman, 'is part of the price Mr Scargill must pay for borrowing money in cash from a trust fund and generally conducting his affairs and the affairs of the NUM and the IMO in the unbusinesslike manner in which they have been conducted.' Lightman applied the same criticisms to Heathfield's loans from the IMO for home improvements.

The next year, 1986, Scargill at last took up the seat on the TUC General Council which had always belonged to the NUM President until Scargill's day. When he was first elected, he spurned it as one of the trappings of office, taking him to a place where he might be contaminated by the compromising habits of the TUC. Now he was glad enough to have it, but it did not last. He stayed on the General Council for only two years, because the NUM declined so catastrophically that after that its numbers no longer entitled it to an automatic seat.

In January 1986 Margaret Thatcher suffered her first major cabinet crisis. Defence Secretary Michael Heseltine backed a European consortium's rescue package for a company called Westland Helicopters, while the Prime Minister favoured an alternative deal proposed by the American Sikorski Fiat group. Heseltine, finding himself isolated and ignored in the Cabinet over a matter concerning his own department, dramatically walked out. Thatcher was attacked for allowing the US Air Force to use British bases to launch bombing raids on Libya.

Later that year came the worst nuclear accident ever, at the Chernobyl nuclear power station near Kiev: a devastating blow for those who had argued against coal on the grounds that nuclear energy was clean and safe. The case for nuclear against coal had yet to be made.

Ian MacGregor did not get his wish to stay at the NCB, now renamed British Coal. MacGregor, in ways that neither man would ever acknowledge, was rather like Scargill. Scargill left, in John Monks' words, no space for those on the other side of the table to operate in; neither did MacGregor. Just as Scargill was convinced that his way was the herald of a better world, MacGregor was an early exponent of the view, so common among businessmen of the 1980s, that management must be free to do whatever it liked, business people were the saviours of humanity, and market forces were the only way forward for a civilized society. For him, as for Scargill, his beliefs were absolute, and the smallest deviation was betrayal. He enjoyed boasting about taking the miners' leaders to the Ritz Hotel. He would not have understood anyone who questioned the moral worth of material success.

Like Scargill, he was arrogant, fond of calling himself 'Big Mac'. But unlike Scargill, he was a big-picture man, uninterested in detail, which is why ministers were forced to hotfoot it to his flat towards the end of the strike to stop him signing a document presented to him by the wily and underestimated Norman Willis, which, though MacGregor had failed to notice the fact, gave much more ground to the NUM than the union's parlous negotiating position justified.

MacGregor, unlike Scargill, was saved from his own incompetence during the strike by good staff work and the support of ministers who were much brighter than he was. By the end of the strike, those ministers had seen through him. He felt insulted that in 1986 the government drew his contract to an end. David Hunt was instructed to seek out Robert Haslam and persuade him to take the job of running British Coal. Walker thought this emollient man would get on better with the miners once the strike was finished. MacGregor was touted for several jobs, including head of the National Health Service, but nothing came of any of it. Knighted in 1986, he devoted his energies to chairing

Religion in American Life, famous for its slogan 'the family that prays together, stays together'. He died on 13 April 1998, aged eighty-six.

One of Haslam's first communications was a request from Arthur Scargill for a one-to-one meeting. Haslam agreed with some misgivings, wondering what it was about; he feared the NUM President might be going to try a dramatic initiative about one of the many problems in the industry. He was wrong. Scargill simply wanted to tell him that he was having some difficulty selling his old house in Barnsley in order to move into Treelands. Might British Coal be interested in buying it? No, they wouldn't, said the astonished Haslam, and the meeting came to an end.[3]

MacGregor had, however, played a crucial part in destroying what was left of the NUM's power and influence. It was under him that the NCB became a willing, secret partner to help create a break-away union in Nottinghamshire and other moderate areas. Files now held at the National Archives show how MacGregor and other top officials aided and guided the new organization.

Backing MacGregor was the helpful and detailed legal advice from lawyers in Fountain Court, where the role of a young, ambitious barrister became crucial to the enterprise. Working alongside Conrad Dehn throughout the strike and its aftermath was Charlie Falconer, former flatmate and close friend of PM-to-be Tony Blair, later to become Lord Chancellor under Blair's patronage. The brief for the UDM was Igor Judge, now Lord Judge, the Lord Chief justice

Falconer's advice – given either jointly with Dehn or sometimes solely to the NCB's legal department – played a crucial role in the creation of the Union of Democratic Mineworkers (UDM), which was to become a running sore to the NUM for the rest of the century, until most of the membership of both organizations was snuffed out in the 1990s by a further wave of closures. For Falconer the work was particularly lucrative as he went on to advise the privatized British Coal before joining the Blair government in 1997.

The story of the UDM began with the threat of expulsion for the Nottinghamshire area of the NUM after it refused to adopt new rules in

January 1985 when miners were still on strike. The new rules were designed to give greater authority to the President and National Executive. On 10 January 1985 an executive meeting of the NUM decided to call a special conference for 29 January to expel Nottinghamshire from 1 February.

The opportunity to create weakness and division was not lost on the NCB. Four days later Ned Smith prepared a secret memo[4] to Jim Cowan, the NCB Deputy Chairman, outlining what the NCB should do in the event of a request for recognition from a new breakaway union in Notts. He told Cowan that the NCB legal department had already stated that it might be legally advisable to grant recognition to the new union – and, of course, it would help greatly in the main task of weakening the NUM. Recognizing the UDM might be in breach of national agreements with the NUM, but the agreements would not be legally enforceable by the NUM.

The new organization, Smith wrote, was expected to represent North and South Nottinghamshire and Bolsover but could extend to South Derbyshire and Leicestershire. His report recommended limited recognition in Nottinghamshire. However, he warned that no official announcement should be made before 29 January, when the NUM conference took its decision on Nottinghamshire, so that the NCB should not be seen to be interfering in union affairs. He did, however, toy with the idea of discreetly making the Board's intention known to moderate delegates in advance, in the hope of encouraging them to defy the NUM. He wanted to make it clear to the Nottinghamshire moderates that recognition was a technical possibility.

The NUM did not expel the Nottinghamshire miners in January, but expulsion was still likely when, on 18 March, Roy Lynk, leader of the dissident Nottinghamshire miners, officially representing NUM Nottinghamshire and calling himself Acting General Secretary, met the directors of North and South Nottinghamshire NCB to ask for the NCB to implement its promised 5.2 per cent wage rise in return for a lifting of the overtime ban.

None of this had been agreed by the NUM executive, and for Lynk to go to the employers with a deal was a massive breach of union discipline, of the sort that would have been unthinkable a few months earlier. Lynk compounded his sin by asking the NCB for help to stop intimidation of working miners by returning strikers; he also wanted the NCB to curtail weekend working so that moderate members could attend NUM branch meetings in Notts, and vote against continuing the strike.

The NCB legal department privately suggested that only by breaking away from the NUM could Nottinghamshire secure the 5.2 per cent rise officially, though payments might be made on account.[5]

On 8 July, with the strike well over and the NCB in vindictive mood, Roy Lynk formally applied to the Nottingham Coal Board to have negotiating rights, having severed Nottinghamshire's connection with the NUM nationally on 6 July. By then the NUM executive had voted narrowly to fire Lynk.

NACODS asked the Coal Board to delay, and the NUM General Secretary, Peter Heathfield, objected in the strongest terms to Lynk being given what he asked for. Lynk received advice from Hopkins, his Mansfield solicitors, that the NUM could not undermine him by forcing entire local Nottinghamshire branches to rejoin en bloc. His solicitors described any decision by the NUM to force branches to rejoin en bloc as 'rather like the Government of Taiwan passing laws which are said to affect the whole of China, but which are in fact only valid in Taiwan.'

But the NUM decided against using such tactics. Instead it took the breakaway group to the courts. An in camera hearing was held on 10 July in London, and effectively the NUM won. Roy Lynk had not balloted his own members properly to change the rules and privately admitted he had been 'precipitate' in breaking away from the NUM. A private note from the NCB lawyer to MacGregor warned: 'In reality, [the judgement] does mean that the question of whether Notts have yet broken away is very much in doubt and also, probably *sub judice.*'

The court case left the NCB in a mess. It could not do as it wished and start negotiations with the breakaway union. A memo of a meeting held by the Board's legal department and its legal advisers, Dehn and Falconer, shows that, on the same day as the court hearing, action to recognize the breakaway miners was secretly being prepared. But the Board did not dare to be seen to do it. The memo concluded: 'Counsel both stressed that it was absolutely fundamental that the Lynk Union was not seen as a Board creation. They considered that the ultimate risk was an action by the National Union against the Board. That being so, it was even more imperative that, if there was any doubt as to whether the Nottingham Union was still part of the National Union, the board should not be seen to be negotiating with it at the moment.'

But the NCB was not going to give up. What happened next was that the NCB drew up a plan to create a legal entity for the future UDM in secret, while pretending to have no official contact with it. The secret instructions prepared by Dehn and Falconer included advice on what consultations the board could have with NUM (Notts) before the creation of a separate organization, and whether the breakaway group should merge with another union like the small Colliery Trades and Allied Workers Association (CTAWA) or become an independent organization.

Their advice was that the board should write to Lynk to clarify the situation; and that it should avoid formal consultations at that stage, because these consultations could become public, and 'would give the impression . . . that the Board was either actually advising Mr Lynk, or the Executive Committee was planning a joint strategy with them' – which is, of course, what was going on, but they did not want the public to know about it. However, there was no harm in having informal talks with Lynk, with the aim of setting up formal consultations once Lynk's organization had seceded from the NUM and become a separate body. That would save time later, because informal talks can cover exactly the same ground as formal talks. Dehn and Falconer suggested 'an off the record informal discussion on a counsel-to-counsel basis with counsel instructed by the board'. They added: 'The surest and most effective course to pursue for those members of the union who are dis-satisfied with the NUM, would be to resign from the NUM and form a new trade union, which, if its membership was sufficient, the Board could proceed to consult.'

On 22 July a secret memo from Marilyn Stanley of the NCB's legal department to MacGregor[6] shows that Dehn and Falconer were helping to draft the exact words of a letter to Lynk. Mrs Stanley, who had been brought in by MacGregor to take charge of the legal department's han-dling of the dispute, noted: 'I advised Counsel [Dehn and Falconer] that Mr Lynk was anxious not to receive a letter from the Board which appeared to cast doubt on what he was doing. Counsel have revised the draft letter to take some account of this . . .'

On 29 July Dehn and Falconer explained how to secede from the NUM with the greatest safety. They warned that if the Notts NUM was to amalgamate with anybody else without first changing its rules, the NUM had a good chance of winning a High Court action against them. But if they changed their rules before amalgamation, 'the Notts union would probably be able to fight off successfully any challenge to the validity of such an amalgamation'. The NCB helpfully showed this advice to the leaders of the Notts NUM. So the breakaway organization, which theoretically had nothing at all to do with the NCB, was secretly privy to the Board's confidential legal advice.

Meanwhile the NUM failed to capitalize on its victory. On 7 August it lost a court case to the Notts NUM when Mr Justice Tudor-Price declined to restore the old NUM leadership in Nottinghamshire. A month later the rebel leaders, with secret legal help from the NCB, put their plan into action. On 16 September Lynk sought negotiating rights in the next pay round, due to start on 15 October, to get representation for Notts members.

The next day Falconer advised getting a resolution before the Board by 4 October, in advance of any decision by Notts, to enable them to negotiate with any new unions that could be set up. Between then and 2 October there was enormous activity at the NCB, preparing draft let-ters to go to Lynk, a draft press statement and a letter to be sent to other unions recognizing the new union for wage talks. It included lengthy advice from Dehn and Falconer[7] on how to justify negotiations with the breakaway union, including asking Lynk to write a letter requesting one-off negotiations. The advice also raised the question whether Notts could be given favourable treatment during negotiations to encourage the union through incentive schemes. It concluded that the Board must be very careful not to refer to the legal relationship between Notts and the NCB in any statement. The line should be that the Board is taking this step for 'urgent practical reasons'.

If the NUM had known all this, they could have derailed the pro-ceedings, because Falconer and Dehn knew they were finding a way to get round the rules in order to start negotiations with the UDM before a proper legal ballot was held. If Scargill or Heathfield had used a loyalist NUM member to bring a case against the NCB they could have won. But MacGregor was willing to take that risk. On 3 October he took the momentous decision to recognize the breakaway Notts area NUM – what was to become the UDM – in pay negotiations due to begin on 15 October.[8]

He was typically forthright in his internal letter to Kevan Hunt: 'For avoidance of doubt, I hereby authorize you to conduct with Mr Wheeler on behalf of the Board the wage round for the coming year for the Notts Area in the terms of his proposed letter to Mr Lynk should the board, having considered any reply received from the National Union, wish to commence negotiations.'

The letter from Wheeler to Lynk, sent the same day, contained all the key advice from both internal and outside lawyers. The key phrase read: 'In the light of this current position, the Board are minded to com-mence negotiations in the current wage round with the present leadership of the Notts area separately from the National Union and I would like to make it clear that there is no question of any Notts miner ending up as a result with terms less favourable than those that may be agreed with the National Union.

'The decision is without prejudice to the present conciliation machinery and to what is to happen when your Union has completed its formal separation from the National Union or amalgamated with other groups. I am not expressing any view on the legal issues involved.'[9]

Peter Walker endorsed the strategy on the same day. The collusion between the breakaway union, the NCB and the government was complete. The only worry expressed by the government was that such action could be interpreted as breaking the spirit of Attlee's 1946 Act which nationalized the coal industry, by arbitrarily changing the terms of the negotiating machinery. Here Falconer came to the rescue with a carefully written letter on 7 October.[10] The NCB had simply to state that it had no intention at this stage of changing the national negotiating and conciliation machinery, so it was not required under the Act to consult people in advance to talk to the breakaway union. So when NUM General Secretary Peter Heathfield wrote to MacGregor's deputy Jim Cowan to protest on this very issue on 8 October, the answer was already prepared.

Heathfield protested again on 16 October, but by then pay negotiations had begun which led to an incentive pay award for UDM members. The breakaway union was also balloting members in Nottingham and South Derbyshire and the CTAWA.

But the NCB were worried that without the results of an official ballot the NUM could still take action to stop the negotiated deal because the breakaway group did not legally exist. However, the NUM did not wake up to this and on 31 October all the NCB's worries were over. The three groups – Nottingham, South Derbyshire and the CTAWA – voted to set up a new union. Lynk wrote as General Secretary designate of the UDM requesting official recognition from the Certification Officer.

A month later, internal legal advice to MacGregor said that once the new union was registered, the NUM would cease to have a place in Notts and South Derbyshire: 'a clean and undeniable break' would have been made. The NCB strategy had triumphed, and the UDM started to recruit outside its Nottinghamshire and South Derbyshire strongholds. The Board was delighted and when the NUM branch secretaries of two collieries, Daw Mill in Leicestershire and Agecroft in Lancashire, persuaded their members to quit the NUM for the UDM through a pit ballot, they received warm personal letters from Kevan Hunt, head of the NCB's industrial relations.

MacGregor decided to help the breakaway union by starting informal discussions with other unions on new negotiating machinery. Letters went out on 11 November, the warmest to the UDM. However, another row broke out over the decision of the NUM to hold a political ballot of its members in December, which was strongly opposed by the UDM.

In the triumphalist spirit in which it had greeted its victory over the NUM, the government had taken the fight to the unions and the Labour Party. It had embarked on a plan which seemed to promise all sorts of good things, from its point of view: embarrassment as well as impoverishment for the Labour Party, as well as a public reminder that Labour was, as Ministers always put it, in the pockets of the union barons. They had decided that if those trade unions affiliated to the Labour Party wished to continue to pay money into a political fund for the benefit of the Labour Party, they must regularly seek permission of their members to do so in a ballot. It did not matter that members could opt out of the political levy, and it did not matter that companies donating to the Conservative Party were under no such requirement to ballot their shareholders.

The unions had responded by setting up a Trade Union Co-Ordinating Committee chaired by Bill Keys, now retired as General Secretary of SOGAT and, though not a well man, seeking an outlet for his restless energy. His job was to run the political fund campaigns inside the unions. In the end, Keys delivered large majorities for allowing all the unions that had political funds to keep them, which was perhaps the only victory the unions scored during Margaret Thatcher's premiership after their great defeat in the miners' strike. But in December 1985 it was far from clear that Keys was going to be able to deliver that victory.

The NUM saw the political fund ballot as a way of trying to regroup in Notts and South Derbyshire by using it to recruit back miners who had defected to the UDM. By law the NCB would have to provide facilities at the pitheads for the rump of NUM members to vote. Once they provided such facilities, the NUM could use these facilities also to try to recruit UDM members back into the NUM. So this piece of legislation, designed to attack and damage the unions, could provide the instrument which allowed the NUM to get back into Nottinghamshire.

For this reason, MacGregor wanted to refuse facilities for the NUM in Notts and South Derbyshire to vote in the NUM's political fund ballot, and the UDM naturally supported his position. They could foresee their hard-won membership ebbing away just as they had launched their new organization.

Keys was quickly on the case. He was in the extraordinary position of insisting on an anti-union law being carried out to the letter by an anti-union employer, but such paradoxes did not trouble him. How could the NCB possibly obstruct a ballot required by law? he asked with manufactured indignation. 'This would be the first occasion on which any employer has sought to obstruct the working of the 1984 Trade Union Act in this way.' He sent a copy to the Certification Officer, who was just about to rule on the UDM.

Both letters were faxed to Falconer marked 'urgent'. His advice was clear: Keys had the law on his side. If the NCB was caught failing to comply with the law and the NUM took them to a tribunal 'it is 99 per cent certain we will lose'. The NCB's internal advice on 29 November warned that if they lost a case 'the board might well have to pay for a re-run of the whole national ballot if the Certification Officer held it to be invalid because of our actions . . . The public relations effects of all this would be little short of catastrophic.'

He also warned that it would be dangerous to allow the UDM to exclude the NUM totally from Nottinghamshire pits while the ballot was taking place, and that the NCB had to be careful not to act in a partisan way over the ballot 'to prevent the NUM from supporting the Labour Party'. This, said Falconer, would damage the NCB and perhaps the government'.[11] However, the NUM, though it may have won back a few members, did not manage to use its access to cause major damage to the UDM.

On 4 December the Certification Officer recognized the UDM as a trade union, despite a last-minute objection from the NUM. Kevan Hunt wrote to Peter Heathfield saying that the existing machinery was to be reformed to allow UDM representation. It was the end of the NUM as the dominant union in its industry.

Thus by the time Margaret Thatcher called another general election, in 1987, the NUM had been so marginalized that the NCB could afford to ignore it, and ostentatiously to take more notice of the new UDM, which was – though a polite fiction was always maintained – little more than an NCB puppet.

The 1987 election produced another landslide for Mrs Thatcher, and a far more surprising one than in 1983. In 1983 the Labour Party had been led by the elderly Michael Foot, who had been characterized by the press, unfairly but effectively, as senile and out of touch; it ran one of the most incompetent election campaigns any major British political party has ever run; and the election came in the wake of a military triumph in the Falklands. In 1987 Labour was led by the young, charismatic Neil Kinnock; its campaign was the first (and easily the best) to be orchestrated by Peter Mandelson, with the help of media gurus who produced, among other things, probably the best party political broadcasts that British politics have ever seen; and there was no Falklands factor. Yet the result was only marginally better than 1983. On 11 June 1987 Margaret Thatcher swept back into Downing Street with a majority of 102. No one seriously doubted that the miners' strike was one of the most important factors. It had frightened people badly, for they had seen a glimpse of civil war; and it had exposed the deep and bitter divisions in the Labour Party.

After the election, Kinnock was in the blackest of depressions. It took him a year to recover; there is a sense in which he has never recovered. The wounds of his long and acrimonious battle with the Bennites, and the now ferocious media campaign waged against him, went very deep in this complex and sensitive man, and the ebullience that came naturally to him in 1983 was starting to sound very forced. His conclusion from the defeat was that Labour had to change its policies even more thoroughly than it had already done, in order to make itself electable; and he knew this meant another few years of infighting and blood-letting. It also meant isolating – cauterizing – the Scargill factor.

This became even more necessary in 1990, when the *Daily Mirror* published its famous allegations against Scargill (see Chapter 6), allegations that were disowned twelve years later by the editor who published them, Roy Greenslade. During the strike, according to the *Mirror*, Scargill not only received money from the Libyan leader Colonel Gaddafi but misused it to clear his home loan from the NUM, and Peter Heathfield and Roger Windsor similarly misused the money for their own benefit.

The *Mirror*'s main source was Windsor, who had fallen out with Scargill, leaving the NUM's employment in 1989 to live in France. 'I left because of the way Scargill was treating the UDM. I felt there was a more intelligent way to deal with the split in the union,' he says. The *Mirror* paid Windsor £50,000 for the story, and the same sum to Scargill's former driver Jim Parker, who had been Scargill's close friend, supporter and admirer before turning against him.

Their evidence by itself was not enough for the *Mirror* to consider the story libel-proof. So Terry Pattinson, the industrial correspondent whom Windsor had approached in the first place, persuaded the NUM's Finance Officer Steve Hudson to drive to London overnight to confirm the story on tape. Hudson was not paid. Since then he has refused to discuss the matter with anyone.

Heathfield, it's said, broke down in tears at the NEC meeting which discussed the report, and his health never recovered. The abuse heaped on his head during the strike had not affected him in this way, but the unhappiness of being believed to have defrauded his members – which would be a betrayal of everything his life had been about – was very great. Scargill, in a different way, is said by his friends to have been permanently psychologically scarred as well.

Greenslade expected Scargill to sue. Pattinson was sure he would not. Pattinson was right. The man who used to boast that he had launched nineteen libel actions against journalists and won them all simply denounced the *Mirror*'s 'vicious lies'. But things had changed. Time was when the NUM executive, faced with a choice between the word of Arthur Scargill and that of a tabloid newspaper which wanted to disparage him, would not have hesitated for a moment. Now, doubtless with heavy hearts, the NUM executive voted to set up an enquiry under a distinguished lawyer, and Gavin Lightman QC was commissioned to do the job.

In Labour movement circles, how you view the Lightman Report depends on whether you are among Scargill's admirers, like Ken Capstick, Alain Simon, Seumas Milne and Tony Benn; or his detractors, the fiercest of whom are either the closest admirers of Neil Kinnock or the many old friends of Arthur Scargill who have fallen out with him. The pro-Scargill camp is furious that Lightman spoke so ill of their man. Seumas Milne, the only journalist Scargill trusts, calls the report 'littered with errors . . . highly political . . . unexpectedly hostile'.

The anti-Scargill camp feel Lightman missed a chance to nail the NUM President, and question whether he had sufficient evidence to acquit Scargill of the charge of misusing the money.

Both views are unfair. The Lightman Report is precise, remorselessly logical and so clearly written that a non-lawyer has no difficulty following it. Lightman seems to have done as thorough a job as was possible when key players refused to co-operate with him – for the *Mirror* team and Roger Windsor refused to see him, and Alain Simon gave only limited help. Lightman does acquit Scargill of the most serious charge against him, that of taking for himself the money meant for his hard-up members. But he paints a ghastly picture of a leadership which, from about summer 1984, clearly, at the kindest estimate, lost its way, and never, in the intervening years, found it again: a leadership that was centralized around Scargill and his closest associates, from which Mick McGahey was largely, and even Peter Heathfield partly, excluded.

Each step this leadership took created its own unforeseen disasters, to which the NUM President responded with another convoluted step which brought its own consequences. The blizzard of overseas bank accounts; the fatal blurring of the distinction between money that belonged to the union, to the International Miners' Organization and to Scargill and Heathfield personally; Scargill's dual role as President both of the NUM and the IMO; all these factors left them open to accusations of all sorts of impropriety, and created a rumour factory which did further damage to their already dreadfully weakened union.

It was four years since the Receiver had been discharged on 27 June 1986, but Scargill was still spending his days twisting and turning, creating yet more elaborate schemes in order to try to undo the damage created by the last one. In 1989, after Windsor left the NUM and Scargill knew that the *Daily Mirror* had IMO bank statements, Scargill created two more secret bank accounts in Germany, Lightman reports.

Part of the trouble was that Scargill had acted without taking qualified advice from lawyers and accountants. The Miners Action Committee Trust Fund, created at the height of the strike in October 1984 to receive donations and loans without having them taken by the sequestrator, was constituted by a deed 'drafted by Mr Scargill without any legal advice shortly after the sequestration order, and backdated to before sequestration', according to Lightman. The trust deed constituting the Miners Research, Education, Defence and Support Trust (MIREDS), based in Ireland and also designed to receive funds and save them from sequestration, can no longer be found: Scargill told Lightman that it was destroyed in 1987 because it was not anticipated that it would be needed again. Was MIREDS' money the NUM's money or the IMO's money? Scargill says it was the IMO's. Lightman says that if it received funds aimed at supporting British miners, which it did, then that part of its money at least belonged to the NUM.

During the strike, Scargill's methods of handling and accounting for the vast sums of cash that were being brought to him from all quarters were so inadequate that 'there is now no way of ascertaining what amount of cash may have passed through Mr Scargill's hands'. Lightman wonders why the National Executive was never told what was going on, why it all continued, and why records were still not kept, after the

Receiver was discharged and the reason for the secrecy had therefore disappeared.

Of course there are all sorts of wild rumours – we heard several of them, from several sources, while researching this book, and the reader is welcome to take a guess at their nature – and, while most of them are probably false, Scargill has only himself to blame for them. The same can be said of Peter Heathfield, who comes out of the Lightman Report with his reputation for integrity badly dented. He apparently told the QC that one reason for not telling the NEC about £580,000 held in the MIREDS account was that the national officers needed to get the NEC to accept the need for economies and rationalization, and they had therefore to convince NEC members that the union was in real financial trouble. If NEC members had known there was £580,000 that they had a call on, this would have been harder.

The report also revealed that, when striking miners were staring starvation in the face, the union was spending £6,560 on improvements to Scargill's home and £13,511 on improvements to Heathfield's. Scargill and Heathfield were not taking their salaries at the time. Nonetheless, it is not surprising that the decision was made not to report these payments to their members at the time.

Scargill and Heathfield told Lightman this was entirely Windsor's idea. This is reminiscent of the suggestion from Seumas Milne, briefed by Scargill, that the visit to Gaddafi was Windsor's idea too. But Windsor was entirely Scargill's creation. While McGahey and Heathfield had their own power bases in the union, Windsor had been taken from obscurity elsewhere and given a job far bigger than anything he had ever had. Scargill made him effectively the second man in the union after himself. He was consulted before the elected national officials McGahey and Heathfield. Windsor never did anything of the smallest importance that Scargill did not wish him to do, and trying to blame Windsor when those decisions exploded in his face does no credit to Scargill.

Another means of avoiding the attentions of the sequestrator was a company called Oakedge, set up by Windsor. In October 1989, just after

Windsor had left the union's employment, Scargill complained to the Fraud Squad about Windsor, citing the dealings of Oakedge. Lightman says he can see no justification for this complaint. Unsurprisingly, the Fraud Squad turned out to be much more interested in the missing Soviet and Libyan money than in Windsor. But Windsor understandably resented it, and it played a large part in his decision to go to the press.[12]

In the year of the Lightman Report, 1990, the future for Neil Kinnock held real hope at last. Thatcher had finally slipped, clinging to the unfair and deeply unpopular poll tax long after it had been shown to be political suicide, and that year she was forced out of office by a Cabinet finally convinced that to keep her was to court electoral disaster. The Conservative Party replaced her with John Major. The polls were, most of the time, showing Labour with a small lead, enough for Kinnock to form a government.

The Scargill factor had been cauterized. The NUM, once the biggest and most powerful union in the land in the days when unions were themselves powerful, was now tiny, powerless and ripe for a takeover in a land where unions had been tamed. The giant TGWU was busily hoovering up small unions, and the best future for the NUM seemed to be as one of the TGWU's many trade groups. But in 1991 negotiations stalled because Scargill insisted on a higher position within the TGWU than TGWU leaders thought the NUM's importance now entitled him to. The NUM therefore remains to this day a tiny and shrinking union of those miners who still keep the faith.

All in all, Kinnock went into the general election on 9 April 1992 with high hopes of forming a government – hopes that looked justified right up to the moment when the results started coming in.

There were all sorts of reasons why an election that was Labour's for the taking slipped out of the party's grasp, and the miners' strike, now seven years in the past, could only have been a small one. But given the narrowness of the result – Major won by twenty-one seats – many people believe that, without the lost year in Labour's recovery, Kinnock would have been Prime Minister in 1992. Here is Kinnock's own view, looking back in 2007: 'All the programme for recovery I was starting to pursue was stalled, not just for 1984–5, but for two years, from about January 1984 to nearly the end of 1985. That was two years in which almost the whole attention of the labour movement was focused politically, emotionally, in one area. Everything was defined by where you stood in relation to the miners' strike.'

The public, he thinks, were being constantly reminded of the winter of discontent. And they were being shown Thatcher in the best light, as an iron lady and a force against disorder. The result of all that, in Kinnock's words, was that 'We did not make the advance in 1987 that we were looking for,' the advance that would have provided a springboard for 1992. The additional twenty-one seats Labour needed in 1992 all had small majorities.[13]

Kinnock does not say it in so many words, and he insists he is not making excuses, but there is no doubt he believes that without Scargill and the miners' strike, he would have formed a Labour government in 1992. He is not alone in this belief.

After the election Kinnock resigned at once, and John Smith became Labour leader. Two years later Smith died suddenly of a heart attack and was succeeded by Tony Blair, who swiftly made it clear that the process of moving Labour rightwards was going to be accelerated. For Arthur Scargill this was the last straw: he resigned from the Labour Party and formed his own tiny grouplet on the far left, the Socialist Labour Party. The far left is, of course, grossly over-populated with tiny, warring grouplets, and Scargill might have been expected to join one of the existing ones, but he chose to form his own, while remaining President of the NUM.

Blair is something that, before the miners' strike, would have been a contradiction in terms: an anti-union Labour leader. Before the strike, Labour, in its darkest hours, for instance after the 1931 general election when it was reduced to a parliamentary rump, had always turned to the unions for succour, support and guidance. The unions had always been Labour's financial bedrock, for, without their money and the people they could put on the streets at election time, the Labour Party could never have fought and won general elections. The Labour Party had been created by the unions to be their political voice. Now, for the first time, it was deliberately distancing itself from the unions, and there was nothing they could do about it. To have a Labour leader who did not feel at home with the unions, who rather disliked them and was not interested in consulting them about anything, was a nasty shock.

Neil Kinnock and John Smith had already forced the unions to accept a vastly diminished role in the running of the Labour Party, but at least by 1994 they thought they had eaten all the humble pie their party was going to force down their throats. They had atoned for the miners' strike, and could begin to poke their heads above the parapet again. Blair's arrival changed all that, and his first major initiative was an indication of the direction of travel: he forced through the repeal of Clause Four of Labour's constitution, which promised public ownership, and he made it clear to the unions that their voice was not going to count for a lot.

Union leaders swiftly began to hope that Blair's majority would not be too large, for then he would have no need of them. Blair's trade union adviser in his first term, John Cruddas, now MP for Dagenham, says Blair's big 1997 majority filled them with gloom: 'They thought, this means the full Blairite agenda, including ditching the unions and linking up with the Liberals.'[14]

Blair may or may not have been right in his view that the public, after the miners' strike, loathed the unions and would not elect a party that was seen to be close to them. What we can be sure about is that, without the miners' strike, no Labour leader could or would have so firmly rejected the unions and all they stood for.

Labour's landslide 1997 victory did not bring the trade unions back to anywhere near the place in the sun they had occupied before the strike. Early in the life of the government, John Monks, now TUC General Secretary, summed it up in one of those great memorable phrases. The unions, and those who had been involved with Labour before Blair, were being treated, he said, as 'embarrassing elderly relatives at a family gathering'.

New Labour, as Blair's Labour Party was known, thought the unions were unpopular, and did not want their government tainted. So in the early days of the Labour government, when it met the TUC, the TUC chiefs would open their newspapers on the morning of a meeting and, with tedious regularity, read the results of a government briefing to the press: whatever it was the unions were going to ask for, the government was not going to give it. Eventually John Monks spoke to Chancellor Gordon Brown about it, and the briefings stopped.

Their lack of influence in the corridors of power was dramatically illustrated from the start. The one big thing they wanted was something it would be easy for the Blair government to deliver. They wanted the European Social Chapter signed, and UK support for additions to it on such matters as maternity benefits and health and safety regulations. Union leaders thought that that much, at least, they would get.

They were to be cruelly disillusioned. The Confederation of British Industry met Blair and extracted a promise from him. Though Blair had to sign the Social Chapter – it was a manifesto pledge he could not safely dishonour – he promised that he would block any additional pro-worker or pro-union amendments to it, if the CBI asked him to. The unions did not even have the chance to plead their case: the meeting with the CBI was secret, and they did not know about it. So the TUC continued to besiege the government with requests that Blair was already pledged to refuse.[15] That was the measure of their place in the land under a Labour government. The movement of Ernest Bevin and Jack Jones found that hard to accept.

CHAPTER 11

NOT AN INDUSTRIAL DISPUTE, BUT A WAR

In politics, you seldom get everything you want. Both sides generally come away with something. But war is all or nothing. Once both sides have thrown their armies at each other, they quickly get past the stage where they can settle for less than total victory or total defeat. That is one of many ways in which the miners' strike was closer to a civil war than to an industrial dispute. The return to work was unconditional surrender, as unmistakable as a defeated army throwing down its weapons – or, perhaps more accurately, a besieged city opening its doors to the invaders because there is not a scrap left to eat and the alternative is to die of starvation.

The police – better armed, better equipped, better dressed, better trained, better organized, better led, and most of all better fed – had defeated a brave and proud enemy. By the end, police were pushing pickets around at will. It was not just defeat: it was humiliation, and the men's noses were rubbed in it every day for the last six months of the strike.

To the victor the spoils. What did Margaret Thatcher, Ian MacGregor, Peter Walker, Norman Tebbit and their colleagues win at such a high financial and human cost?

At the end of the strike, the government was in undisputed command of both battlegrounds: the coal industry and the field of industrial relations. The miners' union, the unions generally, were defeated. These two victories were enduring. They have not been overturned in the twenty-five years that have elapsed.

Were these victories worth having? Britain produces far less coal than it used to. Total domestic production has fallen steadily, following the sharp dip that coincided with the strike. In 1980, the UK produced 130.1m tonnes of coal; in 2006 that figure was 18.5m tonnes. The coal mined in Britain in 1980 produced the same amount of energy as 78.5m tonnes of oil; in 2006 that figure was 11.4m tonnes of oil.

The number of people working with coal in one way or another, in terms both of the headline figure and of the proportion of jobs available in the energy industry, has fallen dramatically. In 1980, around half of the 600,000 people employed in energy production in the UK were working with coal. Today, the total number of people employed in the energy industry is about a quarter of the 1980 figure, and those working with coal represent a tiny fraction of that number.

It could be argued that the decline of the coal industry is no bad thing. Burning coal emits more CO_2 per unit of energy than its competitors, oil, gas and nuclear. If coal had not been reduced in the energy mix, Britain could not have met its commitments under the Kyoto protocol. But, in a sense, that is beside the point, because a greener energy industry formed no part of Margaret Thatcher's objectives in 1984–5. Anyway, we still burn a lot of coal. Coal-fired power stations are still common in the UK. Solid fuels accounted for 16 per cent of the UK's energy use in 2004. The difference is that now we have to import the stuff from Norway, Russia, South Africa, Australia and Poland – even though there is hundreds of years' worth of coal under our feet. In 1948, the Conservative opposition used to call Britain 'an island built on coal' and ask why Labour could not prevent the nation freezing during that year's dreadful winter. We are still an island built on coal, but we cannot any longer get it out of the ground. We have six pits, down from 186 pits at the time of the strike. The 170,000 miners are down to fewer than 3,000. Vast coal reserves have been sterilized underground in mines that are now shut and filled in, for the government ensured that many closed pits could never be reopened, by filling them with concrete.

Over 90 per cent of the UK's 2004 net energy imports consisted of solid fuel, and the UK is expected to import 90 per cent of its fossil energy in 2020. Coal is no longer an asset – it simply contributes to the huge trade deficit that currently plagues the UK.

And what we import is the least environmentally friendly coal. Dave Feickert, one of the NUM head office team in 1984–5, is now a mine safety adviser working in China and New Zealand as well as Europe. In China, he works alongside some of the former scientists and engineers from the Coal Research Establishment and the Mining Research and Development Establishment, both closed by the Thatcher government. The UK clean coal combustion programme, the most advanced in the world in 1984–5, was closed a few years after the strike. Feickert points out that China now has 80 per cent of the world's clean coal power plants, whereas the UK does not have a single one.

Thatcher could close the mines safe in the knowledge that the country was sitting on vast amounts of natural gas out in the North Sea. But that would not always be that case, and today Britain has used about three quarters of all known North Sea gas reserves. Harold Wilson used to say that whoever is elected when the oil money flows will be in power for a generation. It came too late to save Wilson and Callaghan's Labour governments. Instead, it was the basis of the prosperity that helped give the Conservatives eighteen years in power, and Tony Blair another ten. But now it's more or less finished. The gas is running out, but all the infrastructure has been put in place for the economy to be powered by gas that comes from the North Sea.

The oil boom is also on the wane. After a spike in 2000, domestic production of petroleum in 2006 was lower than in 1980. Alongside the decline of coal, this means that Britain now produces fewer energy products domestically (in terms of millions of tonnes of oil equivalent) in 2006 than it did in 1980. We have already seen gas and petrol price hikes as Britain imports more and more, but in the long term this provokes a far more fundamental problem: we will need to buy our gas from Russia and our oil from the Middle East – not places Britain wants to be in hock to.

This does not mean, of course, that the once vast and vital coal industry could have continued as it was. The industry that maintained the country throughout the first two thirds of the last century, the one industry that had to be kept going in 1939–45 if the war was to be won, had seen its best days and needed to contract. But once jaw-jaw was decisively rejected for war-war by the generals, the industry was never going to be contracted, only devastated. And the benefits of this are not clear. It's at least arguable that, by winning the right to do this, Thatcher simply won the right to condemn her country to long-term impoverishment.

But surely at least she was right to curb the unions? Surely they were wrecking the country, calling everyone out on strike, taking us to hell in a handcart? And surely we are all better off now that the Labour Party has liberated itself from the unions? Well, not entirely. First, union power was never as great as it was cracked up to be. It suited union leaders to overestimate it, and it suited the unions' enemies to do the same. Seven years before the strike, when they were at their most powerful, the unions, with Arthur Scargill to the fore, had tried hard to force a small employer in North London to treat its staff properly – and failed. The Grunwick affair was one of those times when things would have been a great deal better if unions had been *more* powerful rather than less. There are and always will be greedy and exploitative employers, and unions provide the only protection people have from them.

As for the Labour Party, it is certainly the case that the balance of power between the Party and the unions changed after the strike, and nine years later the change was hastened by Tony Blair. The unions used to be the senior partner; now the Labour Party is, so much so that it does not mean a lot to say that Labour is the party of the unions. Old Labour's ambition was to achieve 'a fundamental and irreversible shift in the balance of wealth and power' between rich and poor. New Labour has achieved a fundamental and perhaps irreversible shift in the balance of power between trade unions and the Labour Party.

For the first time, Labour leaders seem almost ashamed to admit they even know union leaders. When the government does something that the unions like, union leaders are forced to avoid cheering, for fear of being heard in Middle England. In 1997, Gordon Brown's former adviser Charlie Whelan telephoned the white-collar union leader Rodney Bickerstaffe to ask him to condemn Gordon Brown's first budget, to reassure Middle England that Brown was at loggerheads with the unions.

Union leaders today are genuinely puzzled about why unions can never be seen to achieve anything. If they boast of an achievement, they are punished swiftly and severely. The Communication Workers Union made triumphant noises about fending off privatization, and before it could draw breath the Post Office was turned into a plc.

Take the minimum wage. The TUC wanted £4 an hour. The government decided on £3.60 for those over twenty-one, a 'development rate' of £3 for eighteeen to twenty-one-year-olds, and no minimum wage at all for sixteen- and seventeen-year-olds. John Monks, the TUC General Secretary, nailed a smile to his face and said what a historic milestone it was. He admitted only to a little disappointment that the government had been even stingier – or more prudent, as it's known in the trade – than its own Low Pay Commission recommended.

Monks' famous sang-froid hid bitter union resentment, especially about the treatment of young people. Unions understand where that leads. In London's East End between the two World Wars, sweatshop owners used to employ boys between the ages of fourteen and eighteen, when they were fit and agile and would work for next to nothing. When they started to need enough money to keep a family, they were thrown back onto the streets to starve, and their employers started again with new fourteen-year-olds. That is what happens when young people's labour can be bought cheaply and unions cannot protect them.

To have so diminished the unions that they stay diminished twenty-five years later, even after ten years of Labour government, is certainly an achievement of sorts. How much it actually improves our quality of life or our success as a nation, and whether this achievement is worth the price the nation paid for it, is, at the very least, debatable.

The price was paid by everyone, but especially, of course, by miners – those who struck and those who worked – and their families. Many miners might have been happy about contracting their industry, if care were taken to ensure that there was alternative employment. Instead, they suffered near-starvation, violence and, perhaps most important, the bitterest of humiliations. We have told stories in this book of miners being rescued by their wives from a severe beating from the police, but we might pause for a moment to consider what that does, psychologically, in a community where a man thinks it his duty to protect his wife, not the other way round.

The scars in mining communities have not healed. Pit villages became lawless and dangerous places after the strike: in some in Yorkshire you could buy heroin cheaper than in Leeds. Now they have call centres and distribution centres. Isn't that good? No, say the people from the villages whom we speak to. 'It's all crap jobs, and what will happen when they go to Asia?' was a typical comment.

Photographer Peter Arkell, who took thousands of pictures of the great strike, was commissioned a few years later to take pictures of the protests against the M3 extension near Winchester, and was saddened to see former miners, whom he had last seen on the picket line fighting the police, working as security guards, wearing uniforms and attacking anti-motorway protesters. Later, in 2005, he went back to Yorkshire pit villages and found they had not forgotten: 'They still don't speak to scabs.'

Perhaps the most hopeful initiative is happening on Arthur Scargill's doorstep, in Grimethorpe, Yorkshire – and his daughter is at the centre of it. The closure of the Grimethorpe pit near Barnsley in 1993 was iconic: it was the base of the famous Grimethorpe brass band, and the inspiration for the 1996 film *Brassed Off* with Ewan McGregor, Tara Fitzgerald and Pete Postlethwaite. After the closure Grimethorpe became, quite quickly, the poorest village in the EU and the second sickest town in Britain. Drug abuse and the crime that fuels it became major problems. The police struggled to regain authority after the strike, but

242

they were not trusted; anyway, before the strike the tight communities had done a good job of policing themselves. Unemployment was far beyond the official figures and a whole generation of youngsters was lost to drugs and despair. Those who had never worked were affected worse than those who had been made redundant.

In recent years, local GP Dr Margaret Scargill has been behind a remarkable experiment, the Oaks Park primary care centre, built at a cost of £3m, the brainchild of her husband Jim Logan, a former colliery manager who has made a study of the Cuban health system. Logan believes the Cubans do one-stop-shop healthcare better than anyone else in the world and, now that the British government is trying to provide bigger units for better-resourced primary care, the Cuban example is one it ought to follow. The idea is to improve public health by offering a range of primary care treatments locally, rather than sending people to hospital.

The centre brings together a range of NHS services and also caters for wider social needs, such as housing and benefits. Its GPs are familiar with the health problems of a former mining community, such as respiratory diseases and heart problems. The centre also provides chiropody, dental services, ophthalmology, pharmacy, dietetics, midwives, community psychiatric services and physiotherapy. Dr Scargill advised on the centre's design as one of its six resident GPs.

Did it have to be like this? There was going to be at least some contraction in the mining industry, but did it have to turn into a civil war whose consequences we are still living with? Journalist Seumas Milne says the strike was entirely unavoidable from a miner's standpoint, and so was the course it took. He thinks the rundown of the pits would not have been more humane without the strike, and that is demonstrated by the way the UDM was treated. An orderly retreat would not have worked.

Milne has a point about the UDM. Once it had served its purpose, that of undermining the strike, it was cynically abandoned, and its representations on behalf of doomed pits were ignored. In 2002 the union that had been formed to break the strike was itself forced to call a strike to combat widespread compulsory redundancies planned by the now privately owned UK Coal. The NUM's General Secretary in Nottingham, Keith Stanley, said current workplace laws meant non-UDM miners had no right to strike because they had not been balloted, and the NUM did not instruct its members to observe the UDM's picket lines. The NUM did not ballot on strike action because it was still in talks with UK Coal.

But on the wider issue Milne is wrong. Even given the positions of both sides at the start – the government's view that a rapid rundown was essential, the NUM's determination to defend jobs – there is a great deal that could have been done to prevent the prolonged tragedy we have described in this book.

From the government side, this was admitted to us by the most unlikely figure: Norman Tebbit, who during the strike was the hard-line Trade and Industry Secretary, regarded as one of Thatcher's 'bovver boys' with an uncompromising attitude towards the Left. He now feels remorse. Perhaps mellowed by age (he's seventy-seven), he regrets the damage that was done after the miners' strike to working-class communities through the huge programme of pit closures.

He still blames Scargill for the strike, but admits that the closure programme went too far, though he says ministers had little choice in many cases, with pits flooded or unusable in the wake of the strike. 'Those mining communities had good working-class values and a sense of family values,' he says. 'The men did real men's heavy work going down the pit. There were also very close-knit communities which were able to deal with the few troublesome kids. If they had any problems they would take the kid round the back and give them a good clip round the ear and that would be the end of it.

'Many of these communities were completely devastated, with people out of work, turning to drugs, and no real man's work because all the jobs had gone. There is no doubt that this led to a breakdown in these communities, with families breaking up and youths going out of control. The scale of the closures went too far. The damage done to those communities was enormous as a result of the strike.'

This happened partly because the Prime Minister thought she was on a crusade against an Antichrist. After vanquishing the Argentinians, she was going to vanquish 'the enemy within' – the name she gave to thousands of British citizens who wanted, whether misguidedly or not, to be allowed to go on earning their living in the hard, dangerous but productive way that their fathers and grandfathers had done.

Feeling this, she also felt that there was no point in testing the water and finding out whether a more gradual rundown of the industry might be acceptable, or whether alternative work might be found. Her job as she saw it was to make preparations with military precision, fight the fight with military ruthlessness, and take every ounce of the spoils of victory; and that is what she did.

'I was so disappointed when they called that strike off. We were within striking distance, if you'll forgive the pun, of bashing them into the ground.' That was Arthur Scargill, twenty-four years on and just after his seventieth birthday, on 12 January 2008, talking to ITV Yorkshire. His rather supine ITV interviewer did not ask him why, in that case, he had not prevented the strike being called off, as he had the power to do simply by using his casting vote as President. Nor did he ask for any evidence that the NUM was winning. Scargill avoids talking to journalists who might be inclined to ask such questions.

In November 1984, with the strike clearly going nowhere and the drift back to work well under way, he told cheering miners in Porthcawl, in one of the very last of those great, rousing, barnstorming speeches which still have the power to thrill when you hear them played: 'Can you say to your son or daughter: in 1984 I took part in the greatest struggle in trade union history. I fought to save your pit. I fought to save the jobs. I fought to save this community. And in doing so I pre-served my dignity as a human being and as a member of the finest trade union in the world. I'm proud to lead you. The miners united will never be defeated.' As he said the words, the miners, who were not united, were on the verge of being defeated. If Scargill knew it – and how could he not have known it? – he should have been looking for a way out, as his hero A.J. Cook would have done.

Cook's words to a union conference as the 1926 strike was failing, which we quoted in Chapter 1, serve as a rebuke to Scargill: 'It is not cowardice to face the facts of a situation, and I say that a leader who leads men blindly when he knows different is not only a traitor to himself and his own conscience, but he is betraying the men he is leading.'

When Scargill's loyal members – and he had oceans of loyalty in the NUM to call upon – heard him speak as he did in Porthcawl, with that utter confidence, they thought he must have a strategy. He let them go on thinking it. But it wasn't true. He had no strategy at all. Instead, he delivered the then powerful trade union movement, bound and gagged, into the hands of its enemies. Never has anyone done so much harm to his own side.

His own union was destroyed. It was big, united and powerful before the strike, and small, divided and weak after it. The jibe of his enemies has force: that he went into the strike with a big union and a small house, and came out of it with a small union and a big house. Mick McGahey knew, and could admit to himself, how much damage had been done. The result of the strike, he said years later, was 'to destroy trade unionism not only in mining but in Britain.'[1] Privately he blamed Scargill, but he kept that for secret conversations with the likes of Bill Keys and Neil Kinnock. Talking to one of the authors shortly before he died, he refused to mention Scargill, only saying: 'I believe, and I accept my responsibility in this, that we underestimated the Conservative government's determination to use the state machine against us. In order to dismember the welfare state they had to break the trade union movement, and they needed to break the miners first.'

Scargill himself tends to wander off into accusations of betrayal by other trade unions who failed to come to his support. His faithful former PA and press officer Nell Myers says: 'He hasn't changed his mind about anything because he has been proved right all along – look at what has happened to the mining communities.' She means that this has happened because other unions did not support Scargill; not that this has happened partly as a result of Scargill.

Perhaps the most sophisticated defence of Scargill's handling of the strike comes from his friend and supporter in the NUM Ken Capstick, and it is only fair to quote it at some length:

> I believe we were right and I think history has proven that . . . We are importing something like fifty million tonnes of coal into Britain and if we stop burning coal today, the lights would be out in the morning . . . If you've got a lad in a school playground who's going to be attacked by a bully and instead of just taking his beating, he decides he is going to fight back – he may still lose because the bully might be bigger than him, but his victory is in the fact that he fought back. That's his victory and I believe the victory for us, as Arthur often puts it, was in the struggle itself. The only thing Arthur could depend upon were his leadership abilities. I would say that keeping us on strike for twelve months showed he had enormous leadership abilities. What were Thatcher's leadership abilities? . . . She could stop your wages, she could threaten to close your industry down. She could cause mayhem in your communities and your families, she could use every piece of state apparatus to drive you back to work, like police on horseback charging through your village, charging into your house on horseback.

The victory was in the struggle itself. Scargill believes this because he represented something genuine in the trade union movement of the time: the belief that unions were a force for revolutionary change in society, and trade unionists had a duty to struggle for it permanently. So a union leader who believed in compromising with the class enemy was not just mistaken: he was a traitor to the cause. It is summed up in the title of Seumas Milne's book *The Enemy Within*. The title refers, of course, to Thatcher's famous words about the miners, but it has another meaning. Scargill was an authentic product of the feverish self-absorption of the left in the trade unions in the late seventies and early eighties. They too thought that the real enemy was the enemy within – the right wing of their own movement.

So Scargill thought his real enemies were men like Neil Kinnock and Norman Willis, and that, having defeated the right wing in his own union, there was little else to defeat. All that was necessary now was for the true believers to claim the inheritance that had so long been denied them by the likes of his right-wing predecessor, Joe Gormley. He described those who opposed the candidature of Tony Benn for Labour deputy leader as traitors and saboteurs. He can be measured and humorous about Margaret Thatcher, but not about Neil Kinnock.

Dave Feickert puts it like this: 'Arthur was a unique version of the typical British trade union militant of the time. These no longer exist. I had been one of them, too, but the difference between him and McGahey, Heathfield and all the others and me, is that we believed in making alliances to win, even if they were not with people with whom we agreed about the number of angels on the pin-head.' One of the distinguishing marks of such people was an almost morbid fear of being outflanked on the left, of meeting someone who could claim to be more left-wing than they were. They played slightly childish games of lefter-than-thou.

For such a leader, it was vital to have astute, powerful, competent people around them who could challenge them. Scargill surrounded himself with Nell Myers, a press officer who loathed journalists, hero-worshipped Scargill and doubled as his PA; and Roger Windsor, who had never been much more than a bookkeeper for a small organization. The two other national officials, Mick McGahey and Peter Heathfield, both had to put up with being consulted less than Myers and Windsor.

The shame of it, says the TUC's John Monks, is that there were some good, experienced trade union officials in the NUM head office, upon whose advice Scargill could have relied. Monks cites Dave Feickert, Mick Clapham and Steve Hudson. Windsor, says Monks, was not as good as any of them, but he enjoyed the importance Scargill thrust upon him. Monks thinks Windsor made it harder for Bill Keys and Norman Willis to sell a compromise deal to Scargill. 'He made things worse all the time, echoing Scargill and winding him up, saying things like "We can't have that, can we?"' says Monks. Feickert calls Windsor 'Arthur's dirty tricks man'.

Our researcher Dan Johnson, who grew up in Scargill's village of Worsborough and has studied the strike and Scargill's personality, believes Worsborough is key to the man. Scargill, he says, has a natural suspicion of anything and anyone from further away than Sheffield. 'I should think he couldn't wait to move the headquarters of the union up north when he became President and I wouldn't be surprised if he had to be talked out of locating it in Barnsley,' says Johnson. Today, what is left of the NUM does have its headquarters in Barnsley.

This helps explain the misjudgement that caused Scargill to concentrate all his forces on Orgreave. He was sure that the trade unionists of the Socialist Republic of South Yorkshire would come out in strength and help him win the strike. Johnson adds that Scargill, despite appearances, is insecure, and may have known at some level that he was getting it wrong.

In twenty-five years he has never once owned up to having lost the strike. The fact that he can talk today of having been on the brink of victory makes him a figure of fun. The late John Lyons, then leader of the Engineers and Managers Association, called Scargill 'vain to the point of incoherence'. John Monks, more instinctively kind, calls him 'a force of nature – we had not seen his like before. His school was not a negotiating school. He never compromised. He said, "I only compromised once and I regretted it."'

All of which perhaps makes him sound like a fool, and he was not a fool. His speeches were polished, certain, strong and inspiring. He had all the bureaucratic skills, says John Monks, who had the opportunity to see him at work. Give him a complex paper and he could grasp all the main points very quickly. This put him at an advantage over Peter Heathfield and Mick McGahey, who struggled to keep up with him.

Since he has never admitted that the strike was lost, it is not surprising that in the quarter century that has elapsed he seems, like the

Bourbon kings in 1815, to have learned nothing and forgotten nothing. Hence the sad, almost farcical business of the money, where what he thought was his cleverness resulted time after time in his looking ever grubbier, and where a little professional advice from lawyers and accountants might have saved him no end of trouble. (We are making the assumption that he is innocent of wrongdoing, which we think he probably is, but his convoluted method of running his, the NUM's and the IMO's affairs has left him unable to demonstrate it.)

He is no more intelligent than he used to be about the media, which is a shame because he has natural talent as a broadcaster. In 1993 he gave an interview to Hunter Davies for the *Independent*. Quite why he agreed to see Davies is unclear, since he was obviously resentful of the journalist throughout their meeting, sullenly refusing to sit on the sofa instead of his chair for the photographer, avoiding questions when there was no point in doing so, needlessly insulting his guest, and ensuring a hostile article.

'It was like dealing with a child, an only child, used to getting his own way,' wrote Davies. 'Several times he trotted out 10-minute speeches, such as on the harassment he had to put up with in 1990 when the *Daily Mirror* had a campaign against him, all unfair, all unproved, but all well known. When I tried to get him off the subject, he said I'd brought it up. I said I didn't. Thus we wasted another 10 minutes.'

He saw Hunter Davies, but about the same time turned down an interview with his old left-wing chum Paul Routledge, who was working on a biography. They had once been close, and now were not on speaking terms. He sent Routledge an extraordinary letter, which is worth quoting in full, partly because it illustrates the strange habit he has of referring to himself in the third person:

> I was not surprised to hear that you were writing a biography of Arthur Scargill – I had already been told that by three different sources.
>
> I explained that I was not prepared to assist or give approval in any way to a project of this kind and that on previous occasions I have

refused to give approval or assist other journalists in writing a biography of Arthur Scargill.

The fact we haven't exchanged a word between 1985 and the Labour Party Conference in Blackpool in 1992, together with the vitriolic and inaccurate articles you wrote at the time of the smear campaign by the *Daily Mirror* and Cooke Report, does not help.

I have thought over your request for a general interview but feel in the circumstances it would be unwise. It would undoubtedly be used as an occasion for gleaning information towards the production of your book.

A professional PR adviser would probably have told him to see Routledge but stay away from Davies. But it seems to be Scargill's way to become very close to people, as he did with Routledge, then cut them off entirely and for ever because of some slight or another.

His personal life seems to have unravelled. He parted from his wife many years ago, and is now apparently not on speaking terms with her, though she too lives in the small village of Worsborough. Nor is he on speaking terms with his only daughter, her husband or his grandchildren, all of whom also live nearby. How his family estrangements happened, we do not know. Scargill is credited with a number of affairs, but there is no evidence. Today he is close to Nell Myers. Anne Scargill would not talk to us about her husband: 'It's too painful. I'm not washing my dirty linen in public. I'll take it to the grave with me.'

Dave Feickert says: 'Arthur is now a sad, lonely sixty-nine-year-old [this was in 2007], who does not speak to his ex-wife or his only child or her children. He has a most terrible ability to cut off his friends, through apparently profound disagreements. I have always refused to play this game. I became a Quaker during the civil war of 1984–5 and do not believe, like Quakers generally, that one should do this. So I always chat to him when I see him at NUM events, but we usually talk about our health problems – i.e. I listen to his!'

Of the acolytes – Roger Windsor, Nell Myers, Maurice Jones, Jim Parker – only Myers is left to him. The other three now hate him; hate is not too strong a word. He refused to go to his daughter Margaret's wedding, so she contacted Rodney Bickerstaffe, an old family friend. In happier days the Bickerstaffes and the Scargills saw a lot of each other, and had regular meals together as a foursome. She asked Bickerstaffe to give her away, and he agreed, making the speech at the wedding that would normally be made by the father of the bride. Scargill was not there.

The union could have lived to fight again, been reunited, secured some sort of negotiating position that would have allowed it to protect its members, says Feickert, but failed to do so because Scargill 'never recovered psychologically from a defeat he could never acknowledge'. Yet the miners followed Scargill, especially in Yorkshire. The man had charisma. And he has his supporters to this day, who will not hear a word against him. Neil Kinnock puts that down to people trying to avoid 'a spiritual implosion' by admitting they were wrong. The pride of the mining communities makes it hard for them to admit that Scargill was not the superman they thought. The union was a major part of that pride, with its history, traditions and status. Outsiders sometimes wonder whether miners in Barnsley resent Scargill's comparative wealth and his big house. They do not. That is how they believe the President of their union ought to live.

There are those who, even today, feel that they are somehow betraying something if they allow themselves to be critical of Scargill. Rodney Bickerstaffe is like that: he is normally an affable, communicative man, but getting him to talk about Scargill was like drawing teeth. At one point, more to try to get him talking than for any other reason, we said: 'He's a vain and silly man, isn't he?' No, no, said Bickerstaffe, he's not a silly man, we shouldn't call him silly, we'd damage our book if we did; and he chuntered on like that for several minutes, perhaps hoping we would not notice that he had failed to challenge the word 'vain'.

On 27 May 2002 former *Daily Mirror* editor Roy Greenslade disowned the corruption story that Roger Windsor had given his paper twelve years before. In an article in the *Guardian*, he mused on whether Windsor was MI5's man in NUM headquarters – carefully, because Windsor had already successfully sued the *Daily Express* for saying he was.

It had been rumoured for years. The former head of MI5, Stella Rimington, fuelled the rumour with the answer she gave to the *Guardian*: 'It would be correct to say that he, Roger Windsor, was never an agent in any sense of the word that you can possibly imagine.'

This neither fingers Windsor nor absolves him: it just muddies the waters, and that is how spies operate. They like to spread uncertainty and distrust. These things are the air they breathe. Rimington ensured that suspicion will forever linger over Windsor which, assuming he is not guilty of spying on the NUM, he will never be able to shed. Greenslade, too, is content to leave in the air the thought that Windsor might have been the security services' mole in the NUM.

Windsor wrote a rather sad open letter to Rimington in a clumsy and forlorn attempt to clear his name of the charge; naturally, it went unanswered. In it, after recounting events that we know did happen, he made the sensational (and unsubstantiated) charge that Scargill was still seeking Libyan funding after the strike was over. He seems to have been desperate to clear his name, for he then wrote to renegade spy David Shayler. According to Shayler's partner, Annie Machon, Windsor believed Shayler could exonerate him, which was never very likely since Shayler did not join MI5 until 1991.

Having done so, he handed all his papers to one Malcolm Lister, the architect who designed the building in Sheffield to which Scargill moved the union from its former London home, and was also responsible for the improvements to Scargill's house. Lister, who came from a Yorkshire mining family, admired Scargill and felt honoured to work for him. But his hero-worship turned eventually to loathing, as it did with so many others.

For what it is worth, we agree with the conclusions reached by two journalists who investigated the matter in some depth soon afterwards, Paul Brown and Kevin Cahill. There certainly was a security services spy in the NUM, and probably more than one. We do not know who it was. But it is unlikely to have been Roger Windsor. He is too obvious a candidate.

As for the money, the final word goes to the novelist Marina Lewycka. In her novel *Two Caravans*, she has her young Ukrainian hero remembering 'the solemnity with which his parents donated their gold wedding rings to buy food for the British miners. What happened to all that money? The Ukrainian miners could certainly do with it now'. Marina Lewycka was born in a refugee camp after the Second World War, of Ukrainian parents. And she is married to Dave Feickert.

When Arthur Scargill asked that meeting in Porthcawl in November 1984, 'Can you say to your son or daughter: in 1984 I took part in the greatest struggle in trade union history . . .', he was borrowing from the famous First World War propaganda poster showing a shamefaced man who does not know how to answer his children when they ask, 'What did you do in the war, Daddy?'

An even more obvious First World War reference was offered during the strike by the electricians' union leader, Eric Hammond, who called the miners 'lions led by donkeys', the phrase used about British soldiers in their putrid trenches.

The Great Strike for Jobs, as it is known in NUM folklore, was far more a civil war than an industrial dispute: not just because it was all or nothing, and not just because the two armies clashed with a violence hardly ever seen in British politics. It also shares the defining characteristic of a war. It is politicians who declare war, lead rival armies, cheer and inspire soldiers. But it is ordinary men and women who fight, are hurt and die.

That's why we find looking back on the First World War so shocking. We no longer care about Kitchener and Haig, Asquith and Lloyd George, Clemenceau and the Kaiser. What makes that war so extraordinarily vivid is that it left a whole generation deeply and irreparably damaged. They trusted their leaders, and those leaders let them down.

The miners trusted Arthur Scargill with their homes, their families, their future, their safety, everything they had, and he let them down, bravely shouting, 'Onwards and forwards, brothers, the future lies ahead,' without thinking through the dangers and hardships into which he was leading them.

The nation trusted Margaret Thatcher. She convinced people that she was fighting an Antichrist, that unless the miners were brought down and humiliated Britons could not sleep safely in their beds, that our economic security depended on destroying the power of the unions and a rapid shutdown of the coal industry. Her legacy from this strike is a fractured society that took years to heal (and in mining communities has still not healed) and an energy crisis.

Neither Thatcher nor Scargill paid the price for their war. Neither has ever once acknowledged even the smallest error. In that, they really are like the politicians and generals who fought the First World War and were memorably excoriated by Siegfried Sassoon:

> If I were fierce, and bald, and short of breath,
> I'd live with scarlet Majors at the Base,
> And speed glum heroes up the line to death . . .
> And when the war is done and youth stone dead,
> I'd toddle safely home and die – in bed.[2]

Abbreviations

ACAS	Advisory, Conciliation and Arbitration Service
ACPO	Association of Chief Police Officers
ASLEF	Associated Society of Locomotive Steam Enginemen and Firemen
ASTMS	Association of Scientific, Technical and Managerial Staffs
BACM	British Association of Colliery Managers
CBI	Confederation of British Industry
CEGB	Central Electricity Generating Board
CGT	Confédération Générale du Travail
COSA	Colliery Overmen and Staff Association
CPBF	Campaign for Press and Broadcasting Freedom
CPGB	Communist Party of Great Britain
CTAWA	Colliery Trades and Allied Workers Association
DTI	Department of Trade and Industry
EMA	Engineers and Managers Assocation
FBU	Fire Brigades Union
FOI	Freedom of Information
GMB	General, Municipal, Boilermakers and Allied Trade Union
IMO	International Miners' Organization
ISTC	Iron and Steel Trades Confederation
MFGB	Miners' Federation of Great Britain
MIDAF	Miners Defence and Aid Fund
MIREDS	Miners Research, Education, Defence and Support Trust
MoD	Ministry of Defence

MTUI	Miners Trade Union International
NACODS	National Association of Colliery Overmen, Deputies and Shotfirers
NALGO	National and Local Government Officers Association (now called Unison)
NCB	National Coal Board
NCCL	National Council for Civil Liberties
NEC	National Executive Committee
NGA	National Graphical Association
NHS	National Health Service
NRC	National Reporting Centre
NUJ	National Union of Journalists
NUM	National Union of Mineworkers
NUPE	National Union of Public Employees
NUR	National Union of Railwaymen
ORC	Opinion Research and Communications
PSI	Public Services International
PSU	Police Support Unit
SOGAT	Society of Graphical and Allied Trades
SWP	Socialist Workers Party
TGWU	Transport and General Workers' Union
TUC	Trades Union Congress
UDM	Union of Democratic Mineworkers
WFTU	World Federation of Trade Unions
WRP	Workers Revolutionary Party

CHAPTER NOTES

PREFACE

1. *Morning Star*, 7 June 1989.

CHAPTER 1: THE SHADOW OF 1926

1. Perkins (2006).
2. Ibid.
3. Beckett and Beckett (2005).
4. Perkins (2006).
5. Marquand (1977).
6. Brown (1986).
7. William Keegan, *Observer*, 5 January 2003.
8. Davies (1987).
9. Ibid.
10. Ibid.
11. Crick (1985).
12. NUM website.
13. Hennessy (1993).
14. Routledge (1993).
15. Ibid.
16. Ibid.
17. Ibid.
18. Ibid.

CHAPTER 2: ENTER THATCHER, STAGE RIGHT, AND SCARGILL, STAGE LEFT

1. Beckett (2006).
2. Goodman (1985), p. 21.
3. MacGregor (1986).
4. Ibid.
5. Ibid., p. 110.
6. Routledge (1993).
7. Ibid.

CHAPTER 3: THE GREAT STRIKE

1. *TGWU Record*, May/June 2005.
2. Interview with Trevor Bell.
3. Wilsher, MacIntyre and Jones (1985).
4. Callinicos and Simons (1985).
5. National Archives, released under the FOI Act.
6. Released under the FOI Act.
7. Cabinet Office document released under the FOI Act.
8. Ibid.
9. Interview with Peter Walker.
10. MacGregor (1986).
11. Martin Kettle in Fine and Millar (1985).
12. Jones (1985).
13. National Archives, released under the FOI Act.
14. National Archives, Coal 31/394.
15. Goodman (1985).
16. *Guardian*, 3 June 1985.
17. Jones (1986).
18. Ibid.
19. *Guardian*, 3 June 1985.
20. Jones (1986).
21. Ibid.
22. Milne (1994), p. 41.
23. MacGregor (1986).

CHAPTER 4: THE BATTLE OF ORGREAVE

1. Kinnock Papers.
2. Beckett (1995).
3. Ottey (1985).
4. Callinicos and Simons (1985).
5. Kinnock Papers.
6. *The Miner*, 2 April 1984.
7. Bill Keys' diary.
8. Interview with John Lyons.
9. *The Times*, 16 April 1984.
10. Bill Keys' diary.
11. Wilsher, MacIntyre and Jones (1985).
12. *The Times*, 5 April 1984.
13. Abdel-Rahim (1985).
14. Home Office document released under the FOI Act.
15. *The Times*, 18 April 1984.
16. Routledge (1993), pp. 148-9.
17. Kinnock Papers.
18. MacGregor (1986).
19. Jackson and Wardle (1986).
20. Ibid., p. 32.
21. Routledge (1993).
22. *The Miner*, 2 June 1984.
23. *The Miner*, 15 June 1984.
24. Callinicos and Simons (1985).
25. Jones, Petley, Power and Wood (1985).
26. Nicholas Jones, *Free Press*, May 2004.
27. Home Office document released under the FOI Act.
28. Jackson and Wardle (1986).
29. *Guardian*, 19 June 1984.
30. Ibid.
31. Jackson and Wardle (1986), pp. 23–4.
32. Callinicos and Simons (1985).

CHAPTER 5: THATCHER AND THE ENEMY WITHIN, SCARGILL AND GENERAL WINTER

1. Goodman (1985).
2. National Archives.
3. National Archives, released under the FOI Act.
4. Document released under the FOI Act.
5. National Archives, Coal 26/1410.
6. Goodman (1985).
7. Patrick Wintour, *Guardian*, 20 July 1984.
8. *The Times*, 20 July 1984.
9. Ian Aitken, *Guardian*, 20 July 1984.
10. Document released under the FOI Act.
11. Document of 22 August, released under the FOI Act.
12. Bill Keys' diary.
13. Goodman (2003).
14. Interview with Geoffrey Goodman.
15. Goodman (2003).
16. Callinicos and Simons (1985).
17. Document released under the FOI Act.

CHAPTER 6: PIT MANAGERS, MOSCOW GOLD AND A FATAL LIBYAN KISS

1. Interview with Kevin Barron.
2. Nicholas Jones, *Free Press*, 28 April 2004.
3. David Jenkins, *The Calling of a Cuckoo*, London, Continuum Books UK, 2002.
4. Report of press conference at York, *The Times*, 27 September 1984.
5. Document released by the Cabinet Office under the FOI Act.
6. National Archives, Coal 31/394.
7. Goodman (1985), p. 139.
8. Interview with Tim Bell.
9. Document released by the Cabinet Office under the FOI Act.
10. Document released by the Cabinet Office under the FOI Act.
11. Goodman (1985), pp. 146–8.
12. Routledge (1993).
13. Kinnock Papers.
14. National Archives, Coal 31/445.

15. Milne (1994).
16. Document released by the Cabinet Office under the FOI Act.
17. Document released by the Cabinet Office under the FOI Act.
18. Document released under the FOI Act.
19. Milne (1994).
20. Bill Keys' diary.
21. Routledge (1993), p. 178.
22. Interview with Ken Cameron.
23. Milne (1994).
24. Interview with Roger Windsor.
25. Milne (1994).
26. Ibid., p. 50.

CHAPTER 7: THE COLLAPSE OF GENERAL WINTER

1. Bill Keys' diary.
2. Ibid.
3. *Scottish Miner*, November 1984.
4. MacGregor (1986).
5. Bill Keys' diary.
6. Kinnock Papers.
7. Ibid.
8. Ibid.
9. Callinicos and Simons (1985), p. 180.
10. Stead (1987), p. 62.
11. Winterton and Winterton (1989), p. 124.
12. Ibid.
13. Kinnock Papers.
14. Ibid.
15. Stead (1987), p. 62.
16. Witham (1986), p. 153.
17. Miller (1986), p. 53.
18. Milne (1994).
19. Interview with Alain Simon.
20. Milne (1994).
21. Anne Suddick, BBC News UK, 4 March 2004.
22. Stead (1987).

CHAPTER 8: ELEVENTH-HOUR TALKS

1. Bill Keys' diary.
2. Routledge (1993).
3. National Archives.
4. Ibid.
5. Bill Keys' diary.
6. Beckett (1995).
7. Milne (1994).
8. National Archives, released under the FOI Act.
9. Bill Keys' diary.
10. Routledge (1993).
11. MacGregor (1986), p. 348.
12. Interview with Peter Walker.
13. MacGregor (1986), p. 349.
14. National Archives, Coal 31/438.
15. Bill Keys' diary.
16. Document released under the FOI Act.
17. Nicholas Jones, *Free Press*, May 2004.
18. Document released by the Cabinet Office under the FOI Act.
19. Document released under the FOI Act.
20. Bill Keys' diary.
21. Goodman (1985), p. 182.
22. Bill Keys' diary.
23. National Archives, Coal 31/438.

CHAPTER 9: THE BITTER END

1. Bill Keys' diary.
2. Goodman (1985).
3. Ibid.
4. Routledge (1993).
5. Ibid.
6. Bill Keys' diary.
7. Interview with John Monks.
8. *Strike: When Britain Went to War*, Channel 4, 2004.
9. Routledge (1993).
10. Williams (1987).

11. Wilsher, MacIntyre and Jones (1985).

12. Salt and Layzell (1985).

13. *Sunday Times*, 4 August 1985.

14. Document released under the FOI Act.

CHAPTER 10: THE POST-STRIKE WORLD: LOST MONEY, LOST INFLUENCE, LOST REPUTATIONS

1. Interview with Ken Cameron.

2. Lightman (1990).

3. Routledge (1993).

4. National Archives, Coal 31/443.

5. National Archives, Coal 31/443; memo Marion Stanley, NCB legal department.

6. National Archives, Coal 31/444.

7. Ibid.

8. Letter to Bert Wheeler, director, Nottinghamshire area NCB, National Archives, Coal 31/444.

9. National Archives, Coal 31/444.

10. Ibid.

11. Ibid., Coal 31/465.

12. Lightman (1990).

13. Interview with Neil Kinnock.

14. Francis Beckett and David Hencke, *The Survivor: Tony Blair in Peace and War*, London, Aurum, 2005.

15. Ibid.

CHAPTER 11: NOT AN INDUSTRIAL DISPUTE, BUT A WAR

1. *Independent*, 15 April 1998.

2. 'Base Details', in *Counter-Attack and Other Poems* (1918).

BIBLIOGRAPHY

BACKGROUND

Beckett, Clare (2006) *Thatcher*, London, Haus Publishing

Beckett, Francis (1995) *Enemy Within: The Rise and Fall of British Communism*, London, John Murray

Beckett, Francis and Clare (2005) *Bevan*, London, Haus Publishing

Brown, Gordon (1986) *Maxton*, London, Mainstream

Campbell, John (2003) *Margaret Thatcher – Volume Two: The Iron Lady*, London, Random House

Crick, Michael (1985) *Scargill and the Miners*, Harmondsworth, Penguin

Davies, Paul (1987) *A.J. Cook*, Manchester, Manchester University Press

Francis, Hywel (1984) *Miners Against Fascism*, London, Lawrence and Wishart

Francis, Hywel, and Dai Smith (1980) *The Fed: A History of the South Wales Miners in the Twentieth Century*, London, Lawrence and Wishart

Gerwyn Thomas, William (1976) *Welsh Coal Mines*, Cardiff, National Museum of Wales

Goodman, Geoffrey (2003) *From Bevan to Blair: Fifty Years' Reporting from the Political Frontline*, London, Pluto Press

Hennessy, Peter (1993) *Never Again: Britain, 1945–51*, London, Penguin

Jones, Nicholas (1986) *Strikes and the Media*, Oxford, Blackwell

Lowe, Jeremy Burman (1977) *Welsh Industrial Workers' Housing, 1775–1875*, Cardiff, National Museum of Wales

McIntosh, Ronald (2006) *Challenge to Democracy: Politics, Trade Union Power and Economic Failure 1973–77*, London, Methuen

Marquand, David (1977) *Ramsay MacDonald*, London, Jonathan Cape

Perkins, Anne (2006) *A Very British Strike: The General Strike 1926*, London, Macmillan

Routledge, Paul (1993) *Scargill*, London, HarperCollins

Scargill, Arthur, and Peggy Kahn (1980) *The Myth of Workers' Control*, Leeds and Nottingham, the Universities of Leeds and Nottingham

Watters, Frank (1992) *Being Frank: The Memoirs of Frank Watters*, Barnsley, Monkspring Publications

THE GREAT STRIKE 1984–5

Abdel-Rahim, Moira (1985) *Strike Breaking in Essex: The Policing of Wivenhoe and the Essex Ports During the 1984 Miners' Strike*, London, Canary Press

Barnsley Miners' Wives Action Group (1984) *We Struggled to Laugh*, self-published

Beaton, Lynn (1985) *Shifting Horizons*, London, Canary Press

Beynon, Huw (ed.) (1985) *Digging Deeper: Issues in the Miners' Strike*, London, Verso

Callinicos, Alex, and Mike Simons (1985) *The Great Strike: The Miners' Strike of 1984–5 and Its Lessons*, London, *Socialist Worker*

Coventry Miners' Wives Support Group (1986) *Mummy . . . What Did You Do in the Strike?*, self-published

Dolby, Norma (1987) *Norma Dolby's Diary: An Account of the Great Miners' Strike*, London, Verso

Douglas, Dave (1985) *Tell Us Lies About the Miners: The Role of the Media in the Great Coal Strike 1984/1985*, Doncaster, Direct Action Movement of the International Workers Association

Fine, Bob, and Robert Millar (1985) *Policing the Miners' Strike*, London, Lawrence and Wishart

Goodman, Geoffrey (1985) *The Miners' Strike*, London, Pluto

Holden, Triona (2005) *Queen Coal: Women of the Miners' Strike*, London, Sutton Publishing

Jackson, Bernard, and Tony Wardle (1986) *The Battle for Orgreave*, Brighton, Vanson Wardle

Jones, David, Julian Petley, Mike Power, and Lesley Wood (1985) *Media Hits the Pits: The Media and the Coal Dispute*, London, Campaign for Press and Broadcasting Freedom

Jones, Mark (1985) *Killed on the Picket Line 1984: The Story of David Gareth Jones by His Father*, London, New Park

Lightman, Gavin (1990) *The Lightman Report on the NUM*, Harmondsworth, Penguin

MacGregor, Ian (1986) *The Enemies Within: The Story of the Miners' Strike, 1984–5*, London, Collins

McHugh, Phil (1985) *For the Protection of Miners: North East Lancashire and the Miners' Strike 1984*, Preston, Lancashire Association of Trades Councils

Miller, Jill (1986) *You Can't Kill the Spirit: Women in a Welsh Mining Village*, London, Women's Press.

Milne, Seumas (1994) *The Enemy Within: The Secret War Against the Miners*, London, Verso

National Council for Civil Liberties (1984) *Civil Liberties and the Miners' Dispute*, London, NCCL

Ottey, Roy (1985) *The Strike: An Insider's Story*, London, Sidgwick and Jackson

Reed, David, and Olivia Adamson (1985) *Miners Strike 1984–1985: People Versus State*, London, Larkin

Salt, Chrys, and Jim Layzell (1985) *Here We Go!: Women's Memories of the 1984–85 Miners' Strike*, London, London Political Committee

Scargill, Arthur (1990) *Response to the Lightman Enquiry*, London, Campaign to Defend Scargill and Heathfield

Seddon, Vicky (ed.) (1986) *The Cutting Edge: Women and the Pit Strike*, London, Lawrence and Wishart

Sheffield Policewatch (1984) *Taking Liberties: Policing During the Miners' Strike April–October 1984*, Sheffield, Policewatch

Simons, Mike (2004) *Striking Back: Photographs of the Great Miners' Strike 1984–1985*, London, Bookmarks

Stead, Jean (1987) *Never the Same Again: Women and the Miners' Strike 1984–85*, London, The Women's Press

TUC (1984) *General Council's Report*

Williams, Jon (1987) *Hanging on by Your Fingernails: The Struggle at Lea Hall Colliery 1984–87*, Nottingham, Spokesman Books

Wilsher, Peter, Donald MacIntyre, and Michael Jones, with the *Sunday Times* Insight Team (1985) *Strike: Thatcher, Scargill and the Miners*, London, Andre Deutsch

Winterton J. and R. (1989) *Coal, Crisis and Conflict: The 1984–5 Miners' Strike in Yorkshire*, Manchester and New York, Manchester University Press

Witham, Joan (1986) *Hearts and Minds: The Story of the Women of Nottinghamshire in the Miners' Strike 1984–85*, London, Canary Press

INDEX

Abbreviations used in index
    NCB – National Coal Board
    NUM – National Union of Mineworkers
    TUC – Trades Union Congress